FIFTEENTH
CENTURY
ENGLAND
1399–1509

FIFTEENTH CENTURY ENGLAND 1399–1509

Studies in Politics and Society

EDITED BY
S.B. CHRIMES, C.D. ROSS
AND R.A. GRIFFITHS

SUTTON PUBLISHING

First published in 1972 by Manchester University Press

Second edition first published in the United Kingdom in 1995 by
Alan Sutton Publishing Limited, an imprint of Sutton Publishing Limited
Phoenix Mill · Thrupp · Stroud · Gloucestershire · GL5 2BU

First published in this edition in 1997

British Library Cataloguing-in-Publication Data
A catalogue record for this book is available from the British Library

ISBN 0-7509-1540-4

Cover illustration: detail of Edward IV being presented with a book, c. 1470–1. (Jean de Waurin,
'Chronique d'Angleterre', Flemish, 15th cent., *BL, MS Royal 15 E IV, fo. 14*)

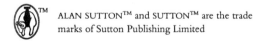

ALAN SUTTON™ and SUTTON™ are the trade
marks of Sutton Publishing Limited

Printed in Great Britain by
WBC Limited, Bridgend.

Contents

Foreword to the First Edition

The seven papers published in this volume are substantially as read by their authors at a colloquium held at University Hall, Cardiff, on 24–28 September 1970. This colloquium, sponsored by myself, Dr C. D. Ross and Dr R. A. Griffiths, and supported by the University of Wales and University College, Cardiff, was attended by fifty specialists in British fifteenth-century history, drawn from twenty-nine universities and other institutions in the United Kingdom and North America. Dr Griffiths, assisted by Dr R. S. Thomas, acted as honorary secretary and treasurer, and the success of the colloquium owed much to his efficient and zealous efforts. The three sponsors have jointly acted as editors of this volume, and Dr Griffiths has also compiled the index.

Four discussion sessions followed the paper readings, introduced and presided over by Professors J. S. Roskell (for papers 1 and 2), J. R. Lander (for papers 3 and 4), A. R. Myers (for paper 5) and Glanmor Williams (for papers 6 and 7). These discussions were lively and fruitful. Notes of them taken at the time by Miss Susan Taylor, Mr R. G. Davies, and Dr R. S. Thomas were made available to the contributors to this volume, who have taken them into account and have added references and bibliographical information in the notes appended to their papers.

It is hoped that the publication of this volume, for which we are greatly indebted to Manchester University Press, will bring to a wider public acquaintance with current trends of scholarship and the advancing bounds of knowledge of a period which used to be called, but can hardly continue to be called, the 'Cinderella' of the centuries of English history.

S.B.C.

University College, Cardiff
April 1972

Foreword to the Second Edition

In the two decades since S. B. Chrimes wrote the original Foreword to this collection of essays, the fifteenth century in English – nay, British – history has attracted some of the most talented and lively young historians working in Britain. The Cardiff colloquium and the publication of its proceedings proved to be an important catalyst in making a wider public aware of their scholarly achievements, including some new approaches to their subject, as Chrimes had hoped. The success of that first colloquium was such that further colloquia have been held at regular intervals since 1970, with particular efforts made to encourage the participation of younger scholars and senior research students. Although he was not able to attend more than one or two of the subsequent colloquia, Chrimes gained considerable satisfaction from the outcome of the venture at Cardiff, which coincided with his approaching retirement from his Chair of History in 1974.

The genesis of the first colloquium was a happy conjunction of factors. In 1970 Professor Chrimes was nearing the end of his academic career and since the death of K. B. McFarlane in 1966 he could be fairly described (by A. R. Myers) as the doyen among fifteenth-century English historians, particularly on the constitutional and political side. Looking back over the generation since the publication of his *English Constitutional Ideas in the Fifteenth Century* (1936), he was struck by the great strides that had been made in the study of a century which, when he began his studies, had seemed to languish, almost neglected, between the achievements of medieval administrative and political historians of T. F. Tout's generation and the flowering of Tudor history. He recalled that when he embarked on his study of John, duke of Bedford, at King's College, London, in 1928, there had been difficulty in finding him a suitable supervisor; eventually, he was assigned to F. J. C. Hearnshaw, an historian of early modern political thought who, as Chrimes remarked, was not noted for his interest in, or knowledge of, the early fifteenth century. He recalled, too, that when he arrived at the Public Record Office to begin his researches, the only other young scholars there with whom he could compare notes on the fifteenth century were K. B. McFarlane and Bertie Wilkinson. All three were to become vigorously independent scholars whose writings have proved extraordinarily influential. Despite the occasional academic spat in reviews or footnotes, each valued approaches to historical study different from his own, and each encouraged (and respected) the work of newer generations of scholars. This attitude, in part, lay behind Chrimes's willingness to host a fifteenth-century colloquium in 1970 – at which Bertie Wilkinson was present.

Chrimes had profound respect for the contribution which McFarlane had made before his death in 1966, not least through his supervision of talented pupils at Oxford. By 1970, one of these pupils, C. D. Ross, was himself supervising pupils at the University of Bristol, where he had taught fifteenth-century history at first alongside T. F. Tout's daughter, Margaret Sharp. In 1970 it seemed to Ross timely that he should bring together his own pupils and those of his contemporaries who were teaching in other British universities, in order to assess the state of fifteenth-century scholarship.

At that juncture, Chrimes had been responsible for advising on the authorship of later medieval volumes in the 'English Monarchs' series which D. C. Douglas had inaugurated in 1964 with the publication of his *William the Conqueror*. As a result, by 1970 work was well advanced on volumes which had been assigned to three of McFarlane's former pupils: A. L. Brown, who had been Chrimes's young colleague at Glasgow (on Henry IV), B. P. Wolffe (on Henry VI) and Ross (on Edward IV); Chrimes himself was nearing the completion of *Henry VII*. The publication of these unique books on the reigns of fifteenth-century kings, with the respective monarchs as their focus, beginning with *Henry VII* in 1972, has transformed the historiographical landscape. In 1970 it seemed an appropriate moment to place some of the emerging conclusions before a colloquium of the authors' peers and their pupils, drawn from Great Britain and North America.

Chrimes's *Henry VII* was not primarily a biography of the king, still less a history of England during Henry's reign. In Chrimesian fashion, it was conceived as 'a study of the impact of Henry Tudor upon the government of England', placing to the fore both ideas and realities in a political, governmental and constitutional context to which Chrimes attached great importance. When *Edward IV* appeared two years later, its focus was different in several significant respects. Leaning decisively towards McFarlane's approach to later medieval society, Ross's book was 'a study in the power-politics of later medieval England . . . the ways and means of gaining and keeping power', in which 'Edward's relations with the English nobility, and especially his use of patronage, occupy a prominent place'. From this point of view, the fulcrum of this present collection of essays, and one of the most frequently quoted subsequently, is the contribution by T. B. Pugh, another of McFarlane's 'retinue' and Ross's earlier collaborator in writing about baronial wealth (and therefore power).

In 1963, Pugh had demonstrated the importance of certain of the Welsh marcher lords and lordships in English political life in the fifteenth century; this and the increased attention currently paid (not least in the University of Wales) to the relationship between Wales and the English state in matters of politics, government and society between the rebellion of Owain Glyndŵr and Henry VIII's Acts of Union suggested that 'Wales and the Marches' should feature in any colloquium to discuss fifteenth-century scholarship. For comparable reasons, the critical importance of the Scottish borderland and of the rival families of Percy and Neville in northern England during the fifteenth century dictated the inclusion of the essay by R. L. Storey, whose studies of the palatinate of Durham and its bishops and of judicial indictments of lawlessness in the north had been partly influenced by McFarlane. These provincial studies have helped to point later scholars towards the fruitful investigation of county (though less so of regional) affairs in the fifteenth century.

Sadly, S. B. Chrimes died in 1984. B. P. Wolffe died in 1988: his *The Royal Demesne in English History* (1971), which was dedicated to the memory of K. B. McFarlane, is a study of the king as landowner and, especially for the fifteenth century, as patron of the entire realm; and his *Henry VI* (1981) adopted a challenging view of the king which is prefigured in this collection. C. D. Ross died in

1986 – five years after the publication of his *Richard III* (1983), which was conceived on broadly similar lines to his *Edward IV*, concentrating 'on the problems of how to gain, and even more on how to keep power in late-medieval England, and on the inevitable centre of these operations, his use of patronage – the main weapon in the armoury of a medieval king'. In both of Ross's books, the 'governance of the realm', as Chrimes understood it, its ideas and realities, was prominent.

T. B. Pugh has continued to advance fifteenth-century scholarship by studies of the nobility and gentry of England and, thereby, of kingship and governance, most notably in *Henry V and the Southampton Plot of 1415* (1988). This is much more than a detailed analysis of an unsuccessful conspiracy, and it ends with a chapter on 'The Place of Henry V in English History' which offers a trenchant alternative to the verdict on the king delivered by McFarlane and his followers. Similarly, his 'Henry VII and the English Nobility' (in *The Tudor Nobility*, ed. G. W. Bernard, 1992), raises the reputation of Henry Tudor as king further than Chrimes had allowed, though ending with the somewhat cautious judgement that 'if ever there was a "New Monarchy" in England, it began and ended with Henry VII'. A. L. Brown's *The Governance of Later Medieval England, 1272–1461* (1989), seeks to explain how the king's government worked 'within a framework of description of institutions', but without forgetting that 'late medieval social structure . . . is integral with its government'. Brown's *Henry IV* is nearing completion; meanwhile, the first essay in this collection is concerned with 'The distribution of political power' after 1399 and with the new 'establishment' on which Henry IV relied. As for Wales and the Marches, R. A. Griffiths (himself a pupil of Margaret Sharp and C.D. Ross) has since sought to enlarge our knowledge of the modes and methods of royal government in the principality of Wales during the later Middle Ages, its impact on local society and the working of the relationship with Westminster and the crown (especially in *The Principality of Wales in the Later Middle Ages*, vol. I: *South Wales, 1277–1536* [1972], and *Sir Rhys ap Thomas and his Family: A Study in the Wars of the Roses and Early Tudor Politics* [1993]). His *The Reign of King Henry VI* (1981) is a study of 'The Exercise of Royal Authority' and, to a degree, offers an alternative view of the unfortunate monarch and his impact on his realm to that of B. P. Wolffe. R. L. Storey, in recent years, has shifted his attention from political society in the fifteenth century to ecclesiastical and educational developments in the later Middle Ages more broadly.

This pioneering collection of essays retains its value: it offers a foretaste of the larger studies of English kingship between Henry IV's usurpation in 1399 and Henry VII's death in 1509, and an introduction to English political society and the important links between the centre, the provinces and Wales. As individual essays and as a collection, the book also provides a framework for the dozen or more subsequent collections of essays on the fifteenth century published by Alan Sutton Publishing Ltd, which in 1995 inaugurated 'The Fifteenth Century Series' as a tribute to the continuing vitality of scholarly study of this most fascinating age.

University of Wales, Swansea   R.A.G.
August 1995

Abbreviations

B.I.H.R.	*Bulletin of the Institute of Historical Research*
B.M.	British Museum
C.C.R.	*Calendar of Close Rolls, 1399–1509* (H.M.S.O., 1927–63).
C.M.H.	*Cambridge Medieval History*
C.P.	G. E. Cockayne, *The Complete Peerage* (new edition, ed. V. H. Gibbs and others, thirteen volumes, 1910–59).
C.P.R.	*Calendar of Patent Rolls, 1399–1509* (H.M.S.O., 1903–16).
D.N.B.	*Dictionary of National Biography*
Ec.H.R.	*Economic History Review*
E.H.R.	*English Historical Review*
H.J.	*Historical Journal*
N.L.W.	National Library of Wales
Proc. Brit. Acad.	*Proceedings of the British Academy*
P.O.P.C.	*Proceedings and Ordinances of the Privy Council of England*, ed. N. H. Nicolas (Record Commission, six volumes, 1834–37).
P.R.O.	Public Record Office
R.P.	*Rotuli Parliamentorum* (Record Commission, six volumes, 1783).
S.R.	*Statutes of the Realm* (Record Commission, 1810–28).

A. L. Brown

Senior Lecturer in History
University of Glasgow

I   The reign of Henry IV[1]

The establishment of the Lancastrian regime

In September 1399 Richard II was deposed and Henry of Lancaster
became king. It had come about with remarkable speed. Richard
was caught unawares and out of England, and his regime quickly
collapsed with virtually no bloodshed. Henry, though he had been
heir to the greatest magnate in England, can have had serious hopes
of becoming king for only a matter of months. The distribution of
political power after the revolution is, therefore, potentially a particularly interesting one to investigate. Richard was accused of arbitrary and oppressive behaviour, and these charges had substance.[2]
He had obviously not governed unaided; who, then, suffered in
terms of office and influence as a result of the revolution? Where
and how did King Henry find support and assistance to retain the
throne? Who were the new men of influence, and which offices
were singled out for change? In short, who were the members of
the new 'establishment'? These are indeed complicated and difficult
questions which call for a number of specialised pieces of research
to evaluate properly the very many facts and figures that it is easy
to collect. I approach them primarily as an historian interested in
central government, in terms of attendance at councils and courts,
of office-holding and gifts made, and by using the records of the
central government. My conclusions are neither surprising nor
clear-cut, but a survey of the evidence is worth making because it
does underline some important features of contemporary society
and Lancastrian politics in the first half of Henry's reign.

Most of the sources used—the Chancery and Exchequer rolls, the
Council records[3] and Exchequer accounts—require no explanation,
but a word of justification is necessary for using the witness lists to
royal charters. These normally contain a dozen or more names and

in bulk they seem to me to be a useful indication of who was about the court and of 'the establishment'. Individually they are too problematical to be useful; the date may be fictitious and it is easy to show that some names are included automatically and that some witnesses could not have been present on a given date. On the other hand, the lists vary considerably; they are not stereotyped and, in general, absences from court and changes in political circumstances are reflected. To take a very simple example: the earl of Northumberland witnessed every Henry IV charter save one down to the 1403 rebellion, and then dropped out entirely until November 1404. Not to labour the point here, may I say simply that, having examined the lists of over half a century, it seems to me that with caution they can be used in this general way to show who was considered important enough by virtue of his status or his relationship with the king to be included as a witness.

Let me begin with the dukes and earls. They were individually the most powerful of the king's subjects and they were given a special pre-eminence by contemporaries. They were the prime politicians of the time, and the dukes and earls closest to Richard were the most obvious sufferers in 1399. We can conveniently identify these as the eight appellants of 1397. When Henry IV became king, two were dead: Thomas Mowbray, duke of Norfolk, had died in exile at Venice, and William Scrope, earl of Wiltshire, had been executed while resisting Henry's invasion. Wiltshire had no children and the earldom given to him in 1397 was annulled, but his father, Richard Scrope of Bolton, and his brother were unharmed. The dukedom of Norfolk, another 1397 creation, was also annulled, but £1,000 was paid for Mowbray's last expenses in Venice, and his son, a minor, was given maintenance and recognised as heir to his father's two earldoms. In fact, he joined the northern rising of 1405 before he came of age and was executed, but his younger brother succeeded to the titles in 1413. The six remaining appellants —the Holland dukes of Exeter and Surrey, the duke of Albemarle, the marquis of Somerset, and the earls of Salisbury and Gloucester —were, however, alive and their past could scarcely be ignored. As the Commons, no doubt 'inspired' to do so, said in 1399, it could not be believed that Richard 'poast avoir fait les ditz mesfaitz sanz counseill dascuns qui furent entour sa persone', and the six were made to answer.[4] Each in turn claimed, some with circumstantial detail, that he was an unwilling partner to the crimes alleged against Richard, the charges and seizures of property from which each had benefited. The farrago of exculpation they produced was accepted, and Henry himself later came forward with the remarkable conclusion that Wiltshire and the two knights, Bussy and Green, who had been executed at Bristol in July and were the only prominent victims of the usurpation, were 'coupablez de toute le male qavoit venuz au roialme'![5] The six lost the new titles with which Richard had rewarded them in 1397 and the grants they had received since the arrest of the duke of Gloucester in 1397, and they were forbidden to give liveries or retain men other than their officials,[6] or to adhere further to King Richard, under pain of treason. But this was a modest punishment, and the reasons are not difficult to imagine. The usurpation had been almost bloodless; Richard's friends had, by and large, not been put to the test of fighting for him; and the lords clearly wanted as little talk of treason as possible. This is, however, in contrast to the savage sentence imposed at the same time on John Hall, valet, who confessed to being an unwilling accessory to the death of the duke of Gloucester.

In practice, of course, the appellants lost heavily in power and influence. They lost the confiscated lands Richard had given them; they lost the concentration of great offices, such as those of chamberlain, constable, and marshal of England, chamberlain of the Household, and military commands in Ireland, the Scottish March, Chester and Wales, Calais, the Cinque Ports, and the Tower, which they had been given; they were swept from all the commissions of the peace into which they had been intruded on a large scale since 1397. Circumstances were clearly very different for them. Salisbury, for example, could not resist a claim by his aunt, the last earl's widow, to be restored to lands in Cheshire and Shropshire which he had seized from her by King Richard's favour, and was obliged to deliver some of his lands to her. In all kinds of ways they must have found themselves at a disadvantage.[7] From the first a distinction seems to have been drawn between the more and the less culpable. The two Hollands—Kent and Huntingdon—Salisbury, and Despenser, if we can accept the evidence of the Chancery rolls, were mollified least. They received scarcely any crumbs in October and November 1399; they were, of course, still under examination, and it was only in December, when they were actually already planning a revolt, that they can be seen to be receiving any favour. Kent then had confirmation of an annuity of 200 marks and a grant of wine given by Richard; he and Huntingdon witnessed two charters dated 10 December; and Huntingdon and Despenser were at a Council meeting on 4 December.[8] These are small things but they are indications that they could have come to terms with King Henry. As we shall see, Henry might have been glad to do so.

In fact, these four rebelled in January 1400, and it is easy enough to understand why. They were probably fearful of what might yet be done to them, and they hoped to recover their position by restoring Richard, for whom they no doubt felt affection. But the rebellion itself lacked strength and organisation.[9] It depended entirely on initial success in surprising King Henry. The leading rebels were these four appellants, Bishop Merks, who had stood up for Richard in Parliament, a few clerks who had been close to Richard, a few knights—most prominently Ralph, Lord Lumley, Thomas Blount and Benedict Sely—and a few hundred lesser men, most of them attached to the leaders or pulled into the rising. The earl of Kent, for example, led his own retainers and apparently press-ganged some of the tenants of his manor of Woking to ride with him. A number of Huntingdon's officers and tenants in Devon raised men or made warlike threats, but not until some days after the main rising had collapsed and probably, as in Chester, because they had been raised by messengers sent out only at the beginning of the rebellion. Militarily it was a small rising, and as so often in the later Middle Ages it is difficult to understand why men took part in so doubtful a venture. Take the knights, for example. Andrew Hake of Gloucestershire had perhaps a motive in that Richard had been generous to him with grants in his last years, and, with no great stake in the county, he had relied on the favour of the king and William Bagot.[10] He certainly had not yet had his grants confirmed by Henry IV. But the same could not be said of Thomas Blount or Bernard Brocas, junior, or Benedict Sely, and particularly not of Ralph, Lord Lumley, the most substantial of the group. Blount had been a Chamber knight in the early '90s but he had not been prominent in the later years. Sely had been a fee'd retainer, a king's knight and marshal of his Household, as well as having a connection with Huntingdon. Brocas was a younger man, the son of one of Richard's retainers. Lumley was a substantial Yorkshire baron apparently with no strong court connections. All were men of substance who had not noticeably suffered under King Henry.

Grants had been confirmed to them; Lumley remained on the commission of the peace and had been appointed a commissioner of array a few weeks before the rebellion. None had any obvious material motive for risking his life in such a venture. The leaders of the plot, the four appellants, these knights and several clerks, were executed, the accepted penalty for failing in a treasonable venture such as this, and so too were a small number of lesser people captured during the main rising. But there was little vindictiveness. The widows and children of the appellants were given back some of their possessions and had grants to maintain them, and their heirs succeeded to their titles and, in time, to much of their lands. This is perhaps not surprising in view of the connections of the noble ladies, one of them the king's sister, and fifteenth-century ideas about property, but there are similar examples lower down the social scale. For example, Bernard Brocas's widow received back all his goods, worth 300 marks, and a third of his lands only a month after the rising, and his son had a blanket grant of his lands eight months later.[11] Mr McNiven has shown that although the Chester rebels were at first to be excluded from the general pardon offered to all subjects, in practice all, even the most incorrigible, were pardoned, almost all of them within months of the rising. The same seems to be true of other areas. There are a good many pardons and restorations to men involved in the main rising, men such as Robert Cokerell of Henley-on-Thames, who rode out with Blount. His messuage, worth 12s a year, and his furnishings are listed in an inquisition of 18 January, but he had a pardon dated 10 February and a grant of his lands and goods on the 11th.[12] William Yarde, a Cornish squire, a servant and retainer of the earl of Huntingdon, and presumably a relative of John Yarde, another of Huntingdon's esquires who was accused of actively promoting a rising, not only obtained a protection from the charges made against him and a pardon, but soon had a grant of land from the king and within twelve months was a king's esquire with an annuity.[13] At Oxford the overwhelming majority of the accused were merely imprisoned and told to have their friends seek a pardon for them from the king.[14] Most did, and the same magnanimity seems to have been shown to others who asked for it. There is the well-known moderation shown to Roger Walden, the former archbishop of Canterbury, and to the former bishop of Carlisle. There is Nicholas Slake, dean of Richard's chapel, who was arrested by the appellants in 1388, again in 1399, and yet again during the January plot in 1400, but was soon King Henry's clerk and receiving grants. And, to anticipate a remark about the Council, even Sir William Bagot, one of the supposed villains of Richard's regime, made his peace and had advances of money against an annuity as early as December 1399, and the annuity itself in 1400, while the family of his fellow councillor Henry Green had several grants. These are examples from the records, and the chronicles too have stories of Henry's moderation. It is difficult to know how much this was due to weakness or policy, but, as we shall see, it was so common that I cannot but believe that it stems also from a genuine magnanimity. Indeed, some of Henry's troubles arose because he was too generous and careless.

The two remaining appellants, Rutland and Somerset, successfully made their peace. Rutland, York's son, had been close to Richard, but he had a claim to forgiveness because he had deserted and because his father was the senior magnate in the realm. Rutland lost his important offices and his gains in confiscated lands, but he soon had significant grants confirmed, and he also was at the Council and acted as a charter witness in December 1399. Even if we discount the story that he revealed the secret of the earls' plot in January 1400, he remained loyal. He joined the Scottish expedition later that year, and he held a series of commands in Wales and Gascony beginning in August 1400. He took part in public occasions, but he seems not to have been trusted. Though he succeeded to the dukedom of York in 1402, he was only occasionally a charter witness or present at the Council before 1406, and he was indeed imprisoned in 1405 for dabbling in a Mortimer plot. He had more influence with Prince Henry than with the king. Somerset, the other appellant, was the king's half-brother. Family connection had not, however, led him to oppose the seizure of the Lancaster property, and even in July 1399 he had taken £200 from the treasurer to raise 300 men to resist Henry's invasion.[15] According to the *Traison* chronicle, the Percies wished him to be executed, but Henry produced a letter which Somerset had written to him in exile to show his secret goodwill.[16] Given the double-dealing of Richard's last years, it is not an impossible story, and Somerset was probably 'on probation' at first. In November 1399 he was appointed chamberlain during pleasure, then in February 1400 for life, presumably because he had shown his loyalty during the earl's plot. He came to be an almost invariable charter witness. This is less significant because he was an official, but petitions signed by him as chamberlain show that he was indeed often at court; he attended the Council occasionally; he served on diplomatic and family missions, such as the return of Queen Isabella; and he held active commands in Calais and Wales until his death in 1410. Large gifts, including some of Huntingdon's property, were made to him, and it seems justifiable to say that he became the magnate closest to the king. Particularly striking is the annuity of 1,000 marks given in November 1401 to Somerset's infant son, Henry, and his heirs male by the king, his godfather. Three years later it was replaced by a £1,000 annuity to Somerset himself and his heirs male to maintain his estate.[17] This indicates a very high degree of favour, and may well have been an irritation to the Percies.

It is a curious irony and an indication of how few there were of the higher nobility to whom Henry could turn in these early years that when the Council was appointed on two occasions in Parliament, in 1404 and again in 1406, only these two appellants and Westmorland, who was not prepared to be an active member, could be found to serve.[18] The king's own sons were still young; the heirs of Huntingdon, Kent, March, Norfolk and Salisbury were minors. York and Warwick had been shown to be weak vessels and while their seniority was recognised, say as charter roll witnesses, they were given little responsibility, and both were dead by 1402. Devon was probably already blind and did not come to Parliaments and Councils. Oxford showed interest only in the recovery of the chamberlainship and died in 1400. Suffolk, whose restoration to his earldom was renewed in 1399 in recognition of his services to Henry since his return, came to Parliaments and Councils but, presumably by his own choice, played little part in national politics: he never witnessed a royal charter nor came to the Council, and he never held a major office. Arundel and Stafford were young men, Arundel still a minor, though he took part in the Parliament of 1399. They could fight, and Stafford was killed at the battle of Shrewsbury, but their use was limited. It was a depleted nobility and Henry did not make new creations, in part probably because Richard's lavish creations were remembered with offence. It is not surprising, therefore, that King Henry relied heavily on the Percies, on Westmorland and on Somerset. Considering the offices and commands taken from the appellants and listed above (p. 3), in 1399 Northumberland became constable and keeper of the West March; his brother; Worcester, remained admiral; and his son, Hotspur, remained keeper of the East March and became constable of Chester and justiciar of north Wales. Westmorland became marshal and Somerset chamberlain. The chamberlainship of the Household and the commands in Ireland, Calais, the Cinque Ports, and the Tower went to trusted knights, a feature I shall return to later.

There is no doubt that though other noblemen sometimes came to court, the men of greatest influence were Westmorland, Somerset and the Percies, though each in a different way. Somerset, as we have seen, was much at court and became intimate with the king. Westmorland, in contrast, does not seem to have been much of a courtier. He was powerful; for example, he came on the Scottish expedition of 1400 with 200 men-at-arms and 1,000 archers. He was one of Henry's first supporters in 1399, but he does not have a prominent part in accounts of the usurpation. He was appointed marshal with the special privilege of carrying a gold rod; in the early years he was almost invariably a charter witness, which he had never been before;[19] he came to the Council and no doubt to court, but far from regularly and it is striking how infrequently he came after the first Percy rebellion in 1403. He was then content to be a great north-country nobleman, warden of the West March and regularly a negotiator with the Scots, coming to Westminster only on special occasions such as Parliaments. This can be seen as merely a decision to concentrate on the affairs of the north, but it is more likely that he was about the court and the council between 1399 and 1403 to safeguard his own interests against the Percies.

It is, of course, the Percies who were of first importance in the early years. In April 1402, for example, the king's marriage contract was witnessed only by Henry Bowet, bishop of Bath and Wells, Somerset, and three Percies, the earl of Northumberland, his brother, the earl of Worcester, and his son, Hotspur, among the lords.[20] Northumberland had been Henry's principal supporter and confidant during the usurpation, and this probably continued in the early years, though it is impossible to describe their relationship in personal terms or to say precisely when or why it broke down.[21] Northumberland was present at most public occasions we know about; he was a regular charter witness; and it is significant that he reported the king's wishes about letters to the chancellor on at least nine occasions.[22] At some periods he came often to the

Council, though his own interests and royal service obliged him to be on the Scottish March for part of each year. He was obviously a man of great influence, well rewarded, and at court a good deal, but it is impossible to be more specific. Hotspur's contribution was mainly military, in north Wales and in Scotland; he was little at the Council and he was never a charter witness, presumably because he lacked status.

The Percy who was most widely useful, and has perhaps been least recognised, is Northumberland's brother, Thomas, earl of Worcester. In 1399 Worcester was a man in his late fifties with a great deal of experience. He had been a commander in France in Edward III's reign and on various campaigns since; he had been successively chamberlain and steward of the Household since 1390; he had been an ambassador and much else. He had not been an appellant in 1397 but he had been proctor for the clergy, and he had been rewarded with a large block of confiscated lands and an earldom. In 1399 he had been with Richard in Ireland, came home with him, and then deserted. But all this was forgotten, no doubt because he was a Percy and because he had Lancastrian connections, for example, as one of Gaunt's retainers and an executor of Gaunt's will. He retained his earldom and the office of admiral, though he ceased to be steward of the Household; he was appointed to further commissions of the peace, and favour was shown to him at once. On 7 November he had eleven patents confirmed and on 13 December received a remarkable annuity of 500 marks in compensation for the Gloucester and Arundel lands he had been obliged to restore.[23] He at once began to serve King Henry. He commanded a fleet of six barges sent to resist the king's enemies in late 1399 and early 1400, though he may not have gone to sea himself.[24] Within a fortnight of the accession he was designated to begin negotiations with France for recognition and for a marriage or truce; he set out on 16 December and was abroad on this mission in the first months of 1400 and again in the early summer.[25] Between embassies he was active at the Council and, according to one of the French envoys, was the leading councillor who dealt with them when they came to see Queen Isabella in October 1400.[26] In the autumn and winter of 1400–01 he was frequently at the Council; in November he was sent on another mission to negotiate with the French; he is mentioned as present at the opening of Parliament in January 1401 and he delivered an answer from the king to the Commons; one of the changes which took place in March in response to criticism of the king's government was his reappointment as steward of the House-hold. Dr Rogers has elucidated this parliamentary 'crisis' and stressed the importance of Worcester, though I would not go so far as to see his appointment as a victory for a faction over an anti-magnate policy.[27] Worcester was already extremely active in Henry's administration, and his appointment seems more likely to have been another indication of the king's intention to provide better government. After the Parliament Worcester's service continued on the old pattern. In April he was again appointed to negotiate with the French; he attended the Council in June; and in late June, July and early August he was engaged in taking Queen Isabella back to France. At this point the nature of his work changed completely. In September–October he probably went with the king on an expe-dition against Glyndŵr because on 21 October he entered into an indenture as lieutenant in south Wales in place of Hugh Despenser, who had just died, and he became master to Prince Henry.[28] He was back at the Council in February–March 1402 and he witnessed the king's contract of marriage on 3 April, but he is known to have attended only one Council meeting for the remainder of the year. Presumably, he now spent most of his time in south Wales and the March; most references are to his service there, and this may explain why he ceased to be steward in June. In December, however, his courtier talents were again used when he went with Somerset to Brittany to bring Queen Joan to England, and he then attended Council meetings until March. He was then certainly in Wales with the prince until immediately before the Percy rebellion in July 1403.[29]

I have described Worcester's career in these years in some detail because he is the least recognised of the Percies. If the family had a grievance against Henry, then Worcester must have felt it keenly because he had served him so consistently. He was probably the most intelligent of the Percies, and it makes one wonder whether his share in the rising of 1403 was greater than has been recognised. It certainly makes it more puzzling.[30] As in the case of his brother and nephew, however, one cannot point to anything in his relations with the king which explains his rebellion. He was not always paid his dues at once and he had some bad tallies, though my impression is that in this respect he was comparatively well-off. He was certainly less at court after the autumn of 1401, but there is no solid evidence that he was less in favour. It is possible that he found his command in Wales a disappointment. He may have been jealous of Somerset, though it is worth noting that the latter had probably more financial grievances than Worcester.[31] One can only say the same of Worcester as of his brother, that he was now less close to the king than he had been, that he had general family grievances on which to dwell, but that he was apparently trusted by the king up to the time of his rebellion. It is important, however, not to be too 'courtier-conscious'. The king needed men like Worcester and Somerset to make his court and service honourable, but offices and missions are only one type of service. Somerset was an illegitimate son, Worcester a younger son, neither with a territorial patrimony to rule. In terms of power they bear no comparison with Northumberland and Westmorland.

It is clear, then, that the Lancastrian 'establishment' among the greater magnates was a particularly small one. There were comparatively few earls of full age in any case, and though a Parliament or Great Council might bring out six or eight, only four were on close terms with the king. The battle of Shrewsbury in August 1403 made Henry's need for the support of great men even more serious. Worcester and Stafford were dead; Northumberland could no longer be trusted and ceased to be a charter witness or a councillor for over a year; Westmorland was now mostly in the north. Only Somerset was really dependable and willing to serve at the Council and in office. York was called upon more, but he was justifiably suspect. Henry had difficulty, as the charter rolls show, in maintaining an honourable court, and the same is true of the Council. This phase lasted until the second half of the reign, when the king's sons and the new earls of Arundel, Kent and Warwick became of service.

In this situation the king could rely more on the barons, thirty-four of whom were summoned to the first Parliament. He did indeed do so, as councillors and charter witnesses, and presumably also as courtiers and confidants. But, though they varied considerably in wealth, they did not have the status of earls; they were not given the same responsibilities; and many were interested only in their own concerns. Professor Roskell has shown that during the reign seldom more than half of the lords temporal attended Parliaments, and the barons were more guilty of non-attendance than the earls.[32] For example, only fourteen or fifteen barons were present at either the Parliament or the two Great Councils in 1400–01. Equally significant, most barons attended Parliaments and Councils occasionally, but only a few were regularly present; only four— Roos, Willoughby, Burnell and Lovell—attended all these three assemblies in 1400–01. This evidence, the charter rolls and the various services performed show that only a small group of barons provided active members of the Lancastrian 'establishment'. The most interesting are Lords Roos and Willoughby. They are mentioned together so often that I feel they must have concerted their actions. Willoughby had been abroad with Henry in 1390–93 and may have been close to the king; this would account for his dismissal from the Council with Henry's knights in 1406. Both joined Henry in July 1399, played a part in the usurpation, and Willoughby had material rewards in the form of the custody of two of the earl marshal's manors even before Henry became king. Neither is prominent in the records of Richard's reign, but both now became common witnesses to royal charters until they died. They stand out from other barons in this, and it is significant in itself because men of their rank had rarely witnessed charters in Richard's reign unless they were office-holders. Both came to the Council occasionally and were nominated members in 1404 and 1406. Roos had a spell as treasurer in 1403–04, audited accounts, and had money to lend the king. Willoughby, with perhaps even greater financial acumen, married Edmund, duke of York's widow, Joan Holland, an heiress in her own right. Neither was a significant office-holder or military commander; they were useful because they were prepared to come about the court and the Council periodically, and—probably even more important—to promote the king's interests in their counties. For example, both came with large contingents on the Scottish expedition of 1400, raised men to resist the northern rebellion in 1405, served on the commission to investigate it, and performed miscellaneous tasks in their localities. Both were added to the commission of the peace in 1399 in all three parts of Lincoln—I suspect, to contain the influence of York and Surrey. In return for all this they had annuities, grants and custodies of lands, though not on a lavish scale. They were useful, trusted courtiers who had thrown in their lot with the king and who must have had influence with him.

The other baronial members of the 'establishment' had rather different careers. Richard Grey of Codnor had not been prominent in Richard's reign but at once begins to figure frequently in the records. He is an occasional charter witness and councillor; he was at once included in commissions of the peace in two counties and in 1401 in two more, though he had been on none before 1399, but it is as admiral, soldier and envoy that he is particularly important. He was at sea in 1400, admiral in 1401, on the Scottish expedition of 1400, and for long periods in Wales, where his service was specially commended by the Commons; he was an envoy, being one of the party who conducted Queen Isabella home; from 1404 until the end of the reign he was the king's chamberlain and much at court, and a member of the nominated Councils in 1406. He was a more substantial and, in contemporary eyes, a more honourable man than Roos or Willoughby, and more generously rewarded. Reginald Grey of Ruthin also joined Henry in 1399. He was quite often a charter witness in the first two years of the reign, which probably means that he came about the court; he served in Scotland in 1400 and then in Wales, but after his capture by the Welsh in 1402 and a 10,000 mark ransom he ceased to be important as a courtier. It is interesting that Roos, Willoughby and Richard Grey, with some others, were permitted to treat with Glyndŵr about Grey of Ruthin's ransom,[33] and there are other examples of the court group acting together. William Heron, Lord Say, is an unusual case. He held his title somewhat precariously in right of his wife, Elizabeth Say, who died in 1399. He is not often mentioned before the revolution, but then began a career—this seems the only word for it—as a diplomat on missions to France, as a councillor and envoy, and to a lesser extent as a commissioner hearing appeals.[34] He succeeded the earl of Worcester as steward of the Household in June 1402, but continued to be abroad on missions, and was replaced in January 1404, the year he died. Say was certainly a loyal Lancastrian after, though not before, 1399, but apparently as a special kind of administrator who received few obvious rewards for being so.

The only other baron who is prominent in these central records is Thomas Neville, Lord Furnival, the earl of Westmorland's brother. In the early years of the reign he was primarily a northern gentleman, who turns up in the records occasionally, for example as a commissioner of the peace, on the March, and being commissioned to take possession of Berwick, Alnwick and Warkworth after the 1403 rebellion. But in the first Parliament of 1404 he was nominated to the Council, where he had never served before; he

became treasurer in December and from the summer of 1404 he was
regularly at the Council until his death in 1407. It is tempting to see
his late-blossoming career as part of an arrangement with his brother
Westmorland, who retired markedly from the Westminster scene
at this time, to ensure a Neville on the March and another at
Westminster to safeguard the family's interests.

Roos, Willoughby, Richard Grey and later Furnival were the
barons most likely to be at court. No other gave anything like
consistent service outside his own locality, though half a dozen
had a special commitment to King Henry. The elderly Lord
Cobham had been able to return from exile in 1399 and was a
frequent charter witness during the first year of the reign, but, to
quote a patent to him in 1400, he was 'so old and feeble that he
cannot labour at his secular business and desires to conform to a
perfect conversation and to have leisure for divine services'.[35] Lords
Lovel and Berkeley did labour a good deal in their localities and came
to court and Council occasionally. Lovel probably enjoyed this, as
he had been doing the same for fifteen years; Berkeley served as
admiral and on several missions. The list can be extended a little,
but the conclusion is clear. Most barons, like most landed gentry,
could be expected to serve on local commissions and come out on
some campaigns—and I am obviously not doing justice to the service
of either earls or barons in the Welsh wars—but few held important offices or major commands or came frequently to court or
Council. Professor Roskell has noted their reluctance to come to
Parliament and I have noticed how few came about the Council.
The majority had probably no close relationship with the king.

The absence of a strong Lancastrian faction among the lords helps
to explain why King Henry relied so much on knights and esquires,
a number of whom he had known well before 1399. This argument
cannot be pressed too far because every king needed the service of
knights and esquires, but in the first half of Henry's reign some of
them were given unusually important offices, and there was a
current of criticism against them, sometimes that they were impover-
ishing the king, more often just that the king relied upon them too
much. There were probably several hundred who had a particular
relationship with the king, ranging from the men in daily personal
contact with him to men who rarely left their counties. One must
try to classify them into groups, but every group overlaps. We are
dealing with individuals who served the king in varying ways as

circumstances and their own inclinations and abilities admitted. The
more clear-cut the classification, probably the less accurate it is.

Some of these king's knights and esquires—more than fifty in the
first half of the reign—came often about the court, though we
know even less about their attendance than about that of the magnates. About thirty-five were strictly Household knights, designated
knights of the Hall and Chamber, or knights rewarded for attend-
ing the king.[36] These men are less prominent in the records than
their equivalents in Richard's reign because Henry made no attempt
to create a Household party or centre, except in the sense that any
honourable Household must have its retainers and organization.
It was not the character but the cost of the Household that was at
issue. The primary responsibility of these knights, some of them
Lancastrian retainers, some not, was presumably to attend the king
personally and fight for him if necessary. My impression is that
though we find references to fees and rewards given to them, some
to their military service and a few to their office-holding in the
counties, they were not much called upon for governmental purposes. Several of the knights of the Hall were old retainers, but the
majority were probably young men, not of the county 'establishment'.

The men I know better are the knights and esquires, seventeen or
so, who came about the court and were close to the king but served
him rather as councillors, officers and commanders.[37] I use membership of the Council as a standard for identifying the group, but this
is of course arbitrary, and there is no absolute division between
the two groups. Indeed, one—Sir John Pelham—falls into both, and
another—Sir John Tiptoft—was a Household knight at the beginning of the reign, then in 1406 treasurer of the Household and a
councillor, treasurer of England, a royal officer and commander,
and embarked on a career which led to membership of the minority
Council in 1422, a peerage and, for his son, an earldom. Yet there
is a meaningful division between the groups. Let me give two
examples of this second group. John Norbury, esquire, as Miss
Barber has shown, was a younger son with few resources who made
his career as a mercenary soldier, became a retainer of Henry and
was with him on his Prussian expedition in 1390–91.[38] He remained
a Lancastrian retainer with a fee; he was in exile with Henry, and
in 1399, even before Richard was deposed, he shot into prominence.
He was appointed treasurer, and later keeper of the Privy Wardrobe

and captain of Guines. Council attendances suggest that until he was replaced as treasurer in May 1401 he spent most of his time in or near Westminster, though he was in arms during the January plot of 1400 and perhaps during the Scottish expedition. From then on he was sometimes at the Council, probably more often than before with the king; he served on some diplomatic missions and on a few local commissions; he may well have served Queen Johanna, whom he had known before her marriage; and he lent the king large sums of money. In 1405 he was ordered by the king verbally to remain with him and not go to Guines, 'considering that his presence would be necessary for good counsel and advice on the king's actions touching the governance of Wales and otherwise'.[39] He was excluded from the Council with the other knights and esquires in 1406,[40] but he remained a friend of the king, who was godfather to Norbury's eldest son; in 1409 he witnessed the king's will. He was, however, less active in affairs of state and probably more of a substantial country gentleman in the estates he had built up in Hertfordshire.

Sir Thomas Erpingham was another Lancastrian fee'd retainer who had fought with Gaunt and with Henry in 1390 and 1392, shared the latter's exile and returned in 1399, and he was one of those who renounced allegiance to Richard at the Tower on 30 September. In August he had been appointed constable of Dover and warden of the Cinque Ports. He became chamberlain of the Household, and the chamberlain's bills which he signed show that he was a great deal at court in these early years. He attended the Council occasionally, so occasionally for a man of his prominence that it seems probable he did not like the work, and my impression is that he did little administrative work either. He was rather a soldier, who later distinguished himself on the Agincourt campaign, and a gentleman fit to be a governor of the king's children, a Household officer—he was steward in 1404 and again between 1413 and 1417, and an ambassador. He was close to the king, and in 1406 the Speaker, Sir John Tiptoft, commended him for the 'molt bone service' he had done to the king 'et plusours foitz sad mys en aventure pur lonur et profite du roy et du roialme'.[41]

These two men served Henry IV in different ways, and one can see variations between the careers of each of these men, but also certain things in common. All had military experience, most a good deal of experience; all were trusted by the king, came to court and were his councillors, and all were well rewarded. At least half were in Lancastrian service before 1399 and several had been in exile with Henry, but this very understandable feature is sometimes exaggerated, for others were men recruited only in 1399. Some, like Sir Peter Courtenay, who surrendered Bristol Castle to Henry and was at once appointed captain of Calais in August 1399, or Sir John Stanley, appointed lieutenant of Ireland, both of them servants of Richard II, served primarily as commanders. Sir Peter Buckton, a retainer of Henry for years and now his standard-bearer, was considered by the Kirkstall Chronicle to be a particularly loved confidant of the king, but he probably served more as an official in the duchy and in Yorkshire than as a councillor and courtier.[42] It is, however, the men at the other end of the scale about whom we hear most in the records, men like Norbury, John Curson of Kedleston in Derbyshire, John Doreward of Essex, or John Cheyne of Gloucestershire, the last two coming into Henry's service only in 1399. They were often at the Council; often at court, if we can judge by the few records we possess of decisions there; often sent between king and Council to explain items of business; sometimes (Cheyne quite often) on diplomatic missions; often on commissions to arrest, enquire, raise troops, in their own counties. Their services are miscellaneous. For example, in April 1402 Norbury, Cheyne, Doreward and Curson, with the earl of Northumberland, four bishops and three others, stood as recogniters for a £2,500 loan to the king.[43] Erpingham, Norbury and Curson, with Roos, Willoughby, Richard Grey and some others, sealed the agreement made at Pontefract between the king and the earl of Northumberland in July 1404.[44] Doreward was once paid because he had been 'sent on divers occasions to us and elsewhere in our realm by our Council on certain most weighty matters touching us and our Council'.[45] There is no doubt that, considering their rank, these men played an unusually large part in Henry IV's government, holding commands and offices that were normally held by their social superiors; they were confidants of the king, available in all kinds of ways to perform commissions, keep government working smoothly, and no doubt to uphold the king in their counties. It is worth recalling the list of offices held by the appellants cited earlier. In 1399 Erpingham succeeded the earl of Wiltshire as chamberlain of the Household, Stanley succeeded the earl of Kent as lieutenant in Ireland; Erpingham succeeded Somerset as constable of Dover and warden of the

Cinque Ports; Sir Thomas Rempston succeeded the earl of Rutland as constable of the Tower and Courtenay succeeded Huntingdon as captain of Calais. It is also of some significance that their successors in these offices, in turn, were Grey of Codnor, Prince Thomas, Prince Henry, the duke of York and the earl of Somerset respectively. There was a subsequent reaction against this eminence. They were never charged with crimes and they remained officers and friends of the king, but after 1406, and to some extent before, they lost appointments and ceased altogether to be councillors. This is significant of contemporary views of social propriety. Later in the fifteenth century, one feels, some of these respectable men might have been given peerages, and historians might now be crediting Henry with a policy of creating a new and counterbalancing nobility!

These fifty or so men who had a close relationship with the king were king's knights and esquires. There was also a much larger body of king's knights and esquires who did not come much to court. I have not gone through the sources systematically to find their names, but there were certainly over 200 men designated at least once in this way in the early years of the reign, many of them receiving annuities of between £10 and £100, and this is apart from those described as 'king's servants' or in other ways. At least fifty of these are specifically said to have been retained by the king for life, and behind this must lie a ceremony of some kind, perhaps even a formal document. Probably all the king's knights and esquires had taken part in some form of oath-swearing, and some or all may have been distinguished by a collar or device like the 'king's livery called "colere"' which was taken from the king's knight Walter Hungerford during the 1400 plot.[46] I must admit that I have merely sampled the very large amount of evidence about these men, who ranged from barons like Henry Fitzhugh to a burgess like John Cosyn of Cirencester, retained by November 1399 with a fee of £10 a year and who played a major part in capturing the earls of Kent and Salisbury, receiving a 100 mark annuity as his reward. My impression is that the primary service Henry expected from them must have been military. A number were appointed captains of castles; we know that some were specifically called out to help suppress risings like that of 1405; and they were summoned along with all the king's other fee'd men to come out armed in emergencies and for campaigns, and were supposed not to receive payment of their annuities unless they had come out, though only about one in

six is known to have served as a captain on the well documented
Scottish campaign in 1400.[47] The striking thing is, however, the
negative evidence that very few served as members of Parliament,
as justices of the peace or even as arrayers, and only a small number
as sheriffs. By and large the retainers were not men of the county
'establishment'. I do not think that any other fifteenth-century king
retained men with fees on this scale. Richard II had done so in the
last years of his reign, and I presume that Henry copied him for
reasons of security, particularly in the first months of his reign.
His father's practice of retaining on a large scale may also have
influenced him. Retaining falls off after that date, but it is an
indication of the respectability and acceptance of the practice that
one suggestion put forward at the time of the Great Council in
February 1400 to deal with disorders in the counties was to retain
'gentz plus suffissantz et de bone fame' with annuities, and there
was indeed a flurry of grants just at this time.[48] There is a large
subject for investigation here, primarily at the county level. Henry
invested a good deal of money in these men, and yet we know
comparatively little that is positive about them. Only in rare cases
were they Richard's retained knights and esquires, though one must
remark again that often Richard's men were employed in other
ways and had grants confirmed to them. A tremendous amount
of shuffling and lobbying must have taken place in the autumn of
1399 as this retinue was formed.

One special advantage Henry enjoyed must also be mentioned.
He was duke of Lancaster as well as king and he inherited the
Lancastrian retinue. This was a particularly large body, which had
a personal loyalty to him and came out the more readily to fight.
It is no exaggeration to say that they were the hard core of his
following, which enabled him to hold on to the throne.[49]

Henry's retaining on a large scale is allied to his liberality—
indeed, extravagance—with pensions and gifts. Sir Robert Somerville and Mr Pronay have shown this in connection with the duchy
and the Hanaper, and the patent rolls show it dramatically.[50] The
rolls for the first year of the reign are approximately twice as bulky
as those of the next largest, the first year of Edward IV. The index
of Warrants for Issues lists 242 pensioners in the Exchequer alone,
as against thirty-one in Henry V's and twenty-seven in Edward
IV's reigns.[51] In 1401 it was estimated that annuities in cash—
that is, apart from grants of land—amounted to £24,000 a year,[52]

and to this must be added another £8,000 or so paid out of the duchy, another indication of its importance.[53] It is, of course, understandable that Henry was generous to his supporters and that he should find it difficult to refuse to confirm Richard's grants. My impression is that about half the grants of Richard's last two years were confirmed, and the great majority of those before. Sometimes they were even increased. But, although this is understandable, the scale of the generosity, the status of the recipients, and the results—in terms, for example, of the Scottish expedition of 1400—suggest that it was not a prudent policy of building up support but rather a combination of necessity, insecurity, generosity and extravagance. It was particularly questionable because Henry had made sweeping promises about good management at his accession. It certainly helps to explain the king's financial worries and why his liberality was frequently a subject of complaint in Parliament.

Two obvious groups remain which I must mention very briefly. First, there are Henry's supporters among the churchmen. He employed a great many, but in this respect also he was at a disadvantage in the early years. To take only the episcopate: Archbishop Arundel, his fellow exile, was apparently close to the king throughout, but until 1406 he was apparently not much at Westminster; he was an automatic charter witness but he did not come often to the Council, and although we know he was consulted a good deal by letter and messenger he seems to have preferred to devote his time primarily to his duties as archbishop.[54] Henry Beaufort, the king's half-brother, was a frequent charter witness from the beginning of the reign and no doubt came to court, but he began to attend the Council only in 1402, and his long governmental career really begins in 1403, when he became chancellor. Skirlaw of Durham, an older man, was the only active episcopal diplomat and councillor at first, and he drops out of affairs after 1401. It was difficult at this time to find bishops to come to the Council, and the other principal charter witnesses were three men of an older generation, Braybrook, Wykeham and Fordham, who were probably not much at court, and Richard's last chancellor, Edmund Stafford. None of these men formed a close relationship with Henry, and it was some years before the new generation of Lancastrian bishops—men like Bowet, Langley and Bubwith—came to the fore. This gap may help to explain the unexplained confidence shown from 1399 in the dean of Hereford, John Prophete, a man with no known prior Lancastrian connection, and the employment of John Scarle, a loyal but relatively insignificant man, as chancellor in 1399.

I must be equally brief with the cognate subject of the professional officers, most of whom were unaffected by the usurpation. The judges and most of the officers and clerks in Chancery, the Exchequer, and the Privy Seal can be seen to have remained in office. The acting clerk of the Council carried on too, perhaps even the secretary, and—surprisingly— Richard Clifford, keeper of the privy seal and an ex-officer of the Household, remained in office with the express commendation of the Commons. The chancellor, Edmund Stafford, bishop of Exeter, was replaced early in the usurpation, but he continued to attend the Council intermittently, was often a charter witness, and was reappointed chancellor in 1401. More surprisingly, the serjeants-at-arms, who had to execute very directly some of Richard's decisions, were almost all retained, though new men were added. There were changes—some probably normal wastage, some certainly brought about by the revolution, though significantly in the less professional offices, such as the minor offices in the courts. In the Common Pleas, for example, the keeper of writs and the chirographer were replaced. William Pountfrett, king's clerk and an old servant of Henry's, apparently took advantage of the accession to ask immediately for the former office, though one of Richard's clerks, Robert Manfeld, had it for life. Almost ten years later Manfeld, who had not been victimized and had his benefices confirmed, recovered the office on the ground that the king had acted in ignorance.[55] This seems simply to be a case of sharp practice, though the long delay in exposing it suggests that a story lies behind it. The office of chirographer, which was a sinecure and could be performed by deputy, was given to Sir Peter Buckton, one of Henry's knights, in place of Henry Godard, esquire, an esquire of Richard's Chamber and retained by him for life. This was clearly another case of spoils of victory, though it is typical that Godard had his old £40 annuity confirmed in 1401.[56] My impression from this and other usurpations in the fifteenth century is that service in the Westminster courts and offices was considered a professional career, not a personal service to the king, and therefore in most cases above politics.

This point is reinforced by the experience of Richard's councillors. Three active councillors, Wiltshire, Bussy and Green, were executed during the usurpation, but none was brought to trial. It is signifi-

cant, however, that while officers who were councillors, such as
Stafford and Clifford, and the master of the rolls, Thomas Stanley,[57]
were accepted by Henry and became his councillors and officers, the
other regular attenders, who were rather administratively minded
retainers, were excluded.[58] The third of the infamous trio, Sir
William Bagot, a councillor, though not an active one,[59] made his
peace but lost his offices and grants. By December 1399, however,
he began to be given advances of money against his annuity, and
was given a £100 annuity in November 1400 until the king provided
for his estate. This delay was probably a test of his loyalty, and by
1402 he was even able to oppose Sir Thomas Rempston, a friend of
the king,[60] though he was never an officer or a man of power again.
Sir John Russell, an elderly man, who had been ill-advised to
receive portions of the earl of Warwick's lands, lost heavily, though
he remained on the commission of the peace in Worcestershire.
This was the same 'decent obscurity' enjoyed by his fellow councillor, Sir Richard Waldegrave.[61] Laurence Dru, esquire, also lost
his annuities as a retainer and councillor, but remained active as a
commissioner in his county and was sufficiently favoured by May
1400 to recover the custody of some land which the king's esquire
Richard Clopton had snatched from him in October 1399.[62] Dr
Ralph Selby had become a monk at Westminster in 1398, but he
perhaps lost an archdeaconry and several benefices he had hoped
to retain, and he apparently indulged his dislike of the usurpation,
because as late as 1409 he was suspected of treasonable correspondence.[63] All these men lost the offices and many of the rewards
they had gained under Richard, and none ever sat on the Council
again. But this was the extent of their downfall, and in most cases
some favour or confidence was shown to them.

The Household was a different case. Many of the lesser servants
stayed on, but all the major officers, steward, treasurer, controller,
and cofferer of the Wardrobe, the receiver of the Chamber, and the
keepers of the Great and the Privy Wardrobes, were replaced—
significantly, by Lancastrians, often men who had served in Gaunt's
or Henry's own households. The reason was no doubt partly
personal and partly political; it was pleasanter and safer in the
delicate circumstances after a usurpation to be surrounded by men
you knew and could trust, and Henry had an obligation to his own
servants. On the other hand, none of Richard's Household was put
on trial. John Stanley, the ex-controller, who had been concerned

with the military side of the Household and the raising of the Cheshire guard, made his peace straight away (probably because he had earlier been a Lancastrian retainer), was soon sent to Ireland as lieutenant, and prospered under Henry. Some, such as John Lowicke, esquire, receiver of the Chamber and keeper of the Privy Wardrobe, or John Macclesfield, clerk, keeper of the Great Wardrobe, retired to obscurity; while others, such as Sir Thomas Brounflete and Thomas More, clerk, made new careers in Henry's service after a couple of years' interval. But this is a field in which we must await Dr Rogers's work.

The political structure of England, of course, depended ultimately on the acceptance and stability of the counties, but this is too vast a theme to consider here. One can readily see the influence of events on county office-holding: for example, the exclusion of the appellants and some of Richard's retainers from the commissions of the peace and the addition of some of Henry's friends in 1399, or the changes in the Devon commission in 1400. But my impression is that this was marginal. Probably the same willing minority of J.P.s continued to do most of the work. Care must have been taken in considering the appointment of sheriffs, commissioners and the like, but crude judgements on this matter are useless. Certainly few of Henry's retainers were appointed, and many of the names are familiar from Richard's reign. The county 'establishment' was almost a law unto itself and difficult to control from Westminster, and this was probably particularly true at this time when the king could rely on few magnates.[64]

What conclusions, then, emerge from this admittedly very general survey? First, though the notorious seizures of property in the previous two years were reversed, there were no widespread dispossessions in 1399. Most civil servants and officials retained their posts, but most of Richard's retainers (using that term in its widest sense)—his earls, councillors, knights, esquires and leading Household officers—were dispensed with, though not victimised. They ceased to be retainers, lost their commands, and saw some of their perquisites transferred to new men, but Henry in general seems to have been generous in confirming grants. No doubt he and his advisers weighed up this problem and one cannot now make a fair assessment of the state of feeling of Richard's supporters, but my impression is that his generosity was too indiscriminate and liberal. The same is true of new grants. Henry himself seems to have been open-handed,[65] and the right balance was not struck between the generosity necessary at a usurpation and the need for the sound, economical government which Henry had promised to provide. One must compare him with Edward IV and Henry VII in this respect, and the comparison is unfavourable. My impression is that he came to the throne an honourable, chivalrous man with old-fashioned ideas and ideals—as witnessed, for example, by his Scottish policy—but that these were not enough for the problems he met.

It is, however, fair to say that in the early years the Lancastrian 'establishment' was decidedly thin among the men who mattered most—the earls, barons and bishops—and this to a large extent for reasons beyond Henry's control. His position was precarious, and this helps to explain his reliance on the Percies (and perhaps even their self-importance), on his knights and esquires, and on the duchy. It may be objected that he did singularly well against rebels. The answer is, I think, that he was fortunate in the circumstances of his own rebellion in 1399 and that he really had to *fight* English rebels only once. That was in 1403, and then he was fortunate as well as decisive. He was in the centre of his support, the duchy, when the rising began, he moved quickly, and he won his only battle, at Shrewsbury, before Northumberland arrived; even so, the issue was finely balanced and could easily have gone the other way.

As far as events in Parliament are concerned, the evidence seems to support a straightforward interpretation, an acceptance of criticisms at their face value. The king's generosity certainly contributed to his financial troubles, and the frequent demands that it must be curbed, culminating in 1406, were amply justified. The criticisms in the Parliaments of 1401, 1404 and 1406 were directed against the king's failures in general, in Wales, on the seas, and against his financial incompetence in particular. The demands were for better government, 'good and abundant governance', rather than for the advancement of any group. The complaint was that the king's administration was not substantial enough and that this brought about weak government. This seems to me to be the best explanation of the change of Household officers and the chancellor and treasurer in 1401, and of the repeated demands for a more substantial Council, culminating in the exclusion of the knights and esquires in 1406. This may appear too administratively-minded a conclusion, but it best explains the absence of scandals or indictments, the fact that the Speakers in 1401 and 1406 were retainers of the king, and the almost complete absence of 'new' men. New men—Henry Beaufort, for example, the king's sons, and some younger magnates—gradually appear on the scene, but it is not until 1406 that a major political upheaval takes place and Prince Henry and a few others agree to try to give stronger government. Even so, factions become important only a few years later. But that is another story altogether.

Notes

1 This paper was prepared as one contribution to the theme of the conference, and it retains its original discursive form, barely touching some issues. I am grateful to members of the conference for their comments, which have improved the paper in many ways.

2 Caroline M. Barron, 'The tyranny of Richard II', *B.I.H.R.*, xli (1968), 1–18.

3 These are discussed in my essay *The Early History of the Clerkship of the Council* (1969).

4 *R.P.*, iii, 449.

5 *Ibid.*, 453.

6 The importance of liveries and cognisances at this period is shown by the severe limitations on them in statutes of 1399 and 1409, and by the considerable number of references to them; in the earls' rebellion of 1400, a king's knight, Walter Hungerford, was stripped of his livery called 'colere', Queen Isabella's servants had King Henry's livery replaced by King Richard's, and an esquire of Huntingdon's was accused of refusing to cease wearing his lord's livery about his neck.

7 *C.P.R., 1399–1401*, 124. Another example, which Dr B. P. Wolffe pointed out to me, is Huntingdon's loss of lands in Cornwall a few days before Christmas 1399. [*Calendar of*] *Inquisitions Miscellaneous*, [*1399–1422*], 58.

8 P.R.O., c53/168, Nos. 10 and 11; *P.O.P.C.*, i, 100. Twenty-four attended this meeting and twenty-five witnessed these charters, both abnormally high figures. The explanation may be that a specially summoned Council or Great Council was meeting in early December.

9 What follows is based on the printed calendars of Chancery rolls, the Pardon roll (c.67/32), the roll of Pleas of the Hall recording proceedings against some of the rebels at Oxford (E.37/28), the large number of local enquiries in *Inquisitions Miscellaneous*, and an interesting article by P. McNiven, 'The Cheshire rising of 1400', *Bulletin of the John Rylands Library*, 52 (1970), 375–96.

10 Hake's wife had a grant of his cattle and goods on 9 April, and he had a pardon on the 21st: *C.P.R., 1399–1401*, 255; c.67/32, m, 19.

11 *C.P.R., 1399–1401*, 207, 386.

12 *Inquisitions Miscellaneous*, 28; *C.P.R., 1399–1401*, 192, 197.

13 *Ibid.*, 204, 367; c.67/32, m. 19, dated 11 April 1400.

14 E.37/28. Most of the accused had pardons during February. *C.P.R., 1399–1401*, 190, 228–9.

15 *Ibid.*, 410–11.

16 *Chronicque de la Traison et Mort de Richard Deux Roy Dengleterre*, ed. B. Williams (English Historical Society, 1846), 39.

17 *C.P.R., 1401–05*, 34, 477.

18 I say *two* occasions in 1404 because it seems very likely that the list of those assigned by the king to be of his Council and printed in *P.O.P.C.*, I, 237–8, refers to a Council nominated in the second (October) Parliament of 1404.

19 He had witnessed only two charters previously, both dated 10 February 1397.

20 G. A. Lobineau, *Histoire de Bretagne*, II (1707), 877. The other named witnesses were the keeper of the privy seal, the dean of the chapel, the secretary and two esquires, John Norbury and Robert Pynart.

21 Dr Bean's analysis of the causes of the Percy rebellion is excellent, but we have almost no evidence about the personal relations of the men involved. For example, there are two letters from Northumberland to the king in 1403 shortly before the rebellion, but none earlier. *P.O.P.C.*, I, 203–5.

22 These are cases where letters under the great seal are warranted 'Per ipsum regum nunciante comite Northumbrie'. Orders brought by intermediaries are rare and nine is a high figure. It may be significant that only one is after June 1401.

23 *C.P.R., 1399–1401*, 110, 178.

24 There are payments to him for a quarter-year's service with 420 soldiers and sailors on Issue Roll (E.403) 564, under 28 November and 23 February. Froissart (*Œuvres*, ed. Kervyn de Lettenhove, XVI, 215–17) has a detailed account of an expedition led by Thomas Percy to pacify Bordeaux in March 1400, but this seems improbable. Sir Hugh Despenser led an expedition there and it looks like a confusion of names.

25 [Exchequer of Receipt,] Warrants for Issues (E.404), box 15, Nos. 33 (dated 12 October), 82, 173 and 185, and Issue Rolls *passim*.

26 Froissart, *Œuvres*, XVI, 366–77.

27 A. Rogers, 'The political crisis of 1401', *Nottingham Medieval Studies*, XII (1968), 85–96.

28 Warrants for Issues, box 17, No. 324.

29 J. H. Wylie, *History of England under Henry the Fourth*, iv (1898), 242.

30 I omit reference to well-known chronicle stories, such as the one that Worcester deliberately misled Hotspur about the king's offer of terms before the battle of Shrewsbury. These stories are difficult to evaluate and this is not the occasion to try.

31 In 1404 Somerset complained that he was due £11,400 as captain of Calais since 1401, almost two years' wages. *R.P.*, III, 434–5.

32 J. S. Roskell, 'The problem of the attendance of the lords in medieval Parliaments', *B.I.H.R.*, XXIX (1956), 153–204.

33 *C.P.R., 1401–05*, 155–6.

34 G. W. Watson, 'William Heron, Lord Say', *Miscellanea Genealogica et Heraldica* fifth series, ix, 232ff. His accounts show that he was on embassies during nineteen months of 1400 and 1401.

35 *C.P.R., 1399–1401,* 225.

36 For example, John Strange's account as controller (British Museum, Harleian MS 319) gives the names of eleven knights of the Hall and Chamber in 1405–06. Dr Alan Rogers's thesis on Henry's Household will add very greatly to this picture when it is published. Some of his materials have been printed in 'Henry IV, the Commons and taxation', *Mediaeval Studies,* xxxi (1969), 44–70.

37 The most prominent were the knights Peter Buckton, John Cheyne, Peter Courtenay, Thomas Erpingham, John Pelham, Arnold Savage, John Stanley, John Tiptoft and Hugh Waterton, and the esquires John Curson, John Doreward, John Frome and John Norbury. There are biographies of several of these in J. S. Roskell, *The Commons and their Speakers in English Parliaments, 1376–1523* (1964), and in a number of Professor Roskell's articles.

38 Madeline Barber, 'John Norbury (*c.* 1350–1414): an esquire of Henry IV', *E.H.R.,* lxviii (1953), 66–76.

39 *C.P.R., 1405–08,* 22.

40 A. L. Brown, 'The Commons and the Council in the reign of Henry IV', *E.H.R.,* lxxix (1964), 24–5.

41 *R.P.,* iii, 577.

42 There is a biography of Buckton in *The Parliamentary Representation of the County of York* (Yorkshire Archaeological Society, Record Series), xvi, 153–6.

43 *C.C.R., 1399–1402,* 563.

44 *C.P.R., 1401–05,* 412.

45 Warrants for Issues, box 17, No. 280, dated 9 November 1401.

46 *C.P.R., 1399–1401,* 385.

47 It would be interesting to know how regularly these annuities were paid and how this was related to services performed. There are certainly some clear cases where the conditions were enforced; for example, the auditor of accounts of the duchy honour of Pevensey had to have a special order to allow an instalment of Sir John Pelham's annuity because he had not been on the Scottish expedition (D.L.42/15, f. 105r.), and fifty-seven members of Queen Isabella's household who had fees or annuities were specifically excused service on the Scottish expedition (*C.P.R., 1399–1401,* 323).

48 *P.O.P.C.,* i, 109.

49 For example, a significant number of the largest contingents on the Scottish expedition of 1400 were led by duchy men such as Sir Henry and Sir Richard Houghton; and another good example is the signet letters sent out in August 1405 to seventy-one duchy men to join a Welsh expedition: D.L.42/16, f. 128r.

50 R. Somerville, *History of the Duchy of Lancaster* (1953); N. Pronay, 'The Hanaper under the Lancastrian kings', *Proceedings of the Leeds Philosophical and Literary Society,* xii, part iii, 73–86.

51 *List and Index of Warrants for Issues, 1399–1485* (P.R.O., Lists and Indexes, Supplementary Series, ix, 2, 1964), 322–3, 328, 345.

52 *P.O.P.C.,* i, 154.

53 Somerville, *op. cit.,* 162–3.

54 This final remark is Dr J. L. Kirby's opinion, based on Arundel's register. I find it surprising that Arundel was present at neither the formal nor the actual marriage of Queen Joanna.

55 *C.P.R., 1399–1401,* 7; *C.C.R., 1405–09,* 428.

56 *C.P.R., 1399–1401,* 16, 545.

57 Stanley was an experienced Chancery clerk and a Lancastrian of sorts, one of Henry's attorneys in 1398 who retained his office in 1399, came very occasionally to the Council, and became chancellor of the duchy in 1405.

58 Apart from the three great officers, the most active attenders at the twenty-one recorded meetings between 1397 and 1399 were Sir John Bussy (present at twelve meetings), Sir John Russell (twelve), Sir Henry Green (ten), Lawrence Dru, esquire (eight), Dr Ralph Selby (eight) and the keeper of the rolls, Thomas Stanley (seven).

59 Bagot was retained to attend the council only in March 1399 (*C.P.R., 1396–99,* 494) and is not known to have attended in 1397 or 1398.

60 *C.P.R., 1401–05,* 96.

61 Roskell, *op. cit.,* 369. He served on occasional commissions after 1399 but apparently lost his annuity.

62 *C.P.R., 1399–1401,* 48, 275.

63 B. H. Putnam, 'The ancient indictments in the Public Record Office', *E.H.R.,* XXIX (1914), 500.

64 Perhaps this is reflected in Philip Repingdon's letter to King Henry in 1401 complaining about lawlessness and disappointment in the counties.

65 Even to the extent in 1400 of giving an allowance of 6*d* a day to Matthew Flynt, 'toothdrawer', in London to attend to poor lieges without fee. *C.P.R., 1399–1401,* 255.

B. P. Wolffe

Senior Lecturer in History
University of Exeter

2 The personal rule of Henry VI

The reign of Henry VI has strong claims to be considered the most calamitous in the whole of English history. It began with a fifteen years' minority: 'Woe to thee, O land, when thy king is a child.' The infant Henry VI succeeded to the inheritance of the united crowns of England and France. But by 1453 only Calais was left, out of all the conquests of Edward III and Henry V. Henry VI had lost the lot, as well as English Gascony, in a series of humiliating military defeats unprecedented since the reign of John. Burgundy, in spite of very strong natural economic ties with England, was now no longer an ally but an enemy. And in 1453, the year when the English were finally thrown out of Gascony, the king himself lost his wits. Two years later began the longest period of intermittent civil war in the whole of English history.

In considering the nature and causes of the collapse of government and political society which followed I think it is unnecessary to look back beyond the period of Henry VI's personal rule. The Lancastrian government of the minority has received an undeservedly bad press from historians. Indeed, if we can rid ourselves of hindsight and cease to regard the minority as the inevitable prelude to what followed, then by contrast with earlier and later English royal minorities, to say nothing of Continental ones, the period from 1422 to 1437 was one of impressive political and social stability. What evidence is there of serious lack of governance during those years? The Lancastrian Council in fact ruled the country surprisingly effectively. They are alleged to have squandered the royal patrimony, but nothing could be alienated until the king came of age. The war continued reasonably successfully. Even the 'alarming if not appalling' financial crisis of 1433, to quote Stubbs's description, only really appears so because of the unique amount of financial information we possess for that year. A single tenth and fifteenth was sufficient to overcome the annual deficit, as Stubbs himself admitted a few sentences later.[1] As for the personal rivalries of Beaufort and Gloucester, which constituted the high politics of the minority, the country could well afford them.

For me, it is in the ensuing period, from 1437 to 1450, that serious problems of credibility arise in the accepted accounts of the political history of this reign. I find it incredible that Henry VI was surrounded by a unique pack of self-seeking knaves, fools or incompetents who brought their country to disaster concurrently at home and abroad; or, alternatively, that one can find the explanation for these disasters primarily in the actions of one single knave, fool or well-meaning incompetent among his subjects—Suffolk, the queen, Adam Moleyns, the duke of York or the duke of Somerset. Equally, I cannot find a satisfactory explanation in a gathering momentum of irresistible forces, political, social or military, either at home or abroad. Nor can I see an explanation stemming from a king who was either a high-minded, sainted recluse, a cypher or a 'nullity'. I do think that Henry VI himself was the essential, unique feature of the reign, and therefore I have tried to look afresh at the powers, aims, actions and character of King Henry VI for the light such an examination can throw on the vexed problems of the origins of the civil wars. I had better state at once my belief that the conduct of the war in France and the problems of government at home were quite inseparable to contemporaries and cannot be considered separately by historians.

Fifteenth-century England was a limited monarchy. The power of the king was limited in two ways: (1) since 1352 some limitation, though not much, had been imposed on the scope of treason and the penalties for treason; (2) more significantly for the long-term future, the king ruled by law and that law was made, not by himself alone, but by the king in Parliament. Nevertheless, a fifteenth-century English king was by modern standards pretty well absolute. His powers, his duties and his responsibilities were enormous.

In many ways, by 1422 the English had already achieved remarkable political maturity, and a great deal of efficient apparatus had been devised and a great number of political conventions developed, which helped the king in his heavy task of kingship. The Lancastrian minority admirably demonstrates how extensive and effective these aids to efficient kingship could be. But when a king came of age, then responsibility and initiative passed to him. The Council from then on drew its powers, its authority, its life-blood, from the aims, character and personality of the king. A weak king meant a weak Council. A weak king with a strong Council was an impossibility in fifteenth-century England.

One of the most recent writers on this period, Mr Kenneth Fowler, in his splendid picture book *The Age of Plantagenet and Valois*, says of Henry VI: he lacked the craft and guile essential to meet the political situation of his day. Here, I think, Mr Fowler shows a fundamental misunderstanding of the vital qualities of later medieval kingship. The really great and successful kings like Henry V and Edward III were successful partly because they were great soldiers in the eyes of their contemporaries, and brave, forceful men at all times, but they were not devious. The successful king was upright, prudent, honourable, just, and not too clever. A deserved reputation for fair and prudent dealing was an essential attribute of kingship. The king personified law and order, truth and justice, and the character and reputation of the man was much more vital than the clothes.

To turn to the much better documented Shakespeare's England to illustrate another vital, related aspect of fifteenth-century English kingship: it is a well-known fact that Englishmen of Shakespeare's day worshipped due order in society and had a mortal dread of disorder and anarchy. Rebellion against an anointed king, let alone regicide, was a heinous sin as well as a crime, odious and horrible to the Elizabethans, not to be thought of. It is perhaps not generally appreciated that a very similar feeling pervaded fifteenth-century England. It is all too facile a view to consider that fifteenth-century England viewed rebellion or disobedience or even opposition to royal authority lightly. The evidence is strongly against such a view. The Tudor chroniclers thought that Richard, duke of York, had been aiming at the throne from at least 1450, and indeed they thought the idea had probably always been in his heart. Yet the facts may have been otherwise. Such an ambition was contrary to all his and his supporters' beliefs, oaths of allegiance and professions of loyalty to Henry VI. The idea of deposing an anointed king was greeted with dismay. Likewise, the rebels of 1450, who called themselves petitioners, were desperately anxious to avoid the stigma of rebellion against their anointed king. They complained that he considered himself above the laws by his own pleasure, but they said that his ministers, not he himself, were to blame for teaching him so. The king could do no wrong.

Again, the dreaded penalties of treason were easily incurred in the mid-fifteenth century for the slightest derogation of kingship, and were thought appropriate. In 1444 Thomas Kerver of Reading, gentleman, was judged to be drawn, hanged and quartered because he said 'Woe to thee, O land, when thy king is a child.' The crowned and anointed king was sacred. Whoever he was, he represented the unity of the realm, the last bulwark against anarchy and the dissolution of society. As Mr Armstrong has demonstrated for us, men abandoned restraint towards the king only in the direst extremities. And even then their words and actions might well backfire. It was essential to preserve the conventional ban on the expression of private enmities in his presence. One could accuse his minister or his alleged favourites in the name of the public weal, but one could not accuse him. Actually to oppose the royal standard on the battlefield was a frightful responsibility. Even as late as 1459, at Ludford, outside Ludlow, when Henry VI took the field in person, the Yorkist forces melted away before him. The mid-fifteenth-century king could himself do no wrong—even if the whole government of the realm was in fact hamstrung by his aims, actions and policies. These attitudes and conventions, I think, help to explain the almost total absence of contemporary criticism of Henry VI himself, not really a saintly nature or one of unquestionable uprightness, though his ostentatious piety may well have helped to ward off criticism in that pious age. Also, he had immense prestige as the son of his father. He was born to the purple, and considerable personal advantages accrued from that.

How much of our view of the personal role of Henry VI in government still stems unconsciously from Shakespeare and the propaganda of early Tudor historiography? May I recall some of the origins of Shakespeare's view of Henry VI and, in general, of that of modern historians?

King Henry was a man of mild and plain-dealing disposition, who preferred peace before wars, quietness before troubles, honesty before utility, and leisure before business; and, to be short, there was not in this world a more pure, more honest, and more holy creature. There was in him honest shamefacedness, modesty, innocency and perfect patience, taking all human chances, miseries, and all afflictions in this life in so good part as though

he had justly by some his offence deserved the same. He ruled his own
affections, that he might more easily rule his own subjects; he gaped not after
riches, nor thirsted for honour and worldly estimation, but was careful
only for his soul's health; such things as tended to the salvation thereof he
only esteemed for good; and that very wisely; such again as procured the
loss thereof he only accounted evil.[2]

It is surely remarkable that Kingsford did not think to question this
picture of Henry VI by Henry VII's court historian, especially since
he attributed Blacman's *Life of Henry VI*[3] to the reign of Henry
VII, when Henry VII was petitioning three successive popes in
vain to get Henry VI canonised so that he could appear as the lawful
heir of his sainted uncle. To this early Tudor period of lobbying
the papacy belongs that other testimony to Henry's sanctity, the
sycophantic *Historia Regum Angliae* of John Rous, with its fulsome
flattery of Henry VII, which also perpetrated the absurd story of
Richard III's having been born a monster with teeth and hair after
two years' gestation.[4]

May we now attempt to judge Henry VI by his actions, working back from the sure ground of Mr Armstrong's first battle of
St Albans into the contradictions of his personal rule? To my mind
the weakness of Kingsford's defence of Suffolk lay not in his
failure to explain away his 'insatiable covetise' (after all, Tudor
historians do not, for example, find it necessary to apologise for
similar traits in Elizabeth's Lord Burghley) but in his inability to
consider that Henry VI may himself have been personally responsible for high acts of state.

The first battle of St Albans was fought between Richard, duke
of York, the premier prince of the blood royal, and his kinsmen
and supporters, the Neville earls of Salisbury and Warwick, on
the one side, and those members of the English nobility and royal
servants who were accompanying the king from London to a
Council meeting at Leicester, on the other. York said that he was
being excluded from the royal Councils principally through the
most prominent member of the Lancastrian house, Edmund Beaufort, duke of Somerset, and that the Council meeting at Leicester
to which he had been summoned was intended to impose upon
him a public humiliation and probably also a charge and conviction
of treason. The actual battle, in which Somerset was slain, was
preceded by elaborate parleys and negotiations conducted through
heralds. York and his supporters received no satisfactory assurances

from the king through these; they would not submit themselves unreservedly to Henry's mercy because, they said, they had been tricked on a previous occasion, and they therefore took him by force of arms and imposed their will upon him. They secured a reluctantly given indemnity for their actions in a Parliament in July 1455 and they ruled the country in Henry's name, not unsuccessfully, until August 1456. For about the first six months of this time Henry appears to have been ill—at least physically and mentally incapacitated. In August 1456 his queen, Margaret of Anjou, carried him off to Coventry, in the heart of the Lancastrian estates, and it proved impossible henceforth to maintain the normal apparatus of political life. This situation led to further armed clashes to retain or to obtain the person of the king, which increased in severity until they were joined without any preliminary parleys and without any mercy being shown to the principal participants. When the Yorkists lost possession of the king's person in February 1461 this led to the dynastic revolution. Such was the first of the 'Wars of the Roses'.

The interesting point here is the Yorkists' claim at St Albans in 1455, just before the battle, that they had been tricked before. The allegation referred to what had happened at Dartford in 1452, when York had appeared with an armed following before the king, expressing similar claims of exclusion from the king's Councils. On that occasion he had surrendered to Henry, appearing unarmed in the royal tent, on a prior undertaking, he maintained, that the duke of Somerset should be removed from the royal presence. There he found Somerset still enjoying the royal favour and was himself conducted, under arrest, to London, where he was constrained to make humiliating submission to the king and to give undertakings for his future good behaviour.

In 1450 there had been a similar occurrence, though conducted with more restraint and less dire consequences. On that occasion, at the height of Cade's rebellion in Kent, York had returned from Ireland, unbidden, to offer his services to his king in a fearful crisis, or so he maintained. He found his entry to the country, and his journey across England, barred by royal agents and he had to force his way into the royal presence. Note that in Henry's reply to York's defence against imputations of treason in 1450 the king said that the murderers of Moleyns had threatened him to his face with treasonable words alleged to have been spoken by York himself.

He named one of them: 'one Wasnes which had like words unto us.'[5] Henry was very credulous, with a ready ear for a sinister accusation.

From 1447 until the birth of Prince Edward to Margaret and Henry on 13 October 1453, York was heir presumptive to the throne. I do not think there is any evidence to suggest that Edmund Beaufort was regarded in that light. And I would here carry back this pattern of related events to Bury St Edmunds in 1447, the occasion which had made York heir presumptive—that is, the death there of his predecessor in that position, Humphrey, duke of Gloucester, the king's uncle. At Bury St Edmunds, where he had gone for the opening of a Parliament, Gloucester had found himself suddenly placed under arrest by the Constable of England on the king's orders, together with various members of his entourage. The shock was such that Humphrey died in his lodgings, under guard, before any charge of treason could be brought against him. It is sometimes forgotten that his followers and his natural son were brought to trial after his death and convicted of coming to the Parliament in arms, conspiring to kill the king and to raise Gloucester to the throne, to release Eleanor Cobham and to make her queen.[6]

The mystery of what went wrong with the government of England, leading to civil war, therefore lies within the period of the personal rule of Henry VI between 1437 and 1450. It was truly personal rule. Baldwin's account of the transference of power from the Council of the minority to the king needs to be revised. If we follow him, it appears that the Council of the minority managed to hold on to some of, if not all, their powers until about 1444, when the young king decided to rely on one principal minister, William de la Pole, earl of Suffolk, and a very few others, and henceforth conducted affairs from the inner recesses of his Household through them. I do not think that the records as printed by Nicolas bear this out. Confusion has arisen because the Council, in 1437, when it had decided that the young king was bound to assume responsibility for the government of the realm, looked around for a written precedent for the commissioning of a new Council by a king and found only one: that of 1406. This was a complicated precedent because in 1406 Henry IV had been ill and had been temporarily *increasing* the powers of his Council. Baldwin knew this well and appears to have assumed that in 1437 something along the same lines must have been intended. But it was not. If the original French instrument of 1406 is compared clause by clause and word by word with its English copy of 1437, it becomes clear that the 1406 precedent is misleading because certain vital extra new clauses were added in 1437, actually giving Henry VI full possession of the normal powers of English kingship.[7] Stubbs, criticised by Baldwin, was in fact correct when he diagnosed a complete transference of power in 1437.[8] Henceforth, the Council could only advise, and could execute policies only when asked to do so. It could not initiate policies and its discretion was confined to routine matters and even then only to those matters on which it was nearly unanimous. Some time about 1444 the Council did indeed try to recover some of its pre-1437 powers, very discreetly and deferentially, because it was collectively horrified at the use the king was making of the prerogatives of kingship. But it failed in the attempt.[9]

I cannot convince myself from the scanty survivals of attendance records at Council meetings, as instanced by Baldwin,[10] that an inner cabinet, *conciliabulum*, clique or court party ran the country from about 1444, either with the king or without him. The original day-to-day minutes of the Council hardly survive at all for this reign after 1444. But this does not mean that they never existed. An important record of what appears to have been one very full vital meeting in 1449 survives in a seventeenth-century copy published by Professor Myers.[11] In any case, what historians have seen as inner cliques meeting to govern the country and ignoring the Council at large might well have been interpreted as hard-working, purposeful conciliar committees if the period had been that of Henry V, Edward IV or Henry VII. Henry VI, in fact, allowed no one, not even Suffolk, any real initiative, and nothing much could be done without him. Was there, in fact, ever a peace party and a war party in the 1440s—or, indeed, ever a *political* Suffolk affinity?

The young Henry began to show a precocious interest in affairs of state from about 1434. Even at the age of ten he was described by his guardian, as 'grown . . . in conceit and knowledge of his high and royal authority and estate, the which naturally causes him . . . to grudge with chastising and to loathe it'.[12] Until 1437 the Council continued to act with the full powers it had enjoyed during the minority. From 1437 until 1444 Henry largely contented himself with exercising personal control of patronage,[13] with giving away the Crown lands. He did not stop doing this in 1444, but from then on he also acquired other definite aims and interests as well. As regards the Crown lands, McFarlane thought he could detect, round about 1439–40, a narrowing of the royal bounty to a Beaufort faction.[14] I have examined 192 grants of royal lands and properties to 169 persons made between 1437 and 1450, but I cannot see any pattern or motive behind them, except that if we exclude nine great lords from the 169 grantees, seventy-four of the remaining 160 were resident members of the king's Household, another fifteen were what one might call country members of the Household, and another twenty-two were government officials with easy access to the Household. When one allows for the minor grants to lesser, unidentifiable people, all one can say is that those who had easiest access to the king benefited most and anyone who had access to him could get something. This unprecedented dispersal of the Crown lands outside the royal family between 1437 and 1450 was accompanied by an extraordinary distribution of honours. Out of seventeen creations of baronies by letters patent or charter before 1500, ten were made between 1441 and 1449.[15] In addition, between the same years five earls, two marquises and five dukes were created.

Abbot Wheathampstead, the verbose and often tedious abbot of St Albans, who is generally considered, despite Yorkist leanings, to have been something of an admirer of Henry VI, is often quoted as an eye-witness who wrote that Henry was *simplex et rectus*,[16] which, I suppose, one must translate in this combination as 'honest and upright'. But this first-hand description was made in a certain context and ought not to be lifted out of that context. It was written some time after Parliament, under York's influence in 1455–56, had passed an Act annulling or resuming all Henry's grants, and the abbot, with the expenditure of much time and money, had just managed to get the abbey's grants exempted.

The most intimate picture we have of Henry VI is that written by his former chaplain, John Blacman. It is a catalogue of his good deeds and habits; but it was probably written at the behest of Henry VII as material for Henry VI's canonisation. According to Blacman, Henry VI showed his disapproval of women with naked bosoms, apparently a fashion in dress from about 1429 according to Thomas Gascoigne. The sight of naked men in public baths similarly incurred his rebuke. He spied on his entourage from a secret window in his chamber lest they should be corrupted by bad company. He was extremely devout. One cannot doubt Henry's unique, obsessive and ostentatious piety, especially when compared with kings like Henry V and Henry VII, who were themselves pious enough by any standards. Witness his extraordinary will, which began to take effect in his lifetime from Michaelmas 1446, with its elaborate curse (Deuteronomy, xxviii) on his heirs and executors should they in any way thwart his wishes, and the instruction to his executors by sale to alienate duchy of Lancaster lands worth £3,395 11s 7d a year from his heirs and successors, kings of England, should they attempt to obstruct the fulfilment of the will.[17] No wonder the Commons in Parliament in 1451 declared it to be 'over chargefull and noyus'.[18] Blacman goes on to say that public business irked him because it took away time from his devotions. This may well have been so; I am not maintaining that he had the gift of application to business, but I think we must agree, if we read between the lines and remember the purpose for which it was probably compiled, that Blacman's description is not the picture of a timid recluse. In those things which interested him, such as the outward forms of conventional moral behaviour, the strict observance of the letter of the law in religious observance and catechising candidates for bishoprics, Henry could be ominously extrovert and censorious.

From 1445 he conceived a new and compelling interest: peace at any price in the French war, perhaps from genuine conviction, but most likely moved by the desires of his new French queen. By 1444 a hopeful, realistic peace policy had at last gained wide acceptance among his chief councillors, even though misgivings in some influential quarters were obvious enough. Kingsford convincingly showed how in Council and Parliament up to June 1445 this general consensus of opinion, embracing Gloucester, York and Suffolk, was founded on a belief that peace negotiations could be, and were being, conducted from a position of strength. This had been the English mood at the truce of Tours (May 1444), obtained by Suffolk. The commander-in-chief in France, Richard, duke of York, another alleged warmonger, was on good terms with Suffolk, the peacemaker, and was using him as an intermediary to arrange a marriage between his eldest son and one of the French king's daughters.[19] The first step towards peace was to be that Henry VI should marry Margaret of Anjou, daughter of Count Réné of Anjou, titular king of Sicily, brother of the French queen, duke of

Lorraine and head of a cadet branch of the French royal family.
The new queen arrived in London in February 1445 amid widespread, spontaneous, approving demonstrations, although she
brought no dower at all to King Henry. The only other official
English policy, cautiously revealed, seems to have been to barter the
English title to the French throne in exchange for the retention of
French territory in full sovereignty.[20] On 4 June 1445 Suffolk received
a singular demonstration of thanks from the Commons and Lords
in Parliament for his 'conservation of the peace in the king's laws
within this realm, in repressing and expelling all manner [of] riots
and extortions within the same', for his knightly courage in the
wars, for his honourable efforts to secure peace, and for the truce,
so beneficial to trade. His efforts to use the truce to strengthen
garrisons in case further negotiations failed was put on record.
Gloucester, that arch-warmonger of tradition, with other lords, rose
in his seat to support the testimonial.[21] The period now becomes
noteworthy for these solemn declarations of intent, responsibility
or non-responsibility in this vital matter. Why should we believe
that they conceal the truth? They ought to be given credence at
least as much as articles of impeachment.

English historians, with their unavoidable hindsight, stress the
basic unreality of Henry V's grandiose French conquests, once the
Burgundian and Armagnac feud which had produced the French
civil war was healed, and once France could realise her full potential. It was a wonder that England held on to her conquests so long.
But French historians jump from the truce of Tours in May 1444
to the reopening of general hostilities in July 1449, and explain that
France needed the five years of truce to build up her strength for
that day. The English, by contrast, did the opposite. Whichever is
correct, English contemporaries traced the immediate causes of what
happened in 1449–50 back no further than 1445. In July 1445 French
ambassadors in London reported the greater warmth which they
received from the king than from his ministers, and they were made
aware that the king was not personally well disposed towards his
heir presumptive, the duke of Gloucester. Although Henry spoke
only four words of French on this occasion, he had other things to
say in English, and the picture here given by the French ambassadors of the king moving about among them is that he was very
much in control of affairs, not a cypher.[22] Henry VI feared his uncle,
it seems, for more than one reason: he feared he was planning to

supplant him and that he might get in the way of the peace. In 1441 the duchess of Gloucester had been tried for treason for alleged attempts, in co-operation with a well known astrologer and a canon of St Stephen's chapel, Westminster, to secure the king's death by witchcraft. Condemning her to perpetual imprisonment, the king was to have her transferred to a more remote and more secure prison in the Isle of Man in 1446.[23]

As for Henry's own French policy, French records show that on 22 December 1445 Henry wrote to the French king secretly and personally, promising him the surrender of Maine and Anjou by 30 April 1446.[24] On 9 April 1446, the day of its dissolution, the chancellor made a solemn declaration in Parliament on behalf of all the lords spiritual and temporal to the effect that God alone and no one of them had prompted the king to arrange a personal meeting with his uncle of France in October to treat for peace, but that they would assist him as far as Parliament would give them the means in furtherance of his blessed intent, but no further. An annulment of Henry V's ban on peacemaking without the assent of the three estates of the realm followed.[25] The next significant event was that Suffolk petitioned for and was granted the opportunity to make a solemn declaration in the king's chamber on 25 May 1447 before the king, eight spiritual and lay peers, including York, 'and others our servants, familiars and domestics then present' that he had never been a party to any proposals for the surrender of the counties of Anjou and Maine.[26] Malicious rumours were stirring, it was said, and the king wished to silence them. Maine and Anjou, the ancient patrimony of the English Plantagenet house, had been effectively reoccupied from 1424. The English Council at first does not seem to have known about Henry's policy or to have been able to face up to recognising it once it did. It was the clear opposite of the official policy, and was not certainly known to them until 27 or 28 July 1447.[27] Even then the surrender was further doggedly resisted by royal officers on the spot, and still appears to have received no support from the new commander-in-chief, the duke of Somerset, by 15 March 1448.[28] The French said they had originally obtained a verbal promise some time before October 1445 that Maine and Anjou would be surrendered.

The duke of York, the English commander-in-chief in France, had been recalled to England in the autumn of 1445.[29] For many months he daily expected to be allowed to return, but in fact he was not, and no new commander-in-chief was appointed for over two years. This in itself is significant enough. Ultimately, when the appointment did go to Edmund Beaufort, duke of Somerset, he did not take up his appointment until March 1448, and apparently even then with no ideas of implementing surrenders in mind. The French king became extremely exasperated with him, finding him more difficult to negotiate with than his more polite predecessor, the duke of York.[30]

The public degradation and the death of the duke of Gloucester in February 1447 had made York heir presumptive. In July 1447 Henry appointed him lieutenant in Ireland to get him out of the way, but York refused to take up the appointment until July 1449.[31] One of the best of the near-contemporary chroniclers, in the so-called Giles's Latin chronicle, which, as Mr Armstrong points out, is not as Yorkist a compilation as Kingsford supposed, states that Henry himself sent York off to Ireland of his own volition to keep him away from his royal presence for a long time. He also says that only Suffolk could influence Henry and that York therefore blamed him, but this does not make Suffolk the prime mover. This same chronicle also puts the responsibility for the treatment of Gloucester on the king—that is, that he had begun to mistrust him, and forbade him his presence from 1445.[32] So does Abbot Wheathampstead when he describes the efforts made in seven successive Parliaments to clear Humphrey's name. Henry, he said, had believed him guilty of assiduously and secretly labouring to encompass his death and usurp the throne.[33] Thus from 1445 there had been four years of vacillation, secret diplomacy, lack of leadership in the field, or of frustrated, hampered leadership, procrastination, countermanding of orders, suspicion and general conciliar confusion. All this embraced Suffolk and, ultimately, when there was one again, the general in the field, Edmund Beaufort.

Some time in 1447 or 1448 the exasperated York brought charges in the Council against Adam Moleyns of slandering him: of saying that he, York, was responsible for the loss of Normandy, and that members of York's council in England, Lord Scales, Sir William Oldhall and Sir Andrew Ogard, were still drawing pay from Normandy while soldiers out there went unpaid. York also complained that when Moleyns had been over in France on embassy for the king he had incited men to come over to England and complain against York.[34] McFarlane wrote about the incident that Moleyns,

Suffolk's right-hand man, flatly denied the accusation in insulting terms. This was the turning point of York's career, he considered. By treating him as an enemy, the court—and he meant here the court party of Suffolk and his colleagues—had made him one.[35] Moleyns, to my mind, convincingly and with much *deference* to York, denied the substance of these charges, though from his answers it emerges that he had said something, but, whatever it was, he claimed it had originated in the execution of a personal command given him by the king. In his answer to the charge he appears to me to have been not an arrogant but rather a frightened man. He also appealed to the lords of the Council then present to declare that they knew that he himself was an advocate of vigorous measures in prosecuting the war in Normandy and that Normandy was not in fact lost even then if vigorous and timely action were taken. The incident is typical of the dissensions and mutual recriminations, accusations of deceit and bad faith engendered by the personal rule of King Henry VI.

In the field, both sides, French and English, broke the truce from time to time: the French first and most conspicuously, perhaps, by investing Le Mans, the capital of Maine; the English in attacking and capturing Fougères, a town on the Brittany frontier. Historians have often seen this as a particularly foolhardy move engineered or weakly approved by Suffolk and Somerset. But the chance survival of a seventeenth-century copy of the minutes of what was probably a very full Council meeting in 1449, published by Professor Myers in 1938 as a parliamentary debate, and subsequently more convincingly described by Professor Roskell as a Council, not a Lords' meeting, happens to show that probably the whole Council, and in any case the fourteen lords named as taking part in the debate, approved of the exploit and probably knew about it in advance.[36]

In 1449, when general hostilities were resumed, Somerset had to surrender Normandy almost at once. In 1450 Suffolk and Moleyns were both murdered. Kent rose in arms. York came back unbidden from Ireland, reached the royal presence only by the use of force and began those charges of the loss of Normandy, directed against Somerset, which ultimately ended in civil war.

Henry VI's own wilful efforts had thus divided, demoralised and hamstrung the English war effort, so that it dissolved in defeat and recriminations. The king's conduct had been simultaneously producing creeping paralysis in the Council and government in home affairs, and a consequent collapse of respect for law and order by the great which would have been unheard of under Henry V.

In his well known chapter in the *Cambridge Medieval History*, McFarlane considered that the assertion of the contemporary chronicler John Hardyng that Henry was unable to distinguish between right and wrong must be rejected. Whatever may have been Henry's shortcomings, McFarlane thought, it was hard to believe that a defective moral sense was ever one of them.[37] How powerful still is Tudor historiography in the matter of Henry VI! I think Hardyng's view has much to be said for it and should be reconsidered. Hardyng is usually especially discredited because he wrote two versions of his chronicle.[38] But he is actually in quite a different category from the sycophantic John Rous, with his separate Yorkist and Tudor versions of his *Rous Roll*.[39] The first Hardyng chronicle was written while he was petitioning Henry VI for a grant of the manor of Geddington in Northamptonshire, which he maintained Henry V had promised him for services rendered and did not live to make effective—it had actually gone to one of Henry VI's squires of the body, Thomas Daniell. This first version does not contain the telling description of the king. But remember what Abbot Wheathampstead said about the danger of maligning the great. In any case, one does not disparage a hoped-for benefactor. The second version, written after 1458 and dedicated to Richard, duke of York, does contain it. But even in the first version, written in the late '40s, Hardyng was very critical of the total lack of governance then prevailing and contrasted it with the happy days of Henry V. His praise for Henry V, not just for what he did abroad but for his effective rule at home, never faltered, and this praise of a Lancastrian king was included even in the so-called Yorkist version.

To return finally to Polydore Vergil. He was a court hireling of Henry VII, but he was also a trained humanist scholar: the first writer with any claims to be a real historian in England since the Venerable Bede. Polydore did in fact put forward another view of Henry VI which he put into the mouth of Richard, duke of York:

He [York] found much fault also with King Henry, saying that he was a man of soft and feeble spirit, of little wit, and unmeet in all respects for the right government of a commonwealth, and therefore that it touched nobility to think of the matter or rather to devise a remedy.[40]

In his British Academy lecture—which, alas, had to be his last word
on the subject—McFarlane said, 'The war was fought because the
nobility was unable to rescue the kingdom from the consequences
of Henry VI's inanity by any other means. It does not follow that
they liked the task.'[41] I might well have taken this as my text,
because what I have said could be taken as a gloss on this word
'inanity'. I do not think it sufficiently allows for the power wielded
by Henry VI or for the perverse wilfulness with which he exercised
it. It was this which dissolved the unity and purpose of the realm
and made all his advisers appear either knaves or fools or both. I am
not saying they were all angels, but I am saying that there was only
one fundamental problem of government between 1422 and 1461:
the character of the king. It took a long time to come to grips with
this problem. An account of this slowly escalating, demoralising
process and the reasons for the delay in reaching a solution tells us
much about the politics of the age and, to my mind, reveals them
as much less sordid than Kingsford supposed. When the problem
was faced up to and reluctantly and ultimately settled, then the
government of England under Edward IV and, more exactly, under
Henry VII could revert to what it had been under Henry V.

The 'Wars of the Roses' were fought by small armies. There was
little plunder or disturbance of the normal economic life of the
countryside. Towns were rarely sacked. Comparatively few people
were killed. They were fought by a fundamentally vigorous, prosperous, expansionist society. After these wars English government
and society were fundamentally no different from what they had
been before them. All this is now admitted. In any case, Kingsford
already demonstrated much of it as long ago as 1925 in his chapter
on the social effects of the 'Wars of the Roses'.[42] These wars must
now also be seen as having a specific, limited cause and a very
limited objective. The basic cause was the political *impasse* created
by the wilful incompetence and untrustworthiness of Henry VI in
that supremely demanding 'age of kings'. The need was simply to
change the government. Had he died a minor, it would not have
mattered. Fifteenth-century England was mature enough to take
minorities in its stride. Had he remained insane, once he had lost
his reason, it would not have mattered. Government could have
managed without him.

This rare but fundamental political and constitutional problem
was still essentially unsolved on the eve of the next civil war nearly

two hundred years later, except that by the time of Charles I the distribution of political power had shifted. Responsibility for the decision to use force in such a rare and desperate situation had by then passed from the heir presumptive to the throne, or from the strongest adult member of the royal family, to Parliament. Nevertheless, the manifesto of the Cade rebels in 1450 already had in it the germ of the later, ultimate solution when it sought to make Henry VI's ministers responsible for his actions. The personal rule of Henry VI from 1437 to 1450 and subsequently demonstrated how disastrously a mid-fifteenth-century king could and did do wrong. Ministers might endeavour to influence his actions, but only his own ability and judgement could control them. England was on the whole extraordinarily fortunate that under the Plantagenets and Tudors this political *impasse* was so very rarely reached. But in the fifteenth century and for a long time afterwards there was still no machinery for changing the government when that government, the king, was adult and responsible for its own actions—except by the so-called 'Wars of the Roses'.

Appendix 1
The transfer of power in 1437

The statement that the actual Bill of 1406 (*R.P.*, III, 572–3) was being used in 1437 is in *P.O.P.C.*,v, 71, dated 12 November 1437. The Council meeting which approved the final version was held on 13 November 1437 with the king present (*ibid.*, VI, 312–15). The 1437 document was an English translation of the French, with a few variations of phrasing of no substance, but omitting (1) reference to the publication in Parliament of the membership of the Council; (2) the specific statement in the king's bill of 1406 that bills endorsed by the chamberlain and letters under the signet directed to the chancellor, treasurer, keeper of the privy seal and other officers should be submitted for endorsement by, or be made by the advice of, the Council, and that these officers should not act without this endorsement. In place of this latter provision a general statement was inserted 'giving them power to hear, treat, commune, appoint, conclude and determine such matters as shall happen for to be moved among them', followed by the same reservations as in the 1406 clause, but with the added reservation of 'other things that stand in grace'. Then follow the additional 1437 clauses with further restrictions not present in the 1406 document. In matters of great weight and charge the Council was to commune them but not to conclude them without the king's advice. In other matters which were within its competence to conclude it must not do so if there was variance of opinion amongst the councillors, for example, half against half, or two-thirds against one-third, in which cases the king must be informed of the diversity of opinions so that he might conclude the matter. In short, the Council had no authority to act in matters 'that stand in grace' and its initiative was confined to minor matters over which it could reach near unanimity.

Appendix 2
Attendance at the Council, 1443–50

Baldwin appears to rely on documents from Nicolas's collection (*P.O.P.C.*) for evidence of the existence of a narrow court party at work within and without the Council from about 1444 to 1450, headed by Suffolk (*The King's Council*, 189–93). But he in fact read into this extremely meagre collection preconceived value judgements about the role of individuals for which there is no evidence here or elsewhere. He *assumed* that Suffolk was responsible for an undertaking to surrender Maine and Anjou given in 1444; that the Council approved this at the time, in spite of the 'war party'; that Suffolk gained a personal ascendency over Henry VI because he alone could free him from the 'yoke' of the duke of Gloucester; that Suffolk was viewed by the lords in general with suspicion; that he chose not to work through the Council; that he had an 'eager partisan' in Moleyns, and that attempts were made from time to time unsuccessfully to attack this 'court party' in the Council.

The *P.O.P.C.* represent the chance survival and haphazard collection of references to forty-two Council meetings between 1 September 1443 and 31 August 1450 (22–28 Henry VI inclusive), an average of six *per annum*. An attendance is stated, or partly stated, in only twenty-three of these; it ranges from three to sixteen, with an average of six. A full attendance is stated in only twelve instances. The meeting places are described simply as at Westminster (seventeen), in the Star Chamber (seven), at the Blackfriars (six), in the king's chamber (one), at Leicester (one), at Winchester (one), at the cardinal of York's palace (one), or not specified. There are one or two documents bearing the royal sign manual and one meeting stated to be held in the royal chamber, but the king is never said specifically to have been either present or not present. The most frequent meetings by regnal years were nine in 22 Henry VI (1443–44), and thirteen in 28 Henry VI (1449–50), but of these nine, three are known only from the endorsement of documents as passed 'by advice of the Council' and twelve out of the thirteen in 28 Henry VI fall into this category. No meaningful conclusions can be drawn from such meagre, incomplete evidence—as is, of course, now recognised for the comparable situation in the Yorkist period.

Notes

1 *Constitutional History* (fifth edition, 1898), III, 121.

2 *Polydore Vergil's English History*, ed. Sir Henry Ellis (Camden Society, old series, XXIX, 1844), 70–1.

3 *Henry the Sixth: a Reprint of John Blacman's Memoir*, ed. M. R. James (1919).

4 *Joannis Rossi Antiquarii Warwicensis Historia Regum Angliae*, ed. Thomas Hearne (1745), 210, 215.

5 *The Paston Letters*, ed. James Gairdner (1910), i, xcv.

6 'Gregory's Chronicle' in *The Historical Collections of a London Citizen*, ed. James Gairdner (Camden Society, new series, xvii, 1876), 187–8; 'Bale's Chronicle' in *Six Town Chronicles*, ed. Ralph Flenley (1911), 121–2; 'Memorandum off the Parlement of Berye' in *An English Chronicle, 1377–1461*, ed. John Silvester Davies (Camden Society, old series, lxiv, 1856), 116–18.

7 *R.P.*, iii, 572–3; *P.O.P.C.*, v, 71; vi, 312–15; and see appendix 1 above.

8 *Constitutional History*, iii, 256; though Stubbs saw the tranference of power as being made to 'the king or the court'; J. F. Baldwin, *The King's Council* (1913), 187.

9 *P.O.P.C.*, vi, cxci, 316–20.

10 *Op. cit.*, 189–93, and see appendix 2 above.

11 'A parliamentary debate of the mid-fifteenth century', *Bulletin of the John Rylands Library*, xxii, (1938), 388–404, and see below p. 42 and note 36.

12 *Paston Letters*, i, 33 (No. 18).

13 Henry Benet's rough minutes of a Council meeting held at Eltham on 30 March 1443 record that when John, duke of Somerset, asked for 1,000 marks of land, 'my said lords being present abstained them in all wise to speak, nor durst not advise the king to depart from such livelihood nor to open their mouths in such matters'. The king commanded he should have 600 marks of land (*P.O.P.C.*, v, 253).

14 *Cambridge Medieval History*, viii, 399.

15 There is a list in *C.P.*, vii, appendix A, 703.

16 *Registrum Abbatiae Johannis Whethamstede*, ed. H. T. Riley, i (Rolls Series, 1872), 247–9.

17 *Collection of the Wills of the Kings and Queens of England, etc.*, ed. J. Nichols (1780), 291–320.

18 *R.P.*, v, 217–18.

19 *Wars of the English in France during the Reign of Henry VI, King of England: Letters and Papers*, ed. J. Stevenson, i (Rolls Series, 1861), 79.

20 *Ibid.*, i, 151.

21 *R.P.*, v, 73–4.

22 *Wars of the English in France*, i, 110–12. Mr C. A. J. Armstrong pointed out that there appears to be no evidence that Henry VI could speak French and that he addressed the French Parlement in English.

23 *P.O.P.C.*, vi, 51.

24 *Wars of the English in France*, ii, part ii, 639–42.

25 *R.P.*, v, 102–3.

26 T. Rymer, *Foedera* (ed. 1704–32), xi, 172–4.

27 *Wars of the English in France*, ii, part ii, 643, 693.

28 *Ibid.*, 704–18.

29 Before 21 September: *ibid.*, i, 163.

30 *Ibid.*, i, 209–20, 243–64.

31 *P.O.P.C.*, vi, 89.

32 *Incerti Scriptoris Chronicon Angliae*, ed. J. A. Giles (1848), 'Chronicon Henrici VI', 33–4, 35.

33 *Registrum*, i, 179; cf. also 'On the mutability of worldly changes', the political poem printed by Kingsford in his *English Historical Literature in the*

Fifteenth Century, 395–7, which alleges that Henry first conceived his suspicions of Gloucester through a bishop who revealed to him something he had heard in the confessional.

34 B.M., Harleian MSS 543, ff. 161r–163r. I hope to publish this document elsewhere.

35 *C.M.H.*, VIII, 404–5.

36 See above, p. 36, and J. S. Roskell, 'The problem of the attendance of the lords in medieval Parliaments', *B.I.H.R.*, XXIX (1956), 188.

37 *C.M.H.*, VIII, 398.

38 The earlier version, B.M., Lansdowne MS 204, was assessed in relation to the later version and partially printed by C. L. Kingsford in *E.H.R.*, XXVIII (1912), 462–82, 740–53. The later version is *The Chronicle of John Hardyng together with the Continuation by Richard Grafton*, ed. Henry Ellis (1812).

39 The Yorkist version was privately printed as the *Rows Rol*, ed. William Courthope (1859). The later version, adapted to suit the reign of Henry VII, is in the College of Heralds and unprinted.

40 *Op. cit.*, 94.

41 'The Wars of the Roses', *Proc. Brit. Acad.*, L (1965), 87–119.

42 *Prejudice and Promise in Fifteenth Century England*, 48–77.

C. D. Ross

Reader in Medieval History
University of Bristol

3   The reign of Edward IV

Of the seven kings who ruled England in the fifteenth century only
Edward IV stands today in substantially higher repute amongst
historians than he did a century, a half-century or even twenty-
five years ago. In place of the temperamental but politically imma-
ture prince portrayed by Commines and later writers we are now
presented with 'a king of iron will and great fixity of purpose . . .
who began to break the teeth of the sinners', a man who possessed
'the ruthlessness of a Renaissance despot and the strong-willed
ability of a statesman', 'an independent and effective man of action',
'an astute and able ruler'.[1] For a succinct summary of the reasons
for this modern reappraisal one can do no better than quote
Professor Chrimes's estimate of Edward's achievements:[2]

> He was to show himself a realist who sought after solid gains rather than
> vainglory. He did much to consolidate the monarchy, to rehabilitate its finances,
> and to restore its prestige. He stopped the process of decay in monarchy and
> government . . . he went far to remedy the 'lack of politique reule and govern-
> ance' which had brought Henry VI to disaster; he was not to be led astray
> by Henry V's martial dreams; he grasped firmly the financial nettles which
> Henry IV had either evaded or sown. He achieved much that Richard II had
> tried but failed to do . . . Edward IV's achievements as man and king were not
> small . . . The foundations of what has commonly been called the 'New
> Monarchy' were laid not by Henry VII, but by Edward IV.

To a large extent, I believe, this reassessment of Edward of York
—now already hardening into the inflexible cement of 'A' Level
orthodoxy—was overdue and well deserved. And yet, if I may sound
a maverick note of scepticism, there is a risk of carrying our current
admiration too far. In particular, there is a danger of investing his
policies with a degree of consistency which they did not possess,
of over-estimating both the degree of his concern with restoring the

royal finances and 'politique reule and governance' and the extent of
his administrative achievements, and of ignoring the extent to which
they depended on the personal whim of a monarch whose judgement
was often far from sound.

As a king, Edward IV had many desirable qualities. He had a
handsome appearance, great personal charm, intelligence, a powerful memory, resourcefulness and self-confidence. He not only looked
like a king, he knew how to behave like one. But his complex
character also contained abundant defects. As well as a sensual
disposition which could afterwards be used to blacken his reputation, he was at various times to show traits of impulsiveness, in-
consistency, irresolution and over-confidence. These failings were
to reveal themselves throughout his reign. For this reason alone,
I do not find it necessary to follow Professor Chrimes in his hypo-
thesis that Edward's later years saw a marked decline in his powers
of judgement and a loss of grip on affairs of state. 'His death,' Professor Chrimes suggests, 'was a crowning mercy, for he had already
reached, if not passed, his zenith as king.'[3] Not only would it be
hard to find contemporary support for this belief, but it is also hard
to reconcile with the claim made by most of his modern admirers
that his later years, especially from 1478 onwards, were the most
fruitful period of the reign in terms of administrative innovation
and reform, especially in the field of finance, where they were stimu-
lated by his growing avarice.

Evidence of Edward's political blunders in the first decade of
his rule is not hard to find. The first clear indication that he might
not be 'the man to give nervous politicians the stability they desired'[4]
comes with his singularly ill-advised marriage in 1464 to the penni-
less widow of a former Lancastrian. Professor Lander has recently
argued persuasively that Edward's union with Elizabeth Woodville
was much less of a political disaster than has commonly been
supposed, and that too much has been made of contemporary
charges that he invited trouble by his inordinate promotion of the
queen's relatives.[5] But on the most charitable view his marriage
was an impulsive and unstatesmanlike act. He acted rashly and he
acted alone, and, as Polydore Vergil aptly remarked, he 'was led
by blynde affection and not by rule of reason'.[6] His later permissive-
ness in allowing the Woodvilles to scoop the marriage market provided the earl of Warwick with a genuine grievance: as father of
the two greatest heiresses in England, he could now find no suitable

husbands for them save Edward's brothers, whose marriages Edward
was not disposed to allow him.

Edward's political conduct in his first decade is also marked by
a lack of consistency. This was noted by K. B. McFarlane in the
king's treatment of political offenders. He observed that it was
typical of Edward IV that his practice touched all extremes, and
added, characteristically, 'to judge from its results its want of consistency was not due to any superior political insight'.[7] A similar
judgement might be passed upon his handling of the notorious case
of Sir Thomas Cook and his fellow London notables, arraigned
for treason in 1468 and eventually subjected to ruinous fines. Edward
had set out, skilfully and successfully, to win the goodwill and
financial backing of the London patriciate, and in the first decade
of his reign he had persuaded them to lend him nearly £40,000—
more than four times as much as they had lent the Lancastrians over
a rather longer period.[8] From the beginning of the reign they had
been the chief financial prop of a needy dynasty. To imperil all this
for the sake of an evanescent financial gain seems astonishing.
His action would be the more understandable had Cook, Sir John
Plummer and Humphrey Hayford, a former sheriff of London, been
guilty of anything serious. Professor J. G. Bellamy has recently con-
tended that we should not be misled by contemporary literary
evidence, especially the highly circumstantial account of the affair
in the *Great Chronicle of London*,[9] into regarding it as a miscarriage
of justice or an act of persecution led by the Woodvilles and the
royal councillor, Sir John Fogge, with the king's consent.[10] Instead,
he tells us, all was done by due process of law. But it is hard to see
that justice was done. The first presenting jury had to be dismissed
because it refused to indict, and a more pliant panel found;[11] the
fine of 8,000 marks imposed upon Cook seems disproportionate to
the offence of which he was apparently convicted (misprision of
treason, not treason proper); the fine was imposed even though
Cook presented a royal pardon covering treason amongst other
offences; and there is at least a suspicion that Chief Justice Markham
was dismissed his post because, by bringing in a lesser verdict, he
incurred the royal displeasure.[12] Whether Edward acted through
greed, or under undue influence from the Woodvilles, the pillorying
of Cook and his fellows would appear to have been at once unjust
and impolitic.[13]

The various errors and omissions of Edward's government,

especially his failure to do much to remedy the abuses which had pro-
liferated under Henry VI, were to cost him his throne in 1470. His
people were disillusioned with him: as John Warkworth observed,
the prosperity and peace for which they had hoped came not.[14] His
recovery of the throne in 1471 was to bring out all his best qualities,
and the successful campaigns of Barnet and Tewkesbury proved
very much a personal triumph for him. But it is worth remembering
that Edward's success owed much to good fortune as well as to his
own undoubted ability and energy. Had his enemies not come
against him singly rather than together; had Warwick not hesitated
disastrously in the early stages of Edward's invasion; had Somerset
not broken from his position at Tewkesbury—the story might have
had a very different ending.

But how much evidence is there for any increase in Edward's
political maturity during the second phase of his reign? Now secure
upon his throne, he had the opportunity to restore the royal finances
and introduce much-needed reforms into the government of the
realm, provided he had the good sense to keep clear of costly and
ambitious schemes of foreign conquest. But in fact he did *not* shun
Henry V's martial dreams. Exactly what Edward hoped to achieve
by his invasion of France in 1475 would be difficult to say with
certainty, but it was certainly not intended to be the bloodless
promenade which it became, nor to end with the English army
rolling drunk in the gutters of Amiens as guests of the wily Louis
XI. It had been preceded by three and a half years of careful and
elaborate diplomatic and military preparation, and only Duke
Charles of Burgundy's defection at the last minute enabled Edward
to extract himself from a difficult situation—with profit if not with
glory. Good fortune rather than good judgement proved his salvation
in 1475. Even at the very end of his reign he could still see his relations
with France in terms of personal revenge upon Louis XI for his
treachery, and the most immediately contemporary and best informed chronicler specifically tells us that in the months before he
died he was once again contemplating an invasion of France.[15]

Edward's later years saw the ruin of his foreign policy, and,
though it must be admitted that his diplomatic situation was far
from easy, his own mistakes of policy contributed largely to this end.
He wobbled uncertainly between the unpalatable alternatives of
supporting a hard-pressed Burgundy against France, and continuing
his profitable alliance with a Louis XI whom he knew he could not

trust. His grasp of the situation seems to have been very much clouded by his growing avarice. To read the details of his diplomacy in these years is to be astonished by his obsession with the idea of arranging advantageous foreign marriages for his children without having to spend a penny himself. It is an ironic comment upon his plans that none of his seven surviving children—two sons and five daughters—was married at the time of their father's death.[16] But his worst error was to embroil himself in an unnecessary war with Scotland, undertaken without clear objectives and for ill-defined reasons of prestige. This is not the place to recount the details, but there can be little doubt that the war with Scotland was essentially of Edward's making. In 1481 large sums were spent in preparation for a campaign which never materialised, and in 1482 even larger sums were consumed by Gloucester's fruitless march on Edinburgh, with the recovery of Berwick as a costly consolation prize. These operations absorbed Edward's reserves of cash, and compelled him to have recourse to benevolences and ultimately to parliamentary taxation. But they proved disastrous also to his Continental diplomacy. He could no longer be an effective support for Burgundy, and he had ceased to be a threat to France. The reconciliation of Maximilian of Burgundy and Louis of France by the treaty of Arras in December 1482, which saw the final defeat of Edward's foreign schemes, owed a good deal to his involvement with Scotland.

Lastly, in this sphere of political management, we come to the difficult question of Edward's arrangements for the government of the realm during the minority of his heir. The failure of the king's efforts to heal the feuds between his leading magnates, and thereby secure an untroubled succession for Edward, Prince of Wales, has long been regarded as a main reason for the bloodbath which followed his death. But Dr E. W. Ives's recent discovery amongst the records of the Augmentation Office of correspondence between Anthony, earl Rivers, and his business agent, Andrew Dymmock, provides fresh, if tantalising, evidence that Edward's own irresolution may have contributed to this end.[17] He had already given full power to Rivers to control the person of the prince, and on 8 March 1483, a few days before his final illness, he also gave him powers to raise troops in Wales 'if need be'.[18] This suggests an attempt to shelter his son behind the Woodville faction. Did he then change his mind and appoint Gloucester protector? Or did he never commit power to Gloucester at all? If he did not, he was inviting trouble, and it says little for his political judgement. Unfortunately, we cannot be sure of the facts, but there may be some justification for Dr Ives's comment that 'no death-bed histrionics could defeat the logic of his own policy. Edward IV was to blame for the faction fight which followed the succession of his young son.'[19]

In recent years Edward's failings as a politician have tended to be overlooked amidst the general chorus of praise for his achievements in domestic government. Most modern scholars would echo with approval Sir Thomas More's weighty epitaph on his work:

In whych tyme of hys latter daies, thys Realm was in quyet and prosperous estate: no feare of outewarde enemyes, no warre in hande, nor none towarde, but such as no manne looked for: the people towarde the Prynce, not in a constrained feare, but in a wyllynge and louynge obedyence: amonge them selfe, the commons in good peace.[20]

Edward's modern reputation rests squarely on his work as a renovator of the royal authority, as a king who brought wealth to the Crown and to his people, as a strong man who kept the peace of the realm. I should like now to discuss certain aspects of his government of England, first and chiefly the crucial question of royal finance, more especially his handling of revenue from land.

There is an obvious comparison here—as in most things—between Edward of York and Henry Tudor. Both were usurpers needing support; both faced repeated rebellions; both were clamped in what Professor Lander aptly calls 'the straitjacket of endowed monarchy';[21] both dealt with Parliaments reluctant to grant taxation save for an invasion of France; both, therefore, had to develop other sources of income in order to maintain their financial solvency. But it is an established fact that Henry VII balanced his books far more quickly: solvent by about 1492, he began to show a sizeable surplus from about 1497, whereas Edward was not free of debt until 1478.[22] Moreover, Henry was successful in raising royal revenue to a much higher level, whilst Edward (in Professor Elton's phrase) 'succeeded in returning to solvency but no more'.[23]

Why was Henry VII so much more successful? Partly because he was more ingenious and more ruthless in his methods, but also, I suggest, because he showed a consistency of purpose which Edward never had. This is where much modern writing tends, in my view, to give a misleading impression. Dr B. P. Wolffe's valuable studies of royal estate management under the Yorkist kings[24] take as their

main theme the proposition that from the beginning of his reign
Edward introduced into the management of the royal estates, including the duchy of York, the earldom of March, and the patrimony
of the Prince of Wales, new and efficient techniques of administration borrowed from methods in use on private estates. These methods
were soon extended to include forfeited estates (the lands of Somerset, Richmond, Northumberland, Wiltshire and Roos are mentioned)[25] and, from time to time, lands in royal wardship during
minority, when these were of sufficient importance. The impression
one derives is of a steady accumulation of the volume of land
under the king's control matched by a systematic policy of much
more efficient exploitation. Both these notions seem to me deserving
of scepticism.[26] It can, I think, be shown that Edward never had
any clear policy of adding to the royal revenue by the accumulation
of land, and there are grounds for questioning whether royal exploitation was very efficient in practice.

Historians have never paid sufficient attention to Edward's splen-
didly fortunate start as king. The great series of attainders in 1461,
involving 113 of his enemies, brought into his hands surely the most
magnificent accretion of landed revenue of the entire Middle Ages.
They included the estates of the dukes of Somerset and Exeter,
the earls of Pembroke, Northumberland, Devon and Wiltshire,
Viscount Beaumont, six barons and some dozens of lesser families.[27]
No wonder the Commons of 1461 were not disposed to vote any
subsidy—nor, indeed, was any asked for: the king now had ample
means to live of his own. Nor was this all. He could now draw
upon the revenues of his own paternal inheritance, the duchy of York
and the earldom of March, and upon the appanage of the Prince of
Wales, forfeited from the Lancastrian Prince Edward, and he enjoyed several valuable wardships, including the estates of Duke
Humphrey of Buckingham, killed at Northampton in 1460. No precise estimate could be given of the total annual value of all this, but
£30,000 would be a conservative guess—or about as much again as
the ordinary annual royal revenue in Henry VI's later years. One
more particular illustration of the size of this windfall is that, with
the exception of Glamorgan and Abergavenny, every major Marcher
lordship in south Wales, from Monmouth to Pembroke, was at the
king's disposal for the first few years of the reign.

Clearly, Edward could not, even had he wished, appropriate the
whole of this vast landed revenue to the royal purse. There were

both family and political pressures upon him to divest himself of large parts of it. He had to provide suitable appanages for his brothers, Clarence and Gloucester. Since he needed political support, he had to be prepared to reverse attainders and disgorge estates to reconciled and submissive Lancastrians. As Professor Lander has pointed out, it was much easier to recover one's estates from the Crown under Edward IV than it ever was under Henry VII.[28] But in fact, in the first decade of the reign at least, such reversals were negligible among the wealthier noble victims of 1461: none of the ducal and comital inheritances I have mentioned was restored before 1470, save Somerset's for a short time in 1463. Much more important was the king's need to reward his supporters and to increase their power in areas which had been strongly Lancastrian in sympathy: some of them were men with little territorial influence of their own. Thus there was ample political justification for the immense rewards showered upon men like William, Lord Hastings, in the Midlands, William, Lord Herbert, in south Wales, and Humphrey, Lord Stafford, in the south-west.[29] There is much less justification for the lavish gains achieved by the Nevill family in the first few years of the reign. Edward was grateful and the Nevills were greedy, and he seems to have been unable or unwilling to resist their continuous demands for royal patronage.[30] The fact remains that, for whatever reasons, a very large part of the lands gained in 1461 had been alienated. Was such lavish alienation politically necessary? Henry VII seems not to have found it so, and he retained large blocks of forfeited or escheated lands under royal control for years at a time, some from the beginning of his reign.[31] But under Edward IV, in the first decade of his rule, neither Exchequer nor Chamber benefited much from forfeitures or wardships. Of the various forfeited estates listed by Dr Wolffe as being placed under the control of specially appointed royal receivers, auditors and surveyors at the beginning of the reign, very little was still being administered by them in 1466.[32] For this reason, whatever new principles of estate management were introduced by the Yorkists, they were not applied to lands gained by forfeiture. And one of the reasons why Edward rewarded his Woodville relatives chiefly with offices, titles and a free hand on the marriage market may well have been that by 1466 he had no more land to give them.

It is abundantly clear that before 1471 Edward had no policy of adding to the revenues of the Crown by retaining his various gains in land. In some respects he went in the other direction, by making permanent alienations from the royal patrimony. Few of his predecessors had disposed of the possessions of the duchy of Lancaster on any great scale, but Edward plundered them for the benefit of his brothers. In 1464 the duke of Clarence was given *in tail male* Tutbury and several other duchy lordships: these were in fact recovered under the resumption Act of 1473, but the alienation was *intended* to be permanent.[33] The duke of Gloucester acquired the lordship of Ogmore *in tail* in 1477, and in 1482 he had a grant *in tail male* of all the duchy manors in Cumberland as part of his great north-western hereditary palatinate, which included the office of warden of the West Marches, then alienated from the Crown for the first time.[34] Sir Robert Somerville observed of these and other alienations of duchy property that 'it was left to the Yorkist Edward to begin in earnest a long process of alienation which, by the time of Queen Anne, had very greatly reduced the duchy's extent'.[35]

How far did Edward's policy towards the accumulation of royal land alter after 1471, when there was no longer the same need to reward supporters or placate opponents, and the king's position was unchallenged at home? Unlike 1461, 1471 brought no great windfall of forfeited estates and wardships. The greatest offender of all, Warwick, escaped attainder, very probably (as Professor Lander has suggested) because the royal dukes of Clarence and Gloucester, as claimants to the inheritance, wanted a more secure title than royal grant.[36] Only thirteen attainders followed Edward's recovery of the throne, and the only magnate to suffer forfeiture was the earl of Oxford. But such as there was Edward lost no time in disposing of. The De Vere lands went to Gloucester, along with other forfeitures, to the value of at least £1,000 per annum. The custody of the Lovell estates was given to the duke of Suffolk, that of John Tiptoft, earl of Worcester's inheritance went to his widow, Elizabeth, and her second husband, Sir William Stanley; the inheritance of John, Lord Wenlock, who had no direct heir, seems to have been given to Thomas Rotherham, bishop of Lincoln, some time before 1475.[37] Neither the royal Chamber nor the Exchequer benefited in any way from the confiscations and acquisitions of 1471.

Still further evidence of Edward's indifference to the possibilities

of increasing his revenue from land comes from the history of the
Talbot estates, in the king's hands during the minority of the heir,
George Talbot, from 1473 to the end of the reign. This was one of
the wardships particularly mentioned by Dr Wolffe as being inte-
grated into 'the Yorkist revenue experiment'.[38] At first they were
largely divided between the queen and William, Lord Hastings,
but by 1478 something approaching two-thirds of the estate (after
allowance for a dower interest) had passed into Hastings' hands.
For this he paid an annual farm of £300, though the lands he held
were worth at least twice as much. Of the part remaining under
royal control, lands worth about £375 in clear annual value were
charged with annuities totalling £200. Thus the total cash yield to
the king's Chamber of a comital estate worth in excess of £1,000
per annum was in the neighbourhood of little more than £450 per
annum.[39]

The first large estate to be appropriated almost intact into the royal
revenue system, whether by way of forfeiture or by way of wardship,
was Clarence's share of the Warwick, Salisbury and Spencer lands,
forfeited on his death in 1478. It was also the only one. In contrast,
one finds Henry VII, after a similar period of eighteen years' rule
administering a whole series of forfeited or escheated estates and
wards' lands.[31] This is one major reason why his land revenue
towards the end of his reign was of the order of £40,000.[40] It is very
doubtful, at least on the basis of the figures provided by Dr Wolffe,
whether Edward's revenue from land reached half that total, even
when allowance has been made for Henry's unusually favourable
family position by 1504.

I have gone into all this at some length in order to emphasise
the dangers of crediting Edward IV with a consistent and determined policy of increasing royal revenues by whatever means were
available to him. In terms of land revenue, at least, financial considerations were constantly subordinated to political expediency,
or to indulge Edward's wasteful generosity towards his friends and
favourites. Had he possessed the political and financial toughness
of a Henry VII, he might have achieved solvency far earlier, and
been a far wealthier king than he ever was.

Much has been written recently in praise of the Yorkist system of
land management. Innovations there certainly were, such as the
appointment of special receivers, auditors and surveyors to replace
the inefficient farming methods of the Exchequer, efforts to in-

crease the royal revenue by the introduction of new rentals and the collection of outstanding arrears, the searching out by special enquiries of concealed or neglected sources of income, especially feudal revenues from wardships, reliefs, marriages, respite of homage, and outlawries. It is, however, generally conceded that what Sir Robert Somerville calls 'this intense activity over feudal dues' belongs mainly to the last four or five years of the reign.[41] But just how effective was all this? Professor Myers believes it was considerable. Commenting on the official progress of the duchy of Lancaster council through Lancashire and Cheshire in 1476, he pointed to the sharp increase in the receipts of Sir Thomas Stanley, as the duchy's receiver-general in Lancashire, which followed it. From £347 in 1476–77, they rose to £800 in 1477–78, and finally climbed to £885 in 1481–82.[42] Can we regard this as evidence of a general increase? In the present state of our knowledge, it is a difficult question to answer. But there are some significant pointers in the other direction. The ministers' accounts for the duchy honour of Pontefract in west Yorkshire show no such increase in the yield of land as did Lancaster. Revenue there remained fairly stable throughout the reign.[43] It is not possible to provide comparable figures of total duchy revenue for the beginning and end of the reign (partly because of documentary deficiencies and partly because of alienations), but Somerville found that in 1463–64 the gross yield of the north parts of the duchy was £7,391; in 1478 it was £6,696— some £700 less.[44] Part of the reason for this decline in revenue may have been the neglect and inefficiency of the duke of Gloucester as chief steward north of the Trent: in 1482 the duchy council roundly told him that he and his deputies, through sales of timber, and other defects, had brought his lordships into great decay.[45] The letter is a remarkably outspoken criticism of a royal duke, but one is entitled to wonder whether Henry VII would have tolerated such a situation over a period of twelve years.

Evidence from other royal estates, or lands under royal control, suggests a similar picture. Figures published by Professor Rosenthal for the lands of the duchy of York show that the duchy lands in Somerset and Dorset produced £348 in 1459–60 and £352 in 1477–78. A group of Yorkshire manors which yielded £117 at the beginning of the reign were yielding £118 in 1483–84.[46] Nor did royal methods of administration lead to any increase in revenue on private estates in the king's hands. For example, the Talbot lordship of

Goodrich, in Herefordshire, fell into the hands of William, Lord Herbert, in 1461, and he retained it to the end of his life. In the three years 1465–68 it supplied Herbert with just over £115 per annum. But after seven years in the hands of royal receivers in the 1470s it was yielding only half as much.[39]

Too often there was a gap between theory and practice in royal estate management. Alongside 'an enterprising and reforming spirit' in the management of the duchy of Lancaster Sir Robert Somerville noted many striking examples of failure to get things done. For example, in an effort to increase revenue from the Yorkshire honours, the duchy council appointed commissioners to make new rentals in 1474, but it found that nothing had been done when it visited the area in 1476. And when one turns to the ministers' accounts one finds that nothing had been done two years after that. In Michaelmas 1480 the officials of the honour of Pontefract were still working on rentals drawn up in 3 Henry VI (1424–25), whilst a few were still using rentals made in 8 Henry V (1420–21).[47]

For contemporary evidence of imperfections in the Yorkist system we need look no further than the well known document in Harleian MS 433, usually attributed to the reign of Richard III, entitled 'A remembrance made, as well for hasty levy of the king's revenues growing of all his possessions and hereditaments as for the profitable estate and governance of the same possessions'.[48] Dr Wolffe, for example, believes that 'it undoubtedly represents a survey of the organisation of the royal revenues as it existed at the accession of Richard III, with some suggestions for improvements'.[49] The faults it lists are, therefore, those of Edward IV's time. Among them it stresses the laxity of accounting procedures at the Exchequer, the fact that stewards of royal lands were often ill-equipped for their posts, and that royal estates, wardships and ecclesiastical temporalities in the king's hands were commonly farmed out, instead of being administered directly for the king's profit. Somerville remarked of this remembrance that many of its regulations bear a remarkable likeness to duchy ordinances of Edward IV's later years: but it was left to Henry VII to make them effective.[50]

One may well doubt whether Edward's government was much more successful in exploiting the king's feudal revenues. Here again the problem was recognised and remedies were proposed, but the arrangements for enforcement lacked teeth. As early as 1471 the escheator in Lancashire was particularly directed to enquire into the

practice of tenants' entering on their inheritances without livery
or licence, but in 1479 the duchy council noted that the practice
continued.[51] Dr Bean found examples where Edward failed to
employ existing powers to prevent tenants-in-chief evading rights
of wardship, so that the Crown lost the wardship of the heir's body
and his marriage as well as the wardship of his lands. At the very
end of his reign Edward endeavoured to deal with the problem of
evasion by legislation against uses. His Bill was designed to apply
only in the duchy of Lancaster, but even so was emasculated before
it reached the statute book.[52] The problem of uses was difficult
indeed, and Henry VII had little more success with it than
Edward.[53]

Finally, I should like to comment briefly on Edward's record in
the field of law and order. Dr Bellamy praises his success 'in
reducing endemic disorder to manageable proportions and thereby
setting the stage for the final assault on local disturbance'.[54] It is,
of course, true that Edward was conspicuously more successful in
preventing the escalation of disorder than Henry VI had been, and
he was able to stifle the quarrels of his great men. It is also true
that the chronic violence and lawlessness of medieval society offered
a peculiarly intractable problem for governments without a large-
scale bureaucracy, a standing army or a police force. Even so, it
would be easy to over-estimate the degree of Yorkist effectiveness
in this matter of peace-keeping. Even in the 1470s there is a disturbing incidence of outrageous crime and sustained defiance of the
government's authority. In 1472 the chancellor's address to Parliament could plausibly propose a foreign war as the only way to deal
with endemic disorder, ending on the despairing note 'it can not
be thought that the rigour of the law for this seson should be the
most convenable remedie'.[55]

Some of the incidents which he may have had in mind—themselves matters of petitions for redress in this very Parliament—recall
the worst disorders of the 1450s. The peculiarly atrocious murder
of John Glyn, deputy to the earl of Wiltshire as steward of Cornwall,
seized by armed men whilst actually presiding over the duchy court
at Liskeard, and afterwards horribly cut to pieces, bears comparison
with the notorious slaying of Nicholas Radford in Devon in 1455.[56]
The long career of lawlessness and terrorism of Sir Henry Bodrugan
in Cornwall recalls the misdeeds of Gilbert Debenham in East
Anglia in Henry VI's later years.[57] In Lancashire there was a

prolonged private war between the Harringtons and the Stanleys in the early 1470s. As late as June 1473 they were still holding Hornby Castle in manner of war in defiance of all royal directives. Only the weight of a powerful commission headed by the duke of Gloucester eventually overawed them.[58] Parliament itself petitioned for action in a serious case of intimidation at Hereford in 1474. Evil-doers indicted for riot and felony had been acquitted in spite of the king's promise that they should be punished, and seventeen of the most substantial knights and esquires of the county openly confessed before the royal commissioners that 'they durst not present nor say the trouthe of the defautes before rehersed, for drede of murdrying, and to be myscheved in their owne houses, considering the grete nombre of the said Mysdoers, and the grete berers uppe of the same.'[59] Lancashire continued notoriously lawless to the end of Edward's reign, reducing the duchy council to despair: its only solution—that the king should visit the area in person—is a sad commentary on the ineffectiveness of normal law enforcement agencies.[60]

The crux of the problem lay in the immunity of the powerful offender, especially those who had the king's support. There was an inherent conflict between repeated demands for *impartial* justice and the king's committed support of the great men to whom he had given the rule of the shires. Bitter complaints against their excesses run through the reign. The Commons in 1467 were particularly outspoken in linking a rising crime rate with the 'heavy lordship' of men in standing with the king, against whom redress could not be obtained.[61] The rebel manifesto of 1469—obviously a partisan document but calculated to appeal to popular grievances— also stresses the malignant effects of the private power of the king's friends: 'they will not suffre the Kynges lawes to be executyd uppon whom they owyd favere unto . . . by the wheche gret murdre, robbres, rapes, oppressions, and extorcions, as well be them, as by thayre gret mayntenaunces of theire servauntes, to us daly done and remayne unpunysshyd, to the gret hurt and grugge of alle this londe.'[62] The Commons of 1472 returned to the same theme.[63]

In this they were beating their heads against a wall. The king would not offend his great men to secure impartial justice, and never paid more than lip-service to the notion of action against the abuses of livery and maintenance, unless people became really obstreperous, or disorder was tinged with sedition. Professor Lander has argued that this was an inevitable consequence of the king's need to have the co-operation of his nobility, and that in this respect Edward IV and Henry VII were very much in the same boat, and followed the same policy. 'The magnate had to be given a fairly free hand in his own district; in return for his loyalty the government did not probe over-carefully into his activities.'[64] Both kings, he argues, were prepared to increase the wealth and influence of those who were loyal in order to secure their control of the shires. But was there not a significant difference of degree? Edward was extraordinarily lavish in delegating local power and influence to his supporters. No man had ever enjoyed the power in south Wales wielded by Lord Herbert in the 1460s. The same is true of Richard of Gloucester in the north in the 1470s. Professor Chrimes would have us believe that by 1483 'there was no over-mighty subject left in England'.[65] But was not Gloucester the mightiest of over-mighty subjects? And was not his great north-country connection, built up with active royal encouragement, a major factor in enabling him to consolidate his hold on the throne? This was part of the price which Edward IV paid for effective political control during his lifetime.

Edward IV's most consistent quality was his determination to be master in his own realm, and in this he achieved considerable success. He died wealthy, respected, and in his own bed. This was no mean feat for a fifteenth-century ruler, and was not achieved without more than his share of good fortune. But he should not be credited with qualities he did not possess. In particular, he should not be too readily regarded as a Mk. I version of Henry VII. The difference in their personalities is profound, and the differences between their policies are hardly less important than the resemblances.

Notes

1 These are the opinions of, respectively, J. R. Lander, 'Edward IV: the modern legend, and a revision', *History*, xli (1956), 52, quoting John Richard Green; A. R. Myers, *England in the late Middle Ages* (1952), 113; G. A. Holmes, *The Later Middle Ages* (1962), 220; B. Wilkinson, *Constitutional History of England in the Fifteenth Century* (1964), 144.

2 S. B. Chrimes, *Lancastrians, Yorkists, and Henry VII* (1964), 111, 124-5.

3 Chrimes, *op. cit.*, 122, 124.

4 K. B. McFarlane, 'The Wars of the Roses', *Proc. Brit. Acad.*, L (1965), 114.

5 J. R. Lander, 'Marriage and politics in the fifteenth century: the Nevilles and the Wydevilles', *B.I.H.R.*, xxxvi (1963), 129–43.

6 *English History*, ed. H. Ellis (Camden Society, 1844), 117.

7 McFarlane, *loc. cit.*, 101.

8 A. Steel, *Receipt of the Exchequer, 1377–1485* (1954), 344–5. Steel believed that London did not lend to the Yorkists until as late as June 1461 (p. 285), but in fact it had already lent them over £11,000, beginning in July 1460 (P.R.O., Warrants for Issues, E.404/72/1, No. 22).

9 Ed. A. H. Thomas and I. D. Thornley (1938), 204–6.

10 J. G. Bellamy, 'Justice under the Yorkist kings', *American Journal of Legal History*, IX (1965), 143–5.

11 P.R.O., K.B.9/319, m. 35–7, 40. Cf. J. G. Bellamy, *The Law of Treason in England in the Later Middle Ages* (1970), 140–1, for the suggestion that there was nothing illegal in the king's labouring a grand jury; but the dismissal of the first jury goes beyond mere labouring; and, to judge from the delay, even the second jury needed a good deal of pressure before it would indict. It also refused to indict other alleged offenders.

12 Bellamy, *Law of Treason*, 168, 222–3.

13 For evidence of the influence of Richard Woodville, Earl Rivers, upon Edward, see T. B. Pugh's contribution to this volume.

14 *Chronicle*, ed. J. O. Halliwell (Camden Society, 1839), 12, and see also the observations of McFarlane, *loc. cit.*, 114.

15 'Croyland Chronicle', ed. W. Fulman, *Rerum Anglicarum Scriptores* (1684), 563. A similar statement was made by Polydore Vergil, *English History*, 171.

16 By 1483 the ten-year-old Duke Richard of York had already lost his child bride, Anne Mowbray (d. 1481). Marriages already contracted for the other children included unions with the heirs of France, Scotland, Burgundy and Brittany. Of these, the failure of the first three was directly due to the collapse of Edward's foreign policy.

17 E. W. Ives, 'Andrew Dymmock and the papers of Antony, Earl Rivers, 1482–83', *B.I.H.R.*, XLI (1968), 216–29.

18 For earlier commissions to array men, see R. A. Griffiths, below p. 161.

19 Ives, *loc. cit.*, 224.

20 *History of King Richard III*, ed. R. S. Sylvester (*Complete Works*, Yale edition, II, 1963), 4.

21 *Conflict and Stability in Fifteenth-century England* (1969), 113.

22 G. R. Elton, *England under the Tudors* (1955), 53.

23 Elton, *op. cit.*, 46.

24 'The management of English royal estates under the Yorkist kings', *E.H.R.*, LXXI (1956), 1–27; also his 'Henry VII's land revenues and Chamber finance', *E.H.R.*, LXXIX (1964), 225–54, and *The Crown Lands, 1461–1536* (1970), especially ch. III.

25 Wolffe, 'Management of English royal estates', 5–6; *Crown Lands*, 57.

26 I should make it clear that it is not my intention to question either the fact or the importance of the administrative innovations described by Dr Wolffe.

27 *R.P.*, v, 476–83.

28 J. R. Lander, 'Attainder and forfeiture, 1453-1509', *H.J.*, IV (1961), 128, 134*ff*.

29 *C.P.R.*, 1461-67, *passim*.

30 For references to some of their gains, see Lander, 'Marriage and politics', 143-4. Contemporary comments on their greed, especially that of George Nevill, may be found in Warkworth, *Chronicle*, 25-6; 'Hearne's fragment' in Thomas Sprott, *Chronicle*, ed. T. Hearne (1719), 299.

31 See, for example, the extract from the General Surveyors' accounts for 1503-04, printed in Wolffe, *Crown Lands*, 142-6.

32 The Somerset and Wiltshire estates mainly went to William Nevill, earl of Kent, and later to Humphrey, Lord Stafford; the Northumberland lands were mainly in Nevill hands; Hastings had many of the Roos estates, and Clarence much of the Richmond lands. This point will be fully documented in my forthcoming book on Edward IV.

33 R. Somerville, *History of the Duchy of Lancaster*, I, *1265-1503* (1953), 233.

34 *Ibid.*, 422.

35 *Ibid.*, 240; and see also his remarks (241-2) on the effect on the duchy of saving clauses in the Acts of resumption.

36 Lander, 'Attainder and forfeiture', 129-30. Though not attainted, Warwick was found guilty of treason after his death under a commission of oyer and terminer in Middlesex and Hertfordshire in 1472 (*C.P.R.*, *1467-77*, 353; P.R.O., K.B.9/41, m. 38). I am indebted to Dr R. L. Storey for drawing my attention to this point.

37 *C.P.R.*, *1467-77*, 297, 310; J. S. Roskell, 'John Lord Wenlock of Someries', *Publications of the Bedfordshire Historical Record Society*, XXXVIII (1958), 48.

38 'Management of royal estates', 6; *Crown Lands*, 57.

39 A. J. Pollard, 'The family of Talbot, Lords Talbot and Earls of Shrewsbury in the fifteenth century', unpublished Ph.D. thesis, University of Bristol (1968).

40 Wolffe, *Crown Lands*, 69.

41 *Op. cit.*, 243.

42 A. R. Myers, 'An official progress through Lancashire and Cheshire in 1476', *Trans. Historic Society of Lancashire and Cheshire*, CXV (1964), 5 n.

43 P.R.O., D.L.29/509/8249; D.L.29/511/8261.

44 *Op. cit.*, 237-8.

45 Somerville, *op. cit.*, 254.

46 J. T. Rosenthal, 'The estates and finances of Richard, duke of York (1411-60)', *Studies in Medieval and Renaissance History*, II (1965), 149-50.

47 P.R.O., D.L.29/511/8261; Somerville, *op. cit.*, 250.

48 *Letters and Papers Illustrative of the Reigns of Richard III and Henry VII*, ed. J. Gairdner (Rolls Series, 1861-63), I, 79-85.

49 'Management of royal estates', 21.

50 *Op. cit.*, 257.

51 Somerville, *op. cit.*, 245-6.

52 J. M. W. Bean, *The Decline of English Feudalism, 1215-1540* (1968), 215-16, 238-42; and cf. 235-6, for his comments on Henry VII's policies in this sphere.

53 As an illustration of this point, Professor Lander called attention to the

findings of Dr E. W. Ives (*E.H.R.*, LXXXII (1967)), that in 1529 and 1540 Henry VIII was prepared to bargain with the nobility for the legalisation of the evasion of feudal dues over two-thirds of their estates; the king was to have only one-third.

54 'Justice under the Yorkist kings', 155.

55 *Literae Cantuarienses*, ed. J. B. Sheppard (Rolls Series, 1889), III, 276.

56 *R.P.*, VI, 35–8.

57 *R.P.*, VI, 136–43.

58 J. C. Wedgwood, *History of Parliament, 1439–1539: Biographies* (1936), 4–6; *C.P.R., 1467–77*, 426–7; *C.C.R., 1468–76*, 244, 315.

59 *R.P.*, VI, 159–60.

60 Somerville, *op. cit.*, 225, 252–3.

61 *R.P.*, V, 618.

62 Warkworth, *Chronicle*, 49.

63 *R.P.*, VI, 8–9.

64 *The Wars of the Roses* (1965), 29.

65 *Lancastrians, Yorkists, and Henry VII*, 125.

S. B. Chrimes

Professor of History
University College, Cardiff
in the University of Wales

4   The reign of Henry VII

The difficulties of getting a detached view of the reign of Henry VII
are considerable, and it is hard to work towards a fresh appraisal
of the realities of the reign, or indeed of the man himself. We are
all too familiar with the extent to which Shakespearean drama
and Tudor propaganda have bedevilled interpretation of fifteenth-
century English history from Henry IV to Richard III. Fortunately,
he did not try his dramatist's hand on Henry VII, but the fact is
that the common efforts at understanding the reign of the first
Tudor have for centuries been dominated, until very recently, by
a literary *tour de force* of great power and persuasive effect, comparable in some respects with Shakespearean plays but composed
more than a hundred years after Henry VII's decease, purporting
to be not drama but sober history, and taken as such for generations
thereafter. This has been the trouble with Francis Bacon's *History
of the Reign of King Henry VII*. Whatever motives moved him
to write this classic work, and however influenced he was by ideal-
istic images of Renaissance princes, he certainly intended it to be
a history, and succeeded in inducing later historians to regard it
almost as a primary authority for the reign. Nearly all subsequent
accounts, until the quite recent, have been highly coloured by his
interpretations of the reign and of the man. This is not surprising,
for Bacon possessed a most powerful and penetrating intellect, and
his English prose style was superb. His honeyed words and striking
phrases remain highly seductive to this day. What is surprising is
that it seems to be impossible to find any substantial study of
Henry VII's reign between 1622, when Bacon's *History* was published, and 1892, when the original German edition of Wilhelm
Busch's *England unter den Tudors, Band I, König Heinrich VII*,

was published in Stuttgart, fortunately published three years later
in English, thanks to James Gairdner, in a translation by Alice M.
Todd. A few years before this, what proved to be the last edition
of Bacon's work was edited with notes by the Rev. J. Rawson
Lumby in the Pitt Press series (1885) until a new edition by R.
Lockyer appeared in 1971. James Gairdner published his *Henry
VII* in the 'Twelve English Statesmen' series in 1889, described
in Conyers Read's *Bibliography* (second edition, 1959) as 'the
standard English Life'. Lumby undoubtedly did a good service
in bringing a text of Bacon into easy reach, but he was after all the
Norrisian Professor of Divinity and not over-qualified to apply
historical criticism to his edition. James Gairdner's services to
fifteenth-century studies were, of course, of fundamental importance,
mainly as an editor of now indispensable texts and documents, but
he remained rather conventional in his treatment of the reigns of
both Richard III and Henry VII, prone as he was to being over-
influenced by Sir Thomas More and Francis Bacon respectively in
his valuable studies.

But it was Busch who not only brought his critical faculties to
bear on Bacon's work but also produced the first substantial study
of Henry VII's reign on the lines of recognisably modern scholarship, at least as understood in the 1890s. His work remains in a
class of its own, invaluable for its detailed survey of many features of
the reign, based on meticulous study of mostly printed sources, and
for its copious references and scrupulous scrutiny of materials. A mine
of information it remains (even if, alas, devoid of an index), but naturally much of Busch's efforts at interpretation smacks of his era and
outlook, and no one now, presumably, would think of Henry VII's
reign as witnessing the establishment of 'an enlightened despotism'.

With the early twentieth century, new notes were struck by
A. F. Pollard's *The Reign of Henry VII from Contemporary
Sources*, in three volumes, which, if it did not do much else,
brought a very considerable and most valuable selection of documents into the purview of students. But the year of publication
(1914) was unfortunate, and the follow-up does not seem to have
been very noticeable. A reprint was produced in New York in 1967,
unfortunately at a very high price. In 1934 K. Pickthorn's *Early
Tudor Government, Henry VII* broke some new ground by making
a fresh approach to questions of government, even if perhaps in
rather a snippety and not very accurate way.

The standard textbooks have until recently remained largely conventional rehashes of Bacon, Busch and some Pickthorn. J. D. Mackie's volume, *The Early Tudors* (1952), invaluable as it was and is for foreign policy, is a case in point, and G. R. Elton's *England under the Tudors* (1955), though fresher, naturally could not give very much space or consideration to the first Tudor king. We have not been well served with selected documentary material for Henry VII's reign since the publication of Pollard's collection. Neither J. R. Tanner's nor G. R. Elton's or C. H. Williams's collections of documents[1] included more than a trifling selection of documents of any kind from Henry VII's reign. But we have, indeed, a good series of printed materials, many of them edited by the indefatigable James Gairdner, in the Rolls series, Record Commission and P.R.O. publications, and some chronicles, the most valuable of which is, of course, Denys Hay's splendid edition of Polydore Vergil.

The fact is that the amount and range of original research in the period remained, and remains, quite inadequate to provide a firm basis for fresh appraisals. We have, however, in recent years seen a considerable number of specialised monographs and articles which are gradually changing our conceptions and bringing us closer to a grasp of more realities. The effect has begun to show in the recent surveys by the present writer,[2] by Dr R. L. Storey[3] and Professor J. R. Lander,[4] and in the analysis by Roger Lockyer.[5] The researches of a number of scholars have brought us into a fair condition as regards Henry VII's financial affairs,[6] his Council[7] and his foreign policy.[8] But we remain weak on a number of important topics—on his Parliaments, his judicature, including that of Chancery, and on much of his administrative machinery. We remain incredibly weak on the biographies of the leading personalities of the reign. It is hard to think of a single useful biographical study of any personage, not even of the highly important John Morton, apart from some valuable sketches of a few individuals provided in the appendices of such works as W. C. Richardson's *Tudor Chamber Administration*.[9] There are, of course, more reasons for the comparative neglect of Henry VII's reign than the obvious fact that it has for long fallen between the stools (or should I say the Chairs?) occupied respectively by medievalists blinkered by 1485 as a *terminus ad quem*, and by Tudorists preoccupied with the rumbustious activities of Henry VIII and his ministers. The fundamental fact is that it has become in recent years increasingly manifest that the realistic history of Henry VII's reign could never be grasped without much more research, not simply into the reign itself, but also into the Yorkist period, itself a monstrously neglected period until very recent years. Many valuable contributions[10] to this field have been made by scholars, some of whom, I am happy to say, are contributors to this volume. Without their labours we should still largely be obliged to intone Bacon and Busch—and see whether any erudite puns or punches could be pulled out of that. It has become abundantly clear that Henry VII's achievements, whatever they were exactly, depended greatly upon Yorkist precedents and efforts in many spheres. Henry VII's activities now appear much less original or innovatory than used to be supposed, and the trend, to some extent, must be towards cutting Henry down to more natural and, I think, more human proportions.

One cannot, of course, refer to more than a few—say, six—points in this paper: (1) the effects of Henry's early life, (2) the king's Council, (3) Parliament and legislation, (4) law enforcement, (5) finance, and (6) the man himself. But I cannot expect to be more than very brief on any one of these topics.

1 *Henry VII's early life*

I am convinced that, in any estimate that may some day be made of Henry VII as man and as king, fuller account needs to be taken of the very peculiar circumstances of his early life. He was born in Pembroke Castle on 25 January 1457, and the first fourteen years of his existence were spent in Wales, nearly all of them in the guardianship of William Herbert of Raglan, a leading Yorkist supporter and Edward IV's favoured key man in Wales. After a very few years he saw little, if anything, of his mother, Margaret Beaufort (who married secondly, before 1464, Henry Stafford, and thirdly, before 1471, Lord Stanley). Henry had, of course, been born after his father's, Edmund Tudor's, death, and his uncle Jasper, to whom he owed so much in later years, was inevitably out of sight at this time. There was, therefore, nothing Tudorish about his upbringing. How far it was really Welsh in more than a topographical sense one hardly knows. Herbert's wife, Ann Devereux (daughter of Walter Devereux, Lord Ferrers of Chartley), looked after him for some years, including the period after Herbert's death in 1469, and she was not a Welsh woman by birth. He must

indeed have been tended by Welsh people, but I know of no
evidence that would enable us to say he ever became seriously Welsh-
speaking. There is no suggestion that he ever visited England,
except once during the readeption of Henry VI. Undoubtedly his
upbringing was in a Welsh environment, and Herbert intended to
marry him off to one of his own daughters. But one must not over-
emphasise the Welshness of his genetics. His father Edmund was
by descent partly Welsh and partly French; his mother, Margaret
Beaufort, might be described as English; his grandfather Owen was
indeed wholly Welsh, but his grandmother Catherine had been
partly French and partly Bavarian in ancestry.

When one bears these facts in mind, and the circumstance that
the next fourteen years of his life were spent in exile, mostly in
Brittany and for a short time in France, and that the all-important
refugees who eventually joined him in exile were mostly from
England, one feels obliged to refrain from overstressing the Welsh
influences shaping Henry's mind and ambitions. In any event, it was
not, of course, any Welsh upsurge that brought Henry to the
gambler's throw that led to Bosworth field. It was the decision of
the French court to use him as a pawn in Franco-Breton politics, to
distract Richard III from his intent to aid Brittany.[11]

It is true that Henry's landing and march through Wales were
unopposed. But he was not exactly received with open arms, and
the extreme caution with which Rhys ap Thomas and other Welsh
leaders meandered towards open support for his cause may well have
obliged Henry to discount the value to him of purely Welsh senti-
ments. Moreover, it was not his purpose to fulfil bardic prophecies
and visions, but to get the crown of England and to keep it. To the
English, Henry's Welsh pretensions can hardly have seemed much
of a recommendation, especially as some of his family connections
had suffered death or forfeiture because of their involvement in
Owain Glyndŵr's rebellion against those Lancastrians, descent from
whom constituted Henry's sole hereditary claim to that crown.
Henry, therefore, when his step-relatives won for him the first, and
nearly the last, battle he ever saw himself, would make some
political propaganda out of his Welsh connections, would use the
Red Dragon banner on occasions, would remember to give small
sums of money to Welshmen about his court with which to celebrate
St David's day, grant favourable charters to some Welsh communities, in time would advance Rhys ap Thomas to be the

dominant figure in Wales, and call his own first-born son Arthur
(as, indeed, Edward IV had so named his illegitimate son). But
all this did not amount to very much of a pro-Welsh policy. His
efforts to bind the lords marcher by indenture to fulfil their duties
are a different matter.

But it is not my purpose to provoke my Welsh colleagues unneces-
sarily. At the moment I merely want to remind us of the very
peculiar, difficult and dangerous circumstances of the first twenty-
eight years of Henry's life and the extreme improbability that he
would ever reach the throne. When he did get to it he had spent
half his life in penurious and very insecure circumstances on the
Continent; he knew hardly anybody in England, and hardly anyone
knew him either. He had never managed any lands of his own, and
had no personal knowledge of government. Not surprising, therefore, that when he got the crown he remained cautious and wary,
suspicious and crafty, obsessed with the real or imaginary problems
of security, preoccupied, 'like a miser' as they said later, with what
Bacon suavely called 'the felicity of full coffers'. Not surprising,
either, that his most trusted ministers and councillors for the rest
of his or their lives were those who had been his fellow exiles or
had shown their hands before the god of battles showed his at
Bosworth.

2 The king's Council

This brings us to the king's Council. On this subject we need not
perhaps altogether share Geoffrey Elton's despondency as revealed
in his article on 'Why the history of the early Tudor Council
remains unwritten'.[12] Much of it no doubt is still unwritten and
much of it is likely to remain for ever unwritten, for lack of
material. However, a good deal has been revealed in recent years,
especially in the indispensable work of the late C. G. Baynes and
Professor W. H. Dunham.[13] We can, after all, get some grasp of a
topic without pretending to full knowledge. I cannot attempt to
summarise all available information here, but there are certain
points that I would wish to emphasise.

Nothing could be more obvious than the essential unity and
flexibility of the Council throughout the reign. The king's Council
was simply the king's Council; there was no Court of Star Chamber,
even though councillors continued to exercise jurisdiction in the
Camera Stellata as they had for generations before. I doubt whether

there were any genuine committees of the Council, even though recognisable groups of councillors existed, such as the Council Learned in the Law, which undoubtedly functioned, even though our information about it is extremely scanty. No statute created any such committee. The Act of 1487 manifestly established a ministerial tribunal, not a conciliar committee of any sort. There was no 'whole', 'privy', 'inner' or 'attendant' council; no offshoots in the north or Wales. The king's Council, moreover, in the sense of 'all the councillors', never met. The total number of councillors identified for the whole reign is 227. Of these, 183 are known to have attended one or more of 135 known meetings of the Council in one form or another spread over twenty-one of the twenty-five years or so of the reign. Of the total number, a rough division into categories has been made: forty-three peers, forty-five courtiers, sixty-one churchmen, twenty-seven common lawyers, forty-nine officials. Some two-thirds of the peerage were present at one or more meetings of the Council over the reign. There is no substance in the idea that Henry VII snubbed the peers; on the contrary, he clearly sought to associate with his government as many of them as he could trust by designating them councillors, even though few of them were given regular jobs. Naturally, nothing like a meeting of all the Council ever took place. At most two dozen or so councillors were summoned and attended habitually or frequently. This was not an inner Council; it *was* the Council in so far as the Council was manifested in a formal meeting. Some at least, but not necessarily all, of these took the councillor's oath. The most regular attendants, as we should expect, were the chancellor, the treasurer and the keeper of the privy seal, a small number of councillors in whom the king reposed special confidence, of whom more anon, plus a varying number of councillors, frequently but not regularly attendant, summoned on grounds we know not what.

There is no great difficulty in determining where Henry looked to obtain trustworthy recruits to add to the nucleus of a Council which he had already formed in Brittany and France and had brought with him. He found a substantial number of them from the ranks of those who had had experience as councillors to either Edward IV or Richard III or both. Where else, after all, could he possibly find men of practical experience as advisers and administrators? Twenty-nine of his frequent councillors had been councillors to one or other of the Yorkist kings; thirteen to both, nineteen to Richard III. Fifteen were near relatives of Edward IV's councillors, and others had had prominent administrative careers under the Yorkist regimes.[14] Not surprising should the regime of the first Tudor turn out to be in large measure a continuation of the Yorkist one.

Once Henry had chosen his principal officers, he trusted them and kept them in office for very long periods. Two chancellors held office for twenty years between them: John Morton from 1486 until his death in 1500; William Warham from 1504 to 1509, and beyond to 1513. Lord Dinham was treasurer from 1486 until his death in 1501, and was succeeded by none other than Thomas Howard, earl of Surrey, for the rest of the reign and far beyond until 1522. As for the keepership of the privy seal, the wily diplomat Richard Fox held it from 1487 to 1516.

There were five councillors who attended council meetings very frequently without holding one of the three principal offices, and who were clearly very high in the king's confidence. All five had in one way or another aligned themselves with Henry before Bosworth. These were Reginald Bray, who in the earliest days of the Buckingham conspiracy of 1483 had enlisted at least two of the others— Giles Daubeney and Richard Guildford; the other two, Thomas Lovell and John Riselly, had joined Henry in exile. All five retained great importance in the regime and great personal influence with the king. In 1497 the Milanese ambassador could describe Daubeney, Bray and Lovell as the leading men of the realm.[15] Venice was informed in the same year that Morton, Fox, Bray and Lovell were the king's principal ministers.[16] Next year the Spanish envoy reported that these four men, together with Daubeney, Bishop Thomas Savage and Margaret Beaufort, were the most influential persons in England.[17] It is remarkable that as late as 1507 Catharine of Aragon could write to her father and say that Daubeney (at this time the king's chamberlain) was the man who could do most in private with Henry.[18] Clearly each of these persons needs closer attention than he has ever received from historians; but we must move on.

3 *Parliament and legislation*

As for Parliament during the reign, there seems to me to be very little of significance occurring in the history of that institution. Parliament as an institution was not in any way notably different at the dissolution in 1504 of Henry's seventh and last Parliament from what it had been at the meeting of the first Parliament in 1485. There were no significant changes in procedure, so far as we know, no change in composition or electoral arrangements; there was a good deal of legislation the importance of much of which appears to have been greatly exaggerated ever since Bacon's eulogy of it. Seven Parliaments during the years 1485–1504 and no more were not very many, about the same frequency as under Edward IV. I wish I could let you know how many weeks, in all, Parliaments were in session, but at the moment Elton says 'perhaps twenty-five weeks',[19] Storey says fifty-nine weeks,[20] whereas I make it seventy weeks. Perhaps there is a job for a computer here.

As yet no one spoke of the 'Houses of Parliament', though references to 'Parliament House' and 'Common House' are quite frequent, and the latter expression had some years earlier come to bear a certain institutional as distinct from a merely locative sense. There was as yet no such term as 'Lords' House' or 'House of Lords', for as yet there was no need for it. The Lords' House *was* the Parliament House. A contemporary expressed the realities very neatly by the phrase 'in the common house beside the parliament house of the king's grace and the Lords'.[21]

I would not wish to get bogged down here in the subject of peerage history, but one should bear in mind that although an hereditary presumptive right to a personal summons had come into existence by this time, the right was still presumptive rather than absolute. Henry VII was prepared to recognise this presumptive right to the extent of summoning a descendant or relative of a person who had some sort of claim, and this kind of summons accounts for at least six of his sparse nine 'new creations', if these be the right words. Only one of these nine was given a barony by charter, and that was none other than Giles Daubeney.[22] It was no part of Henry's policy to reward faithful service by multiplying writs of personal summons. But there was always the Garter, and no fewer than thirty-seven knights of the Most Noble Order were created, more than half of them men who were among his closest associates in war and government.[23]

In the composition of the Lords, the personal summons was the thing that counted most, whether by writ or word of mouth. We should notice that it has been recently pointed out that Henry's first Parliament was perhaps the first occasion on which names were

omitted from the list of summonses on grounds of partisanship.[24]
The number of persons summoned varied from eighty-eight to a
hundred and one. The archbishops and bishops normally numbered
twenty-one, the abbots and priors were constant at twenty-seven;
the lay lords varied from thirty-four to forty-three; the men of law
from nine to twelve. But how many actually attended? Even Professor Roskell is unable to tell us that,[25] but there is good reason to
suppose, as he showed for these and earlier Parliaments, that the
actual attendance was a good deal less than the number of summonses. We must remember, however, that at least five Great
Councils assembled during the reign in addition to Parliament; we
know very little indeed about them but the business done in them
appears to have been of considerable political importance.[26]

As for the Commons, no discernible changes in composition
occurred. The constituencies remained the same, returning seventy-
four knights of the shires and 222 burgesses for the boroughs, 296
members in all.[27] There is no evidence of any attempt or need for
the Crown to 'pack' the Commons. A number of the king's councillors were elected, and the Speakers were clearly regarded primarily
as king's servants, and received rewards accordingly.[28] Not all the
king's measures were exactly popular, and some certainly aroused
criticism and opposition. The nearest approach to a crisis was over
the demand for a customary feudal aid in 1504, but Henry accepted
the alternative offer with a good grace, and the affair blew over.
The king's pleasure, whenever pressed, normally prevailed. None of
the Parliaments failed to assist him financially in one way or
another.

But we must come to the question of law-making by parliamentary statute. Law could, of course, be made by royal proclamation, but none of the sixty-two known proclamations by Henry
VII, so far as I can see, fall into the category of law-making in the
sense of altering the common law.[29]

I reckon that 192 statutes were assented to during the reign, an
average of about twenty-seven per Parliament, a goodly quantity
but not therefore necessarily of the importance that Bacon and others
have imagined. By far the largest category, with thirty-five items,
were Acts of attainder or restitution. Next come thirty-one variegated
items of trade, prices and wages regulation. Twenty-eight are so
miscellaneous as to defy categorisation. Twenty-two were of major
concern to lawyers because they modified the common law. Nine-

teen are of a personal character. Fourteen are concerned with law enforcement, often repeating either themselves or earlier statutes. Thirteen confer or define privileges or pardons. Twelve made fiscal provisions. Seven are largely concerned with the justices of the peace. Six refer to the merchants', especially alien merchants', position. Five relate to Church matters.

Of the twenty-two statutes of substantial interest to lawyers, two are of a general importance: the so-called 'Star Chamber' Act of 1487, which, we all know, had nothing to do with Star Chamber; and the so-called 'De facto' Act of 1495, which, as Pollard pointed out more than forty years ago, said nothing about kings *de facto* or *de jure*.[30] Four statutes touched upon the criminal law; nine related to procedural law; seven modified the land law. All these deserve attention. But there is not much here to justify Bacon's idea that legislation was Henry VII's 'preeminent virtue and merit'.[31]

Nor am I prepared to accept the idea that has sometimes been made much of—that a greater number of official Bills than Commons Bills were presented or that the government largely replaced the Commons as the initiator of statutory legislation. I have little to add on this matter to what I wrote some thirty-four years ago,[32] and I cannot now find space to reiterate it. There was not, so far as I can see, such a thing as an 'official' Bill, but certainly Henry's government initiated a considerable number of measures that became enacted as statutes. We can be sure he did not bother to do this except in relation to the topics that interested his government, and these topics were fewer and more limited than has often been supposed. But of course he assented to many that were initiated by others than himself or his government.

4 Law enforcement

The best introduction to the question of law enforcement was provided by Chief Justice Hussey when he addressed all the justices early in the first year of the reign. 'The law,' he said, 'will never be well executed until all the lords spiritual and temporal are of one accord to execute them effectually and when the king on his part and the lords on their part both want to do this, and do it.'[33] There were plenty of good statutes, he also said, but how to enforce them? That was the question.

The fact seems to be that there was a lack of will to enforce, on the part of the king as well as of others. The king's agents for law enforcement were in any event none too reliable. Many statutes of the reign reveal the shortcomings of justices of the peace, the corruptions of sheriffs and sheriffs' officers, and of jurors. The weakness of the common law courts in the face of the old practices of maintenance, champerty, embracery, the giving of liveries, and of retaining by indenture or otherwise—the very offences which the tribunal of 1487 had been set up to deal with—is obvious. But these offences continued to be legislated against until the last Parliament of the reign, and we can hardly suppose that the tribunal and other courts had met with any great success.

But surprisingly little initiative was taken by the Crown, so far as we know, in prosecuting offenders before the Council in Star Chamber or before the ministerial tribunal, or elsewhere. That more was done in King's Bench is possible, but the only studies of its working so far available[34] are not very encouraging to the idea. But we do know, thanks to another at present unpublished work, that a good many prosecutions were initiated in the Court of Exchequer, though not to any appreciable extent in connection with these offences.[35] Retainder, as Dr Guth reminds us, was a social evil only when it conflicted with the king's interests. Little vigorous repression of it was undertaken either in the Exchequer or elsewhere. His investigation of the plea rolls of King's Bench shows that after 1490 about two actions of this kind occurred per term, but the bulk of these ended in pardon or dismissal. In the Exchequer nine such cases occurred, all after 1501, none initiated by the Attorney-General.

It was infringement of the law relating to customs duties which attracted the most prosecutions, largely initiated by Crown officials. Naturally, illegality in this sphere touched the king's financial interests closely, and this alone provided the motive for prosecution. 'There is,' Dr Guth says, 'very little evidence on the Exchequer record that the Crown was seriously interested in the general enforcement of parliamentary statute.'

We may doubt how far any medieval king expected to be able to enforce penal statutes at all fully. No adequate machinery had come into existence for the purpose. Henry VII's government was no exception to the general rule. It appears to have been no more and no less efficient in this sphere than previous governments. It cannot be accused of any particular ruthlessness or harsh administration in this particular sphere. But that Henry VII was extremely anxious to increase his revenue is not open to doubt. He would therefore encourage prosecutions where hard cash profit could be expected, as in the matter of the infringement of customs regulations. Better still, however, he could compel a measure of law-abiding-ness and also obtain large financial advantages for himself by extracting from some of his subjects bonds, whether obligations or recognisances. Bonds (not, of course, an invention of Henry VII's) were offered or extracted for a great variety of reasons, which we cannot pursue here.[36] The whole subject needs a much more detailed study than it has yet received, but one conclusion seems to be clear. The financial screws by recognisances were tightened to supplement the machinery of the law courts. Much could be done by the king's agents to oblige wealthy law-breakers to come to terms and enter into a bond for the king's pardon, conditional per-haps upon future good behaviour, by a procedure expeditious, largely secret and highly lucrative. Moreover, the operation of this procedure was the king's own personal hobby. All such bonds were given by the king's favour, and all were the result of a bargain entered into with the king's agents or directly with the king himself.[37]

We can perhaps leave these unfortunates to make their bargains with the king's grace, and direct our attention to a few points in the matter of finance generally.

5 *Finance*

There can be no doubt that finance was the matter which, next to his life, throne and dynasty, lay nearest to Henry VII's heart. No grounds can be offered for any revision of the Baconian judge-ment which asserted that 'of nature assuredly he coveted to accumu-late treasure'.[38] This major interest of Henry VII's has also been a major interest of modern historians, and probably more work has been done on it than on any other single theme—far more than one can hope to summarise here. On the subject of Chamber admini-stration of finance so much has been written that I need say nothing on it.[39] A few comments at least are perhaps permissible on some of the souces of Henry's revenue.

I think that Dr Wolffe makes a very valid point in his recent book[40] when he observes that the division of royal revenues into 'ordinary' and 'extraordinary' is one made by historians rather than by fifteenth-century commentators. Fortescue used this distinction with reference to expenses, not revenues. The important difference to the king was the difference between 'certain' and 'casual' revenues. It would be as well if historians viewed the problems from that point of view.

All published accounts of Henry VII's parliamentary taxation must be subject to revision in the light of Dr R. S. Schofield's doctoral dissertation on 'Parliamentary lay taxation, 1485–1547'.[41] Dr Schofield's thorough investigations put the whole of this basic theme on to a sounder footing than exists elsewhere. The most important revelation is perhaps the signficance of the attempts made during the reign to replace the traditional stereotyped fifteenth and tenth by the directly assessed subsidy as the main form of parliamentary grant. This form of grant was a tax fixed at varying rates levied on each individual according to prescribed criteria, with the total yield unfixed and open. Such subsidies had been granted seven times before 1485; two of these were failures and withdrawn, and the others not very successful. Such proposals were viewed with suspicion and hostility by the Commons. The attempt to impose such a subsidy in 1489, modelled on that of 1472, was partially a failure, and in lieu of the large outstanding balance a fifteenth and tenth were eventually agreed to.

In 1497 the Commons ratified a large grant sanctioned by a Great Council, in the novel form of an aid equal in total amount to two fifteenths and tenths, but the usual division of the county total among the vills was abandoned in favour of the assessment of individual contributions. A similar compromise was adopted in 1504, when Henry accepted the Commons' offer of an aid of £40,000 (£10,000 of which he remitted) in lieu of the feudal aid for the knighting of his son and the marriage of his daughter. Both experiments were successful, and led on to the development of the directly assessed, open-ended subsidies aimed at from 1513 onwards.

Professor J. J. Scarisbrick has provided some useful information on the clerical contributions to taxation,[42] but the materials for the reign are very scanty and little precision can be achieved on this theme.

On the subject of loans and benevolences, we are indebted to Dr G. L. Harriss for lucid, illuminating observations.[43] He rightly doubts whether loans invited by signet letters can justly be called 'forced' in the modern sense of the term. For an individual to refuse such a request was doubtless difficult, if not virtually impossible.

But nonetheless these loans were in form made 'by agreement', and there is little or no evidence that the requests, usually modest in amount, were resisted or aroused any particular resentment, and most of the loans were repaid. The extraction of a benevolence, benevolent 'loan', or rather gift, was a different matter. Henry's intention to invade France in person gave him an opportunity in 1491 to levy such a benevolence, as similar circumstances had given the same chance to Edward IV in 1474. The levy was sanctioned in advance by a Great Council and subsequently ratified by Parliament, whilst Richard III's statute was ignored, presumably as being irrelevant. Whether it was Morton's or Fox's fork that came in useful in this connection is not very significant, for this, if it existed, was but an echo of an analogous fork invented by Edward IV in 1473–75.[44]

I despair of saying anything useful in a very short space on the matter of revenues from Crown lands, with all the pertinent accompaniments of attainders, forfeitures, Acts of resumption, and methods of management and accounting, and indeed, with Dr Wolffe contributing, I dare not attempt it. I content myself by referring to his recent book aforementioned, small, inexpensive and invaluable. You will notice, however, his insistence that the story of Henry VII's achievements had its origins in the estates of the house of York and March, and can in fact be told only from 1461, with the accession of the earl of March to the throne.[45]

Revenues from Crown lands were necessarily limited by the nature of the source. More open-ended possibilities could be exploited in the sphere of feudal prerogative rights and in the form of obligations and recognisances. I cannot now say any more about the latter, but some words must be spared for the former. As feudal overlord, Henry VII determined to extract in practice all the financial advantages that his position in legal theory accorded him. Much depended on what the common lawyers could make of the only extant legal statement of the overlord's rights contained in the thirteenth-century text known as the *Statuta de prerogativa regis*. Much of this text, which was not a statute but a declaration of common law, had become obsolete and misunderstood by the fifteenth century, but it provided a solid text which could be reinterpreted, glossed and made to cover all sorts of possibilities conducive to the king's interests. It was assuredly no accident that whilst no readings in the Inns of Court on this text are known to antedate the reign, the first has been dated within the first three years of it, and two very full readings were given in 1491.[46] There was little legal doubt as to the financial obligations of a tenant-in-chief holding land by military service. It might be difficult to identify all who were legally tenants-in-chief, but their total number could readily be increased if the officials applied themselves to it. The *Prerogativa* did not place any limitation upon the all-important phrase 'qui de ipso tenent in capite per servicium militare'. It was open, therefore, to Henry VII's lawyers and officials to bring incorporeal things, such as offices, annuities, privileges, etc, into the picture. The ranks of the tenants-in-chief could be extended to include not only those holding land but also those who held almost any incorporeal thing directly from the king, and it could be presumed that such things were held by military service if there were no specific indications to the contrary. We are frequently told that all this was legal enough. But then, it is the essence of chicanery that it is *not* illegal. The Council Learned in the Law was not learned for nothing.

6 *The man*

I have left myself very little time or space in which to dwell upon Henry as a man. I do not regret this, for I have as yet by no means made up my mind as to what manner of man he was. I would not at all readily subscribe to the commonly received conception of him, largely springing from Baconian appraisals and literary flourishes. The realities of Henry's personal characteristics are not easy to come by. There are few personal touches in the sources, and what there are I have not yet been able to assess.

My tentative impression is that he was probably less successful as king but more human as a man than is usually supposed. I suspect that the penury and insecurity of his early years left their mark upon him for life. However desirable it was for the king to become solvent and affluent, one can scarcely doubt that the lengths to which he himself went or to which he allowed his agents to go in raking in the cash are bound to cloud his reputation. However disturbing the threats from the Lambert Simnel and Perkin Warbeck conspiracies must have been, one feels that he became obsessed with the problem of security, especially in his later years, as manifested by his extraordinary pursuit of the not very fearsome Edmund de la Pole and his brothers. To Henry the spectre of the White Rose was more than a ghost. It was something real enough to shape and condition his diplomacy and commercial policies. It seems likely that his political judgement, so robust and astute in his best years, faltered somewhat as the years passed.

If it be true that a man can be known from what he spend his money on, we are by no means without materials for such knowledge.[47] We note that Henry played cards and tennis, and frequently lost quite a bit of money on these pastimes; he often rewarded his jesters, one of whom was habitually called 'the foolish duke of Lancaster'. He could buy little presents for his queen and pay off her debts. He could give as much as £30 to 'the young damsel who danceth', and £12 to a young maiden who performed likewise. He could give 2s to a 'woman for a red rose'.

He spent more than £200 on the burial of his son Edmund, nearly £600 on that of Arthur, nearly £3,000 on that of his queen. He spent a good deal on musicians, players, athletes, fools and joculars, revels, disguisings, jousts and butts. Above all, he could salt away more than a quarter of a million pounds in his favourite investments —jewellery and plate. Indeed, when his time came on 21 April 1509, that was nearly all he could leave behind him in the way of treasure.

But whatever else this extraordinary man achieved, we cannot deny that he bequeathed also what English history could not readily do without—the Tudor and Stuart dynasties and all that they were to imply.[48]

Notes

1 *Tudor Constitutional Documents*, ed J. R. Tanner (1922; second edition 1930); *The Tudor Constitution*, ed G. R. Elton (1960); *English Historical Documents, 1485–1558*, ed. C. H. Williams (1968).

2 *Lancastrians, Yorkists, and Henry VII* (1964; second edition 1966).

3 *The Reign of Henry VII* (1968).

4 *Conflict and Stability in Fifteenth-century England* (1969), which contains many valuable suggestions.

5 *Henry VII* (1968).

6 See below, pp. 79–82.

7 See below, pp. 72–4.

8 This received extended treatment in J. D. Mackie, *op. cit.*, and five chapters are devoted to it in R. B. Wernham's *Before the Armada* (1966).

9 The fullest account of Sir Reginald Bray's life is contained in this work. Most of the relevant articles in *D.N.B.* are out of date, and many personages are scarcely noticed therein. Valuable sketches of some of the persons are

provided in J. S. Roskell, *The Commons and their Speakers in English Parliaments, 1376–1523* (1965), and J. C. Wedgwood, *History of Parliament, 1439–1509: Biographies* (1936).

10 E.g. B. P. Wolffe, 'The management of English royal estates under the Yorkist Kings', *E.H.R.*, LXXI (1956), and *The Crown Lands, 1461–1536* (1970); J. R. Lander, 'The Yorkist Council and administration, *E.H.R.*, LXXIII (1958); 'Council, administration, and councillors, 1461–85', *B.I.H.R.*, XXXII (1959); 'Attainder and forfeiture, 1453–1509', *H.J.*, IV (1961); *English Historical Documents, 1327–1485*, ed. A. R. Myers (1969), contains in addition introductions to the documents selected and invaluable bibliographies.

11 The fullest account in English of these matters is in J. S. C. Bridge, *A History of France from the Death of Louis XI*, I (1921).

12 *Annali della Fondazione italiana per la storia amministrativa* (1969), 268–96.

13 *Select Cases in the Council of Henry VII* (Selden Society, 75, 1958).

14 See the articles on the Council by J. R. Lander mentioned in note 10 above.

15 *Cal. S.P. Milan*, I, 335.

16 *Cal. S.P. Venice*, I, 256.

17 *Cal. S.P. Spain*, I, 163.

18 *Ibid., Supplement*, 131. According to Bacon (*Henry VII*, ed. Lumby, 142), Perkin Warbeck's proclamation of 1496 included Fox, Bray, Lovell and Riseley, as well as Oliver King and Empson, among the fifteen persons Henry held in trust. In Speed's edition Guildford was also included.

The talents of these five councillors were diverse. Bray and Lovell were chief among financial administrators. Daubeney was a naval and military commander held in high esteem. Guildford had a flair for military engineering, but died on a pilgrimage to Jerusalem. Riseley was a diplomat and French linguist.

Thomas Savage, successively Bishop of Rochester and London and archbishop of York, is reckoned as the first identifiable President of the Council (1497–1502).

19 *The Tudor Constitution*, 228.

20 *Henry VII*, 118.

21 *B.I.H.R.*,III (1925–26), 175.

22 J. Enoch Powell and Keith Wallis, *The House of Lords in the Middle Ages* (1965); *Complete Peerage*, and *D.N.B.*

23 *Complete Peerage*, II, appendix B, 565–7.

24 Powell and Wallis, *op. cit.*, 529.

25 'The problem of attendance of the Lords in medieval Parliaments', *B.I.H.R.*, XXIX (1956).

26 *Bibliography of Royal Proclamations*, ed. R. Steele, I, lxxxvi–lxxvii.

27 J. C. Wedgwood, *History of Parliament, 1439–1509: Register* (1938).

28 Roskell, *op. cit.*

29 *Tudor Royal Proclamations*, ed. P. L. Hughes and J. F. Larkin (1964).

30 *B.I.H.R.*, VII (1929), 1–12.

31 *Henry VII*, ed. Lumby, 74.

32 *English Constitutional Ideas in the Fifteenth Century* (1936), 236–49.

33 Year Books (1678), *1 Henry VII*, Mich. pl. 3. Cf. Chrimes, *op cit.*, 378.

34 Marjorie Blatcher, 'The working of the Court of King's Bench in the fifteenth century', unpublished Ph.D. dissertation, University of London (1936),

based upon the sources for Michaelmas term, 1488. A summary was published in *B.I.H.R.*, xiv (1937), 196–9.

35 I am indebted to Dr Deloyd John Guth, now of Michigan University, for allowing me to use his valuable, at present unpublished, Pittsburgh Ph.D. dissertation (1967) on 'Exchequer penal law enforcement, 1485–1509', and to Professor G. R. Elton, under whose supervision the work was prepared, for his kindness in lending me his copy of it.

36 See very generally Richardson, *op. cit.*, 141–58; F. C. Dietz, *English Government Finance* (1926; second edition 1964), 33–50. J. R. Lander, in his recent most stimulating book (cited in note 4 above), 100, notes that the late K. B. McFarlane, in his review in *E.H.R.*, lxxxi (1966), 153–4, of the *Calendar of Close Rolls, 1500–09* (1963), which contains notices of a remarkable number of recognisances, went so far as to say that 'the point had almost been reached where it could be said that Henry VII governed by recognisance'. I have little doubt that there is much truth in this suggestion, but the whole matter needs a more thorough investigation, and we look forward with impatience to a forthcoming study of the subject by Professor Lander. He will, for example, show that out of sixty-two peerage families existing between 1485 and 1509, only fifteen or sixteen remained free of financial threats by recognisance. It is possible that further study of indictments at common law, such as those being made by Mr A. Cameron (Nottingham), may reveal a greater degree of law enforcement than at present appears. A number of actions, however, were stopped by writ of privy seal, and how far these cases were followed up by the recognisance method is a matter for investigation.

37 B. P. Wolfe, 'Henry VII's land revenues and Chamber finance', *E.H.R.*, lxxix (1964), 246.

38 *Henry VII*, ed. Lumby, 213.

39 The fullest account is in Richardson, *op. cit.*

40 *The Crown Lands*, 16–17.

41 Unpublished Ph.D. dissertation, Cambridge (1964). I am indebted to Dr Schofield, of Clare College, for his generosity in lending me a copy of his work, and to Professor G. R. Elton for his good offices. I understand that Dr Schofield's work is being prepared for publication.

42 'Clerical taxation in England, 1485–1547', *J. Eccles. Hist.*, ii (1960).

43 'Aids, loans, and benevolences', *H.J.*, vi (1963).

44 *English Historical Documents*, iv, 527–8.

45 *Op. cit.*, 50.

46 The fullest discussion is contained in S. E. Thorne's introduction to his edition of Robert Constable's reading, *Prerogativa Regis* (1949).

47 Especially in the Issue Books of the treasurer of the Chamber, extracts from which were printed in S. Bentley, *Excerpta Historica* (1831), 85–133.

48 All the matters in this paper are more fully discussed, together with many others, in my forthcoming book *Henry VII*.

T. B. Pugh

Senior Lecturer in History
University of Southampton

5   The magnates, knights and gentry

I

The magnates of England whose political conduct is recorded by medieval chroniclers in the thirteenth and early fourteenth centuries were all the lords spiritual and temporal of the kingdom. This vague and convenient term meant in that period the bishops and the abbots and priors of the chief religious houses, as well as the earls, barons, knights and other wealthy members of that large but ill-defined social class whom we know as the gentry.[1] Before the establishment of a parliamentary peerage in the later Middle Ages, the ranks of the magnates included all those men among the English land-owning aristocracy who merited a personal writ of summons to Great Councils or Parliaments. By the late fifteenth century the magnates were no longer a large body of more than a hundred of the Crown's important tenants-in-chief.[2] The numerous barons of thirteenth-century England had been replaced, socially and politically, by a peerage which seldom exceeded about sixty families.[3] In 1421 the terms of the treaty of Troyes were ratified in Parliament by 'the three estates of the realm', namely, the prelates and clergy, the nobles and magnates, and the commons.[4] When Edward IV created the marcher lordship of Raglan in 1465 (the last marcher lordship to be established in Wales), he did so expressly in recognition of the valour of William, Lord Herbert, 'whom . . . we have raised to the estate of baron and magnate of our realm'.[5] Barons were magnates, but lesser men could no longer be regarded as possessing that status. By the Yorkist period the lay members of the upper house in Parliament (a relatively small group of great landowners) were the English magnates.

In the Latin annals wrongly ascribed to William Worcester, the magnates of England are mentioned on three occasions.[6] Among the guests present at the lavish festivities which accompanied Archbishop George Nevill's enthronement at York in September 1465 were 'most of the magnates of England, except the king and queen'. The banquet which followed that ceremony was a spectacular orgy of gluttony, and we might expect such an event to be well attended. Warwick and the magnates of England, we are told, were secretly displeased when Queen Elizabeth Wydevill's father, Lord Rivers, was made lord treasurer on 4 March 1466, and they again disapproved six months later when Lord Herbert's heir was made a baron, with the title of Lord Dunster, in view of his forthcoming marriage with the queen's sister, Mary.[7] The anonymous author of this narrative, often cited as one of the best authorities for the history of Edward IV's first reign, has been successful in creating the impression that the English nobility in general shared the political views of Warwick and his associates. There are reasons for doubting whether this was so. Warwick was contemptuous of the Wydevill ancestry of the queen's father,[8] but several of the few surviving English earls were prompt to show themselves more realistic in their appraisal of the new political situation created by the disclosure of the king's secret marriage.

An aristocracy which had already accepted families of such mixed social origins as the de la Poles, the Hollands, the Beauforts and the Bourchiers had no reason to reject the Wydevills once Lord Rivers's daughter, Elizabeth, had become queen of England. Between October 1464 and February 1466 the earls of Arundel and Essex, and Edmund Grey, the newly created earl of Kent, married their heirs to Wydevill wives.[9] Their readiness to contract such marriage alliances with the Wydevills hardly suggests that they viewed with resentment the rapid advancement of the queen's family. Even the greatest of aristocratic houses in late medieval England did not allow social snobbery to impede their chances of material gain. Although Sir William de la Pole (d. 1366) made his huge fortune as a merchant and war financier, his grandson Michael (d. 1415), later the second de la Pole earl of Suffolk, married in 1383 Katherine, daughter of Hugh (d. 1386), earl of Stafford, who was of royal descent.[10] It is true that few English noblemen married into merchant families before the Tudor period, but financial considerations doubtless helped to maintain social barriers. Because it was customary for English barons to give such large sums in cash as marriage portions for their daughters, members of the nobility could marry most profitably

within their own social class.[11] As Warwick, through his grandmother, Joan Beaufort (d. 1440), countess of Westmorland, was a
kinsman of the royal house and a direct descendant of Edward III, he
could afford to regard Richard Wydevill (d. 1469), Lord Rivers, with
patrician disdain, but another aspect of his family history has not
escaped attention by historians and genealogists. Warwick was exceptional among the higher nobility in having a not-so-remote ancestor
who had been a London merchant. His maternal grandfather,
Thomas Montague (d. 1428), earl of Salisbury, was a grandson of
Adam Francis, who in 1352 had become mayor of London.[12]

Warwick's own Nevill dynastic interests were certainly prejudiced
by the brilliant matches arranged for Queen Elizabeth Wydevill's
younger sisters. Early in 1465 the king was responsible for the marriage of the queen's youngest sister, Katherine (who was still a child),
to Henry Stafford (1455–83), duke of Buckingham, a minor in royal
wardship.[13] The pseudo-William Worcester tells us that Warwick
secretly resented Buckingham's marriage[14] and this comment gives an
indication of Warwick's own plans for his daughters, Isabel (1451–76)
and Anne (1456–83), who were destined to become the greatest
English heiresses of their day. Because Warwick had no son by his
wife, the Beauchamp heiress Anne (1426–92), his two daughters
could expect to inherit almost the whole of the enormous possessions
of their parents,[15] and finding suitable sons-in-law of appropriate
rank was a matter which most deeply concerned the earl's prestige.
Between the announcement of the king's marriage in September 1464
and his deposition six years later, every English earl who had a male
heir available to marry chose for him a Wydevill wife.[16] The matri-
monial triumphs of the Wydevill sisters left Warwick unable to find
husbands for his own daughters among the English higher nobility,
unless they married the king's younger brothers, the dukes of Clarence
and Gloucester, and that King Edward would not permit.[17]
Warwick's grievances against Edward IV were far more real and
genuine than his recent critics (including J. R. Lander and
K. B. McFarlane) have been prepared to admit.[18] The marriage
of George, duke of Clarence, with his cousin, Isabel Nevill, which
took place at Calais on 11 July 1469, was the signal for the Yorkshire
rising led by Robin of Redesdale and the resumption of civil war.[19]

Because of the havoc wrought by civil war, the ranks of the great
magnates in the 1460s were much depleted. Before fighting broke
out at St Albans in 1455 there were six English dukes (Buckingham,

Exeter, Norfolk, Suffolk, Somerset and York) and twelve earls (Arundel, Devon, Northumberland, Oxford, Richmond, Pembroke, Salisbury, Shrewsbury, Warwick, Westmorland, Wiltshire and Worcester).[20] In the final phase of Lancastrian rule the higher nobility consisted of sixteen magnate families (two families, the Tudors and the Nevills, both held more than one earldom), but only ten of these great houses still retained their lands after the overthrow of the house of Lancaster. Although few baronial families were extinguished in the male line directly as a result of involvement in the Wars of the Roses, the consequences of the dynastic struggles between Lancaster and York for the more distinguished members of the English aristocracy have been sadly underestimated.[21] Of the sixteen great magnate families which existed in the last decade of Henry VI's reign, only two (represented by the earls of Arundel and Westmorland) were unscathed by the political catastrophes which afflicted English society between 1455 and 1487. The long-lived William (1417–87), earl of Arundel, who held that earldom for nearly half a century, was never very active in war or politics. According to William Worcester, the second Ralph Nevill (d. 1484), earl of Westmorland, was simple-minded,[22] which may help to explain why his career was so uneventful. Earl Ralph's vigorous younger brother, John, Lord Nevill, was an active Lancastrian partisan, slain at Towton.

In Edward IV's first Parliament, which met on 6 November 1461, the seven earls who were of full age constituted the whole of the higher nobility, but only six of them (Arundel, Essex, Kent, Oxford, Warwick and Worcester) attended this session (the earl of Westmorland was absent).[23] Two of these six earls (Henry Bourchier, earl of Essex, and William Nevill, earl of Kent) were new creations, as they had just been promoted by Edward IV from their place among the lesser peers. The penalties of forfeiture and attainder incurred by the leading Lancastrian adherents (the dukes of Exeter and Somerset, and the earls of Devon, Northumberland, Pembroke and Wiltshire) had greatly enhanced the political power of the Nevills. Warwick, with his vast Beauchamp, Despenser, Montague and Nevill estates, now dominated the rest of the English baronage as no magnate had done since Earl Thomas of Lancaster in the middle years of Edward II's reign.[24] The prolongation of the civil war in the northernmost counties for more than three years after Edward IV's decisive victory at Towton on 29 March 1461 worked to the advantage of the Nevills. In May 1464, after the last remnants of Lancastrian resistance had been crushed in the battles of Hedgeley Moor and Hexham, the king rewarded the services of the ablest of his war captains, Warwick's younger brother, John Nevill (d. 1471), Lord Montague, by giving him the earldom of Northumberland forfeited by the Percies.[25]

The civil wars between Lancaster and York brought into existence a new Yorkist nobility during the late fifteenth century. Most of the lords had remained loyal to Henry VI until his cause was irretrievably lost at Towton. In twenty-two years Edward IV created or revived at least thirty-five peerage titles: he made four dukes, two marquises, eleven earls, two viscounts and sixteen barons.[26] Here his practice resembled that of Henry VI, not that of the early Lancastrian kings. Unlike Edward III and Richard II, both Henry IV and Henry V had been reluctant to add to the ranks of the higher nobility. In 1154 there were twenty-two English earldoms, but only seven remained in existence when Edward III supplanted his father in 1327. A high rate of natural extinction, the unwilling-ness of English kings since Henry II to creat new earldoms[27] (except for near kinsmen of the royal house) and renewed political disturb-ances after 1307, culminating in outbreaks of civil war, had combined to make the comital title a rare distinction when Edward II's disastrous reign was at last terminated. During the half-century after 1327 Edward III created or revived thirteen earldoms and Richard II bestowed no fewer than twenty-two titles among the higher nobility.[28] After the royalist revolution of 1397 the upper ranges of the English nobility began to resemble more closely the court of Richard II's French father-in-law; in his hour of triumph Richard created five dukes, one duchess in her own right (Edward I's aged granddaughter, Margaret Marshal, formerly styled countess, now became duchess of Norfolk), a marquis and three earls.

Perhaps because of Richard II's recent excesses, the early Lancas-trian kings showed themselves far more circumspect in their grants of the highest honours, and between 1399 and 1422 there were only six additions to the English higher nobility.[29] Henry IV in 1412 made his second son, Thomas, duke of Clarence, and the youngest of the king's Beaufort half-brothers became earl of Dorset. Henry V created two dukedoms (Bedford and Gloucester, for his younger brothers, John and Humphrey) and revived two earldoms (Cam-bridge and Worcester), both of which were extinct before the end of his reign. It was after Henry VI's coming of age that the first great expansion in the size of the House of Lords (which already existed in fact, if not in name) began. By conferring so many new peerage titles, Edward IV was continuing a recent trend which had commenced in his predecessor's reign.

The Crown was not impoverished by the creation of a new Yorkist peerage. The excessively generous endowment of George, duke of Clarence (who was even given on 30 August 1464, during pleasure, the lands of the earldom of Chester), was exceptional.[30] The Yorkist nobles were either provided for out of the spoils of vanquished Lancastrians or they were not granted lands by the king at all. William Nevill (d. 1463), Lord Fauconberg, did well: he obtained nearly sixty manors and lordships to support his new status as earl of Kent.[31] The Yorkist victory in the civil war had placed at Edward IV's disposal forfeited lands on a quite unprecedented scale. The principal beneficiaries were the king's two younger brothers, the dukes of Clarence and Gloucester, his eldest sister, Anne, duchess of Exeter, three of the Nevills (Lords Fauconberg and Montague, and Warwick was by no means neglected), and Lords Herbert and Hastings.[32] Edmund (d. 1490), Lord Grey of Ruthin, whose treachery at the battle of Northampton on 10 July 1460 gave Warwick the only military victory he was ever able to win,[33] received no lands from Edward IV; his tenure of the lord treasurership in 1463–64 was brief, and he had to wait until 1465 for his earldom. The queen's father, Lord Rivers, was doubtless expected to enrich himself from the profits of the lord treasurership, to which he was appointed a few months before he was made an earl in May 1466. As lord treasurer and constable of England and a member of the king's Council, Lord Rivers had an income of £1,330 per annum from his offices, so he was adequately provided for, quite apart from the dower estates of his wife, Jacquetta (d. 1472), duchess of Bedford.[34] Edward IV created few peerages after his restoration in 1471; in this as in other respects he set a precedent followed by Henry VII. Between the end of the fifteenth century and the accession of James I the parliamentary peerage did not increase in proportion to the growing wealth and population of England.

The Herberts of Raglan were the most remarkable of the new baronial families who owed their rise to greatness to the Wars of the Roses. William Herbert, one of seven barons created by

Edward IV in 1461, was the first Welshman to enter the English
peerage (if we discount Henry VI's half-brothers, Edmund of
Hadham and Jasper of Hatfield, who were naturalised by statute in
1454, two years after they had been granted earldoms).[35] Before
Edward IV's accession in 1461, Sir William Herbert of Raglan was
one of the richer landowners in south Wales, but the Welsh gentry
were not wealthy by English standards. Herbert's income from his
inheritance at Raglan was worth considerably less than the fees he
received as the duke of York's steward of Caerleon and Usk and as
sheriff of Glamorgan and steward of all the earl of Warwick's Welsh
marcher lordships.[36] In a letter written on 20 May 1454 York's chief
steward, Sir Walter Devereux (d. 1459), was at pains to reassure the
duke that his son-in-law, Sir William Herbert, 'saith he is noo monis
mon but only youres'. Despite that assurance, Herbert was wisely
absent from the rout of Ludford in October 1459, but there is no
reason to suppose that he ever lapsed from his Yorkist allegiance
or changed sides.[37] He rendered timely service in helping Edward,
earl of March, to win his first victory at Mortimer's Cross on 3
February 1461, and he was one of the small gathering of notables who
chose Edward of York to be their king in London a month later.[38]

Shortly after Edward IV's accession, Herbert was made chief
justice and chamberlain of south Wales. The persistence of Lancastrian resistance, the rivalry between Edward IV and Richard
Nevill, earl of Warwick, and the rise of a new court party led by
the Wydevills enabled Herbert to gather into his own hands an
accumulation of offices in the principality and the Marches which
gave him more power than any subject had previously enjoyed
there.[39] By the time William Herbert was rewarded with Jasper
Tudor's forfeited title of earl of Pembroke on 8 September 1468 he
had made his family the most powerful in Wales. In less than ten
years this grossly ambitious and grasping Welsh country squire
had turned himself into an English magnate, with an annual income
of some £2,400.[40] Herbert's feud with his former patron, the earl
of Warwick, which began in 1461, was one of the chief causes of
the new outbreak of civil war in 1469.[41] The marriage contract
between Lord Herbert's heir and the queen's sister, Mary Wydevill,
made on 20 March 1466 'at the instance of our sovereign lord the
king and his pleasure', was a treaty of alliance between two upstart
magnate families. Besides Mary Wydevill's dowry of 2,500 marks
(which was still unpaid when both her father and father-in-law were

executed in 1469), Lord Herbert had bargained successfully for other and more immediate gains. He wanted to convert his existing lease of the lordship of Haverfordwest into a grant for himself and his heirs, and he also sought to obtain from the king the reversion of the manor and lordship of Kilpeck, Co. Hereford, and of part of the duchess of Bedford's dower lands in Gloucestershire. Lord Rivers undertook to see that the king made these grants, in accordance with Herbert's wishes, before his daughter's marriage took place, and the grants were all duly made, on 26 September 1466. This document reflects Lord Rivers's confidence that he could induce Edward IV to do exactly what suited the Wydevills.[42]

Edward IV's reliance in the crisis of 1469 on a new court party led by the Wydevills, the Herberts and Humphrey Stafford of Southwick, Co. Wilts. (who had been made a baron in 1461 and created earl of Devon in May 1469), was a singular error of judgement. The defeat of William Herbert, earl of Pembroke's Welsh army by the Yorkshire rebels at Edgecote on 26 July left King Edward in a most humiliating position.[43] He was forsaken by his subjects as no previous English ruler (apart from Edward II in 1326) had ever been, and for two months he had to submit to being Warwick's prisoner. The elevation of lesser peers such as Rivers, Herbert and Lord Stafford of Southwick to earldoms was too radical a break with tradition and, moreover, the king's chief courtiers had done enough to merit their intense unpopularity.[44] There was a new Yorkist nobility in the 1460s and its most conspicuous members were destroyed by Warwick's enmity and popular hatred. The upheavals of 1469 demonstrated that newly created magnates such as Lord Rivers and Humphrey Stafford were quite inadequate to withstand Warwick, because they could attract no binding loyalties on the part of the gentry, the class from which they themselves had so recently sprung.

After his restoration in 1471, Edward IV took care not to repeat these major political blunders, and during his second reign there were few new English earls. Even the faithful William (d. 1483), Lord Hastings, never attained the earldom he had done so much to deserve, although in terms of landed wealth and the size of his retine he belonged among the greater magnates. In October 1472 the king rewarded Lewis of Bruges, seigneur de la Gruthuyse (who had provided Edward with hospitality while he was in exile in the Netherlands), with the title of earl of Winchester. As Lewis of

Bruges held no property in England and soon returned to Flanders, his earldom was simply an inexpensive way of discharging a debt of honour. Apart from this titular revival of the earldom of Winchester, between 1471 and 1483 the upper ranks of the English peerage were augmented only by members of the house of York: the king's own two sons, Richard, duke of Gloucester's heir, Edward (1476–84), earl of Salisbury, and the elder of the king's step-sons, Thomas Grey, Lord Ferrers of Groby,[45] who was made earl of Huntingdon in 1471 and marquis of Dorset four years later. Once the struggle for the crown between the houses of Lancaster and York had finally ended, the older conventions governing the distribution of the higher peerage titles were re-established.

II

During the first quarter of the fifteenth century the body of lords temporal who were being summoned to Parliament seemed likely to remain a small group, permanently fixed and unchanging in composition, and amounting to only about forty magnates. Between the death of Edward III in 1377 and the accession of Henry VI in 1422 there were very few additions to the number of lords temporal in Parliament. Only four of the lay lords summoned in Richard II's reign belonged to families which had not previously been represented in the upper house in Parliament.[46] Although Richard II in 1387 by letters patent conferred on Sir John Beauchamp of Holt, Co. Worcs., the estate of baron, that precedent was not repeated until the promotion in 1441 of Sir Ralph Boteler to baronial rank, with the title of Lord Sudeley. In early Lancastrian England the parliamentary peerage which was becoming established was assuming the character of an exclusive oligarchy, virtually closed to new recruits, even from among the landed aristocracy.

This situation was soon changed by the minority of Henry VI. The Council set up in 1422 to rule England until the infant king came of age included three knights who were not members of the upper house in Parliament, Sir Walter Beauchamp, Sir Walter Hungerford and Sir John Tiptoft, and after 1426 two of these, Hungerford and Tiptoft, were summoned to Parliament as barons. In 1432 Sir John Cornwall, who had been married to the young king's great-aunt, Elizabeth (d. 1425), dowager countess of Huntingdon, was made a baron in Parliament, with the title of Lord

Fanhope. Apart from a few new creations among the higher nobility, neither Henry IV nor Henry V had chosen to reinforce the ranks of the English baronage as present in Parliament,[47] but now, while Henry VI was still a child, new peerages were in effect being called into existence in accordance with the wishes of the king's Council, which was essentially a baronial oligarchy. The most prolonged royal minority in English history and Henry VI's subsequent unwillingness or inability to exercise the Crown's authority in person prevented the upper house in Parliament from developing into a closed corporation. The longest period of baronial government that medieval England ever experienced led to a rapid increase in the number of peers summoned to Parliament. Between the ending of his minority in 1436 and his deposition in 1461, the new titles created by Henry VI (quite apart from promotions within the existing peerage) included three earls, one viscount and twenty-one barons.[48] Perhaps influenced by French usage during the years when Henry VI still had some claim to be styled king of France as well, a more elaborate peerage was now becoming established in England, with new grades of peers. Lord Beaumont was the first English viscount, an honour conferred on him in 1440, and the title of marquis (first created in England in 1385) was revived in 1444 for the benefit of William de la Pole, earl of Suffolk. This lavish distribution of titles, for which Suffolk himself was chiefly responsible in the 1440s, had the effect of clearly distinguishing the lords temporal in Parliament from those below them in the social scale.

In accordance with the terms of the income tax granted by Parliament in 1435, persons of 'the astate of Baron and Baronesse and every estate above' were to be singled out for a separate (and presumably more rigorous) tax assessment made in 1436 by the lord chancellor and the lord treasurer of England. With few exceptions (and some omissions, quite apart from minors in royal wardship), the English baronage as rated for taxation in 1436 was the parliamentary peerage, together with sixteen dowagers.[49] There were some families, such as the Cornwalls of Burford, Co. Salop (descendants of Henry III's younger brother, Richard (d. 1272), earl of Cornwall), and the Hiltons of Co. Durham, who continued to use the style of baron until their lines became extinct long after the fifteenth century,[50] but in politics from Henry VI's reign onwards the English baronage had become synonymous with the parliamentary peerage. In fourteenth-century England some of the lesser magnates present in Parliament were described as bannerets, or knights,[51] but in the later Lancastrian Parliaments all the lords temporal were now recognised at least as barons, and barons made up about two-thirds of the lay lords who had personal writs of summons.

Before the emergence of a parliamentary peerage the social distinction between the English nobility and the gentry did not exist. It was in the early fifteenth century that persons of some social standing began to describe themselves simply as 'gentlemen'; at first, no doubt this meant nobleman (as it had done in the past), but this new usage soon spread and the meaning of the term changed. In an age of social mobility the status of men who had advanced their fortunes might well defy precise classification, and already by 1450 a merchant (or even a yeoman) could be styled gentleman. Hitherto, gentle (*gentil*) had meant noble, and before 1400 gentlemen were noblemen, born and not made.[52] English aristocratic society early in the fourteenth century consisted of some three thousand landowners whose estates were reckoned to be worth at least £20 a year. Amongst these noblemen the earls (of whom only a dozen still survived in 1300) were pre-eminent by reason of their rank; the rest were all lords, or more specifically barons, bannerets, knights or esquires, but they did not yet classify themselves simply as gentlemen in fourteenth-century England.[53]

The establishment of a House of Lords marks the beginning of a new epoch in English social history, because henceforth only peerage families were noble; the gentry were not. If that process was not complete until the late Tudor period, it was already far advanced a century earlier. Although the Commons in Parliament were growing in importance in the fourteenth and fifteenth centuries, as a class the landed gentry did not (as K. B. McFarlane pointed out) 'so much rise (though some did) during the later Middle Ages as fall from the nobility which their ancestors had enjoyed'.[54] Recognition that the peerage had come to constitute a separate estate of the realm has led historians to regard all the landowners immediately below the rank of baron and those above yeoman status as belonging to the gentry, a class not easy to define. Along with gentry families of noble descent in fifteenth-century England were others who had accumulated wealth and acquired gentility (usually based on the possession of land) by prowess in war, success in trade[55] or service in one of the professions, especially the law.[56]

From the taxation returns of 1436, Professor H. L. Gray con-
structed a comprehensive survey of the social structure of fifteenth-
century England, and his statistics concerning the landed wealth of
the gentry continue to command ready acceptance.[57] Below the
rank of baron, he concluded that there were about 183 landowners
(whom Gray classed as 'the richer knights'; although they had not all
been knighted, they were well qualified for knighthood) with taxable
incomes averaging just over £200 per annum. Another 750 prosperous members of the gentry enjoyed annual incomes of between
£40 and £100. Lesser landowners, whose property was worth
between £20 and £40 a year, numbered about 1,200 persons, and
those whose annual income was more than £10 a year (but less than
£20 per annum) were more numerous, probably about 1,600 in all.
By 1530 Garter King of Arms had decided that in order to qualify
for the right to use a coat of arms, the distinguishing mark of
gentility, a man ought to have a freehold income of at least £10 a
year.[58] Some of the minor landowners who described themselves
as 'gentlemen' in 1436 declared that their taxable income was only
£5 per annum, but of course that may have been an under-estimate
of their resources.[59] The size of the gentry—all the landowners
between the baronage and the yeomanry—in fifteenth-century
England has been variously estimated at between 6,000 and 9,000
families.[60] Professor Gray's most significant conclusions concerned
'the richer knights', that group of about 183 landowners whose
total taxable income he reckoned to be approximately £38,000 per
annum. It would appear that these men 'enjoyed nearly as great a
share of the landed income of the realm as did the nobles themselves'.[61] These conjectures, which have profoundly important
political implications, are rapidly becoming established as irrefutable
historical facts. The whole trend of H. L. Gray's figures conveys
an exaggerated impression of the extent of the landed property
held by the gentry, while at the same time making the great magnates seem much less affluent than they really were.[62]

Taxable income in 1436 included life annuities and the fees
received by office-holders. Fourteen peers, whose own incomes were
assessed for taxation at a total of £11,466, had granted life annuities
amounting to £1,779 per annum, and some of the richer gentry
were among the principal recipients of this largesse. If these arrangements were typical, the English baronage as rated for taxation
(forty-two peers and sixteen dowagers) was probably spending

about £7,000 in annuities to retainers, servants, relatives and other dependants, and most of this sum would be reckoned among the taxable incomes admitted by commoners. H. L. Gray reckoned that the total taxable sum received by members of the peerage from life annuities and offices granted by the Crown was rather less than £5,000. The annual value of all the taxable annuities and fees which the king was paying to commoners cannot be ascertained, and we do not know if it was greater or less than the similar payments due to peers (and some dowagers), but it is clear that these tax returns may well conceal a substantial transference of wealth from both the nobility and the Crown to the gentry.[63] Sir William Oldhall (d. 1460), later Richard, duke of York's chamberlain and Speaker in the Parliament of 1450, was receiving £80 per annum from his brother-in-law, Lord Willoughby; perhaps he included that sum in his declared income of £215 3s 4d from property in five counties, but we cannot be sure that he did.[64] The Hampshire knight Sir John Popham (d. 1463), later elected Speaker in the Parliament of 1449, drew two-thirds of his income of £120 from annuities. He had 100 marks per annum granted to him in 1417 by Henry V and another life annuity of 20 marks given him early in his career by Edward (d. 1415), duke of York. Popham was unlucky in that his annuity from the Crown was included in his tax assessment, although it had not been paid for four years.[65] Richard Wydevill, esquire (father of the future Lord Rivers), declared his income from property in Kent and four other counties as £148 a year, but a large part of that was provided by his annuity of 80 marks, charged on the duchy of Lancaster estates.[66] Another duchy of Lancaster annuitant was the Cambridgeshire knight, Sir William Asenhill (d. 1443); his lands in that county and in Yorkshire were worth £95 per annum, but his total taxable income was £140.[67] In Middlesex, William Pope, esquire, had £80 a year wholly derived from offices and annuities; he was receiving £10 per annum from the duke of Gloucester and the rest of his income came from royal grants.[68] The local tax returns which survive for London and fifteen counties[69] list the names of individuals and the totals of their personal tax assessments, without indicating the different sources from which that income was derived. Such detailed information is available only in two files of Exchequer documents[70] relating to the tax assessments of various persons, including a number of peers and peeresses, and we cannot tell how many members of the gentry were beneficiaries in 1436 of annuities granted by the king or other lords.

The financial burdens of a Lincolnshire baron, Lionel (d. 1461), Lord Welles, show how misleading the personal tax assessments of some peers are.[71] Lord Welles, who appears among the lesser barons, with a taxable income of £322 a year, was a man much encumbered with family responsibilities. Although his estates were worth in clear value £604, they were charged with life annuities that cost him no less than £282 a year. He had to support his son Richard, his mother, his brother William, and his sister Katherine, as well as his two aunts, Eleanor and Lucy, and he was still paying off at a rate of £40 a year debts bequeathed him by his late grandfather, John (1352–1421), Lord Welles. Four manors worth £73 6s 8d a year were held for life by Lord Welles's mother, Maud, who had remarried, and this share of the family estates was in the possession of her second husband, John Haytfield, who therefore ranked as one of the richer members of the Lincolnshire gentry, with a taxed income of £100 per annum.[72] Another Lincolnshire baron, Robert (d. 1452), Lord Willoughby, whose landed income was £1,040, was paying annually £360 in life annuities, so he was liable for taxation on only the remaining £680.[73] When Lord Welles's heir, Richard, married Lord Willoughby's only daughter, Joan (who subsequently became sole heiress to her father's estates), the two barons had both settled manors worth £100 a year on feoffees in order to make suitable provision for the young married couple. Because of this marriage settlement and annuities assigned to other relatives of Robert, Lord Willoughby, both the Welles and Willoughby baronies appear in 1436 to be much less well endowed than they really were. Although such information is not available for the majority of peerage families, it is improbable that Lords Welles and Willoughby were the only peers who were obliged to make provision for relatives.

H. L. Gray calculated that the average English baronial income in 1436 was £865 including annuities, or £768 without annuities, and his interpretation of these taxation returns indicated that there were ten very wealthy commoners with incomes of about £557 each.[74] That there were a few landowners among the gentry who were richer than the lesser peers is indisputable; Sir John Fastolf (who died childless in 1459) and Sir John Stourton (who became a baron in 1449) both admitted to possessing £600 a year. In Dorset

(a county for which the local returns do not survive) an income of
£660 (which was therefore taxed at the highest rate payable) perhaps
belonged to Sir Humphrey Stafford (d. 1442) of Hooke, who was ten
times elected knight of the shire; his father's income from their
family estates in Dorset and in the Midlands had been assessed in
1412 at not much less than £600 a year.[75] In Northumberland Sir
Robert Umfraville had £400 a year in 1436, but the rest of these
conspicuously affluent commoners have yet to be identified, and by
a singular coincidence all six of them have to be sought in Devonshire. In that county £3,307 of income was taxed at the maximum
rate of 2s in the £, and that led Professor Gray to assume the
existence of half a dozen non-baronial landowners in Devonshire
whose property was worth on average £557 a year. As the taxable
income of Thomas Courtenay (d. 1458), earl of Devon, was found
to be only £733 a year, it looks at first sight as if the greatest nobleman in the west of England was closely rivalled by several members
of the gentry in his own county.[76]

Such conclusions would be profoundly mistaken. The greater part
of the Courtenay estates were in the hands of the earl's mother,
Anne (d. 1441), dowager countess of Devon; she had fourteen of
her late husband's thirty-six manors in Devonshire, together with a
life interest in all the Courtenay lands in Cornwall and other
properties. In 1432 the dowager countess of Devon had remarried,
and that marriage had probably made her second husband, John
Botreaux, esquire, the richest non-baronial landowner in Devon
in 1436. Moreover, Thomas, earl of Devon's income was assessed
for taxation by the local commissioners in Devonshire, and not by
the chancellor and treasurer in London. The whole of the Courtenay
estates, as held by the dowager countess and the earl, would therefore account for a large part of the £3,307 of income in Devonshire
which had to pay tax at the rate of 10 per cent.[77] Until more is
known of the social structure of fifteenth-century Devonshire we
cannot safely assume (as K. B. McFarlane did) that the 1436 taxation returns 'reveal the existence of some ten commoners whose
landed wealth was not much less than that of the average baron'.
The disparity in resources between Thomas Courtenay, earl of
Devon, one of the most troublesome of Henry VI's over-mighty
subjects, and the Devonshire gentry was far greater than H. L.
Gray's much quoted statistics suggest. Devonshire was one of the
poorest counties in late medieval England, and it is unlikely that

there were members of the Devonshire gentry whose wealth and power could vie with that of a fifteenth-century earl of Devon.[78]

III

The taxation returns of 1436 will not enable us to arrive at reliable estimates of the landed wealth of the English baronage or the gentry, but these records can serve another purpose. The nobility were required to provide the Exchequer with lists of all the life annuities they were paying. Thirteen of these detailed schedules survive; they are the lists delivered to the lord treasurer of England, Ralph (d. 1456), Lord Cromwell, by one duke, two earls and ten barons, and they contain valuable evidence to show how widespread was the practice of retaining for life. Furthermore, we know the total sum (£50) of the life annuities paid by Lord Tiptoft, although the names of his annuitants have not been preserved.[79] Reginald (d. 1450), Lord de la Warr, was apparently exceptional in that he had given life annuities costing £270 to seventy-six persons. These charges consumed over 30 per cent of his landed income and none of his annuitants was a knight or an esquire. The political and military power of a late medieval magnate depended essentially on the following he could recruit among the gentry. These fourteen peers for whom we have information concerning their annuitants constituted one-third of the English lords temporal taxed in 1436. Apart from Lords Welles and Willoughby (whose expenditure was largely incurred by payments to members of their families) and Reginald, Lord de la Warr, only two of these fourteen peers had granted life annuities which amounted to more than 10 per cent of their personal taxable income. John Holland (d. 1447), earl of Huntingdon (and later duke of Exeter) had married as his second wife Beatrice (d. 1439), dowager countess of Arundel; their joint income was assessed for taxation at £1,002, and part of a sum of £160 expended in twenty-six life annuities represented charges which the earl had acquired with his wife's Arundel dower interest. One of the Yorkshire barons, John (d. 1455), Lord Scrope of Masham (taxed at £557 per annum), was paying thirty-three life annuities, at a total cost of £80 a year.

The subsidy levied in 1436 was a graduated tax, the incidence of which fell most heavily on the larger incomes; those over £100 a year but less than £400 were taxed at 8d in the £, while the rate rose to an unprecedented level of 10 per cent on the largest incomes,

amounting to £400 a year or more.[80] It was in the taxpayer's interest
to make a full declaration of all the annuities and fees which he had
granted for life, as the tax on these sums would have to be paid
by the recipient and not by the donor, whose own income was
taxable only in clear value, beyond reprises. The return made to the
Exchequer by Thomas (d. 1460), Lord Scales, indicates the benefits
which could accrue from this concession; his income from estates
in six counties was stated to be £400, but because he had granted
four life annuities, costing in all £24 a year, his taxable income
was only £376. Lord Scales, by avoiding taxation at the highest
rate of 2s in the £, was able to save in tax payment in 1436 more
than these four annuities had cost him.[81]

As a similar tax ha d been collected as recently as 1431, there
was some prospect that such income taxes might become a regular
part of English government finance. Despite the fiscal advantages
which could result from granting annuities for life (instead of
during pleasure or for a definite term of years), it is clear that most
of the fourteen peers for whom evidence is available had not greatly
burdened their family estates with charges of this kind. William
de la Pole (d. 1450), earl of Suffolk, whose taxed income included
the considerable amount of property accumulated by his wife, Alice
Chaucer (d. 1475),[82] was paying £150 a year to four persons; but
pensions to his widowed sister-in-law, Elizabeth, and her daughter,
Katherine de la Pole, accounted for most of that sum. Both these
ladies had become nuns and the £50 a year paid to the former
countess of Suffolk and the annuity of 100 marks enjoyed by her
daughter probably represented a settlement in lieu of the dower
to which Elizabeth Mowbray had been entitled, as widow of Michael
(d. 1415), third de la Pole earl of Suffolk.[83] John (d. 1443), Lord
Tiptoft, with a taxable income of £1,098, was paying annually
£50 in life annuities. John (d. 1453), Lord Talbot (later earl of
Shrewsbury), whose declared annual income of £1,205 included
the £100 a year which he was receiving from Richard (d. 1460),
duke of York,[84] could easily afford the life annuities costing £27
per annum which he had granted to four persons, among whom
was his attorney-general, Richard Legett. Lord Beaumont, whose
income was assessed at £733 a year, had granted life annuities to
only three persons, and they amounted to a total annual charge
of £8.[85]

The giving of cash fees and annuities was not, of course, the

only method of retaining. Like the king, a great magnate had a wide
range of offices in his gift. By appointing stewards, receivers, constables and janitors of castles, keepers of forests, parks and warrens,
he could enlist men in his service; often the fees paid in connection
with these local offices were far in excess of adequate remuneration
for such duties as were performed.[86] A nobleman's affinity included
his household men (who might muster a few hundred persons in the
more splendid baronial establishments), his councillors and numerous estate officials, but in Lancastrian England the leading members
of the higher nobility considered it necessary to pay fees to retain
in peace and in war a sizeable following among the gentry, usually
in those shires where the lord had his principal estates.[87] It has
been calculated that by 1442 Henry Percy (d. 1455), earl of Northumberland, was spending about a quarter of the revenues of his Yorkshire manors in fees granted to his retainers, and it was in that
county that the Percies had their most valuable estates. The earl of
Northumberland's landed income in 1436 was probably as much as
£2,800 a year, but the taxable income which he declared was only
£1,210;[88] the difference between those two sums may perhaps indicate the size and cost of his retinue, as well as fees payable to
household and estate officers. In view of his duties as warden of
the East March on the Scottish border from 1417 to 1434,[89] the earl
of Northumberland doubtless needed a much larger permanent
retinue than most lords whose estates lay south of the Trent. Only
ten peers were found to have taxable incomes in excess of £1,000
in 1436; we have lists of the life annuitants in the pay of five of
these lords (Humphrey, duke of Gloucester; John Holland, earl of
Huntingdon; William de la Pole, earl of Suffolk, and Lords Talbot
and Tiptoft), but we lack similar information concerning the annuitants of the other five leading magnates (Richard, duke of York;
Richard Beauchamp (d. 1439), earl of Warwick; Richard Nevill
(d. 1460), earl of Salisbury; Henry Percy (d. 1455), earl of Northumberland, and Ralph (d. 1456), Lord Cromwell), and they included
some of the most powerful members of the English aristocracy.
Inevitably, conclusions drawn about a minority of the English peerage can have only a limited value, but the cost of life annuities
granted before 1436 by Humphrey, duke of Gloucester, and thirteen
other peers hardly suggests that the English nobility as a class was
spending too much on retainers in the generation before the Wars of
the Roses.

The most interesting of these lists of annuitants is that supplied by Humphrey, duke of Gloucester. Because the income tax of 1436 was confined to freehold estate in England, his tax assessment of £2,243 did not include his annuity of £1,000 a year during royal pleasure, or the revenues from his earldom of Pembroke and his lordships of Cilgerran, Llanstephan and Tenby in Wales.[90] There can be little doubt that the sum of £280 6s 8d which the king's uncle was dispensing in life annuities payable to twenty-three persons[91] amounted to less than 10 per cent of the full income he really enjoyed. His annuitants included his cook, William Hawes (sometime a servant of Henry IV), his baker, John Coventre, the abbot of St Augustine's, Canterbury, and a woman who may have been one of the duchess's attendants. Duke Humphrey's retinue consisted principally of three knights and six esquires. The most expensive of his retainers was Sir John Grey (d. 1439), son and heir of Reginald (d. 1440), Lord Grey of Ruthin, who had 80 marks a year. Grey's long record of war service in France accounts for his election in 1436 as a knight of the Garter, filling the vacancy caused by the death of the Regent Bedford. All three of Gloucester's knights were prominent landowners. Sir John Grey had married Constance (d. 1437), Dowager Countess Marshal, whose estates, worth perhaps as much as £600 per annum, seem to have evaded taxation altogether.[92] Sir Robert Roos (d. 1441), who had an annuity of 40 marks, was almost the richest member of the Lincolnshire gentry, with a taxable income of £165 per annum.[93] Sir Nicholas Thorley (d. 1452), was the second husband of Alice (d. 1452), dowager countess of Oxford, who had her own inheritance besides her dower. Thorley's taxable income of £340 from lands in eight counties must have come mainly from his wife's property, but he was receiving £20 a year from Duke Humphrey.[94] Three of the duke's esquires also had annuities of £20 each; Conan Aske and John Ripley, who declared incomes of £90 and £80 respectively, were well-off in their own right,[95] but John Skelton (d. 1458), retained by the duke since 1423, had not yet succeeded to his father's Cumberland estates.[96]

Needless to say, Gloucester could not claim the exclusive allegiance of all his retainers. William Pope, esquire, had already served the house of Lancaster for more than forty years. Only £10 of his annual income of £80 was provided by Duke Humphrey; the rest was derived from royal grants.[97] The Yorkshire esquire, Ivo de

Etton (who had 20 marks per annum from the duke) was also retained by the king.[98] Although the former lord protector was heir to the throne when Henry VI came of age, his retinue was not large, and, apart from the three knights, it was remarkably undistinguished. Robert Sandford, esquire, of Co. Kent, George Lampet of Thorndon, Co. Suffolk, and Nicholas Wolfe, who were all drawing annuities of £10 a year granted by Duke Humphrey, were persons of little or no local importance.[99] Gloucester's adherents may have been more substantial in 1422,[100] but the ill success of his attempts to take control of the government during Henry VI's minority becomes more understandable if we look at the men who still remained in his service in 1436. Few men of property cared to link their fortunes too closely with those of a royal duke who had shown little capacity for political leadership. The risks were too great. After Duke Humphrey's death at Bury St Edmunds on 23 February 1447, forty-two of his followers, mostly Welshmen, were arrested and imprisoned. Five of them, including the late duke's bastard son, Arthur, were condemned to death in July on charges of treason and they were already strung up for execution at Tyburn on 14 July before Gloucester's enemy Suffolk would allow them to have the benefit of a royal pardon granted by Henry VI.[101]

IV

The three greatest English landowners in the latter half of Henry VI's reign were the dukes of Buckingham and York and the earl of Warwick.[102] The affinity of Humphrey Stafford (d. 1460), first duke of Buckingham, is better documented than that of any other magnate in fifteenth-century England. In 1448 the duke's retinue included ten knights and twenty-seven esquires, many of whom belonged to the Cheshire gentry. Although Buckingham had inherited lands in twenty-two English counties, the west Midlands were the house of Stafford's main sphere of influence. Annuities paid to his retainers, councillors and household servants in 1447–48 cost £452; together with the fees and wages of all the estate officials, these payments amounted to over £900 per annum.[103] The best paid of the duke's retainers was Sir Edward Grey (d. 1457), who succeeded in 1445 to his wife's barony of Ferrers of Groby. He was retained for life in 1440, with an annual fee of £40, which was to be increased to 100 marks when Grey became a baron.[104] Two of the

duke's knights, Sir Richard Vernon (d. 1451) of Haddon, Co. Derby,
and Tong, Co. Salop (who had been Speaker in the Parliament of
1426), and Sir John Constable (d. 1451) of Halsham and Burton
Constable, Co. Yorks., were worth fees of £20 a year, but for the
rest £10 was the customary retaining fee for a knight and the duke's
esquires usually got 10 marks a year.[105] The fee of 40 marks a year
granted to John Bourchier (d. 1474), esquire (later Lord Berners),
was exceptional; he was the youngest of the duke's four half-
brothers.[106] It is unlikely that any of Buckingham's contemporaries
could command a stronger following among the gentry or bring
a bigger private army to a battlefield. During the political crisis
caused by Henry VI's insanity, Buckingham was rumoured in
January 1454 to be having 2,000 badges with the Stafford knot made
for distribution among his followers.[107]

After 1450 Buckingham (like Richard, Duke of York) was facing
serious financial problems; he was owed great sums of money by the
Crown, and the largest of these debts was £19,395 in arrears of
wages due to him as captain of Calais. The income from his Welsh
marcher lordships had drastically declined and the cash receipts
from his estates were probably inadequate to pay for the expenses
of the ducal houshold, which already by 1444 cost annually about
£2,200.[108] This expenditure appears to have increased appreciably a
decade later, partly because the duke now had to maintain another
household for his heir, Humphrey (d. c.1458), earl of Stafford.[109] It is
true that Buckingham's estates were much richer and more extensive
than those of his father, Edmund (d. 1403), earl of Stafford, but in
his later years provision for his large family constituted a heavy
burden, which strained even his resources.[110] Down to 1458 Buckingham tried to keep on good terms with both sides; loyal to the
king, he remained friendly towards his wife's brother-in-law, the
duke of York.[111] By the autumn of 1459 he had joined forces with
York's enemies and his change of front was perhaps the most
important factor which at last made possible the outbreak of civil
war. Buckingham's support enabled Queen Margaret to attack York
and his allies, the Nevill earls of Salisbury and Warwick. Duke
Humphrey's financial difficulties may have influenced his decision
to ally with the court party, but that cannot be proved. His personal
loyalty to Henry VI is likely to have been the chief consideration,
combined with a conviction that the house of Lancaster would once
more triumph over its enemies. Buckingham's share of the spoils

after the rout of the Yorkists in October 1459 included the forfeited lands and goods of Sir William Oldhall and the fines which three others of York's chief adherents (Walter Devereux, William Hastings and Walter Hopton) had to pay in order to obtain the king's pardon.[112] Buckingham was the most distinguished casualty on the royalist side in the battle of Northampton, fought on 10 July 1460. He had done well out of his fidelity to the Lancastrian dynasty and his decision to fight to the death to resist Richard Nevill, earl of Warwick's seizure of power is understandable, but Stubbs's description of him as 'the peace-making duke who fell at Northampton' seems inappropriate.[113]

K. B. McFarlane's study of bastard feudalism was based to a large extent on the affinity of John of Gaunt, whose income and expenditure could not be rivalled by any magnate in fifteenth-century England.[114] The duchy of Lancaster was worth over £12,000 per annum, and, if we include the duke's Castilian pension, his income may have amounted to as much as £20,000 a year in the last decade of his life.[115] Annuities charged on the Lancaster estates were costing over £3,000 per annum in 1394, and the fees paid by the duke were notably generous; one knight got as much as £100 a year and many esquires had 20 marks. In the early years of Richard II's reign the men who had contracted to serve the duke of Lancaster included one earl, three barons, eighty-three knights, and 112 esquires.[116] His retainers were hired to protect the duke's person and property (for at times he was dangerously unpopular); their services were required to uphold his political influence and to further his ambitions, both at home and abroad.[117] No other English noble needed (or could afford) a retinue on such a scale. John of Gaunt was the richest man in England and between 1371 and 1388 he styled himself king of Castile; but above all it was the succession to the English throne that really justified the upkeep of his great retinue in his later years. Richard II was childless, and, if the king left no direct heir, the crown would be won by the most powerful claimant. The annuities and fees paid by John of Gaunt were a sound investment. He created the political following which enabled Henry of Lancaster to usurp the throne in 1399 and keep it in the upheavals that followed. Henry IV's expenditure on retainers was even greater than his father's: annuities absorbed nearly £9,000 per annum of the duchy of Lancaster revenues during the early years of his reign, and these charges were still consuming over

£5,000 a year in the later years of Henry V.[118] In 1401 all the annuities granted by Henry IV were reckoned to be costing £24,000 a year.[119] The first Lancastrian king has often been criticised for his extravagance, but the throne of England was well worth the price he paid for it. After 1399 the Crown was the centre of bastard feudalism because the king's own affinity was far greater and stronger than that of any subject. The Lancastrian party, built up by John of Gaunt and carefully maintained by his son and grandson, was left leaderless in 1422 by the premature death of Henry V. This invincible political connection disintegrated in the nerveless hands of Henry VI.

Numerous duchy of Lancaster valors yield plenty of information about the retainers in the service of John of Gaunt and his heirs. The administration of the York estates may (as K. B. McFarlane imagined) have been just as efficient as that of the duchy of Lancaster,[120] but no comparable series of records has survived. The bulk of Richard (d. 1460), duke of York's inheritance came from his maternal uncle, the last Mortimer earl of March, but a valor made in 1443 shows that these Welsh marcher lordships were not heavily burdened with annuities paid to his retainers. Apart from the enormous fee of £200 per annum paid to John Talbot (d. 1453), earl of Shrewsbury, in 1443 there were only fourteen York annuitants in the Marches, who together cost the duke less than £170 a year.[121] Although Duke Richard was the greatest private landowner in Wales, few of the Welsh gentry were in his pay and his following in the Marches seems to have been less numerous than that of the duke of Buckingham. Before the king's illness in 1453, York had failed to win the confidence of most of his fellow peers, and the influence which he could exert in English politics depended essentially on the support of a small group of devoted followers, men such as William Burley (d. 1458) of Bromcroft, Co. Salop, Sir Walter Devereux (d. 1459) of Weobley, Co. Hereford, Sir Thomas Harrington (d. 1460) of Hornby, Co. Lancs., Sir Leonard Hastings (d. 1455) of Kirby, Co. Leics., Sir Edmund Mulsho (d. 1458) of Cavendish, Co. Suffolk, Sir Andrew Ogard (d. 1454) of Rye, Co. Herts., and Sir William Oldhall (d. 1460) of Hunsdon, Co. Herts.[122] Before fighting was resumed in September 1459 the deaths of several of the richer knights who had been long in the duke of York's service had probably seriously weakened his position, and the rout of Ludford on 12 October exposed the weakness of Duke Richard's power at its

very centre. Among those who defected to the Lancastrians was the
Herefordshire knight Sir John Barre (d. 1483) of Rotherwas, who
had been receiving a life annuity of £20 from York since 1433.[123]
Duke Richard was by far the greatest of Henry VI's over-mighty
subjects, but three generations of the ducal house of York never
attained territorial influence comparable to that enjoyed by the
house of Lancaster.

v

When Edward IV returned to recover his kingdom in March 1471
he landed at Ravenspur, but, unlike Henry of Lancaster in 1399,
he aroused remarkably little enthusiasm in northern England. In
Yorkshire both the gentry and the citizens of York followed the
lead given by the recently restored Henry Percy (d. 1489), fourth
earl of Northumberland. During his exile in the Netherlands in the
winter of 1470–71, King Edward had prepared the way for his
return by sending an envoy, Nicholas Leventhorpe, on a mission
to the earl of Northumberland, presumably in an attempt to enlist
his aid. In this renewed contest for the throne Northumberland was
bound to hope for a Yorkist victory. If the readeption of Henry VI
were to prove lasting, there was always a danger that he might once
again be deprived of his earldom in favour of Warwick's younger
brother, John Nevill, Lord Montague, who had held it from May
1464 until early in 1470. Although the Percy earl had good reason
to favour the ex-king of England, he was unable to provide him
with any active support; Northumberland's own retainers among
the Yorkshire gentry were still Lancastrian in their sympathies.[124]
Even in south Yorkshire King Edward's party gained few recruits,
although the house of York had held estates in that part of the
country since 1347.[125] Until he got safely into the east Midlands,
the region where Lord Hastings's influence was paramount, King
Edward's prospects looked less promising than those of Henry
Tudor in August 1485. He had landed in Holderness with a small
force of no more than 2,000 men and no substantial reinforcements
came in until he was joined at Nottingham by Sir James Harrington
(d. 1487) of Brearley, Co. Yorks, and Sir William Parr (d. 1483) of
Kendal Castle, Co. Westmorland, who brought with them another
600 men. At Leicester Lord Hastings's retainers, perhaps 3,000
strong, rallied to their lord and they made up a large part of the

contingent which enabled Edward IV to enter London unopposed
on Thursday 11 April.[126] Before King Edward could face Warwick's
challenge in battle at Barnet on Easter Sunday, 14 April, Yorkist
magnates such as Hastings and the Bourchiers had to raise an army
for him. Until he decided to return to his Yorkist allegiance early
in April, George, duke of Clarence (who could mobilise a squadron
of about 4,000), probably held the balance between the two sides.[127]
Edward IV owed his final triumph in 1471 partly to Warwick's
mistakes but even more to the failure of his Lancastrian and Nevill
enemies to unite against him.

Even after Warwick's defeat and death at Barnet the Lancastrian
cause was by no means lost. If Edward IV was to retain the crown
which he had so unexpectedly regained, it was imperative for him
to compel Queen Margaret's allies in the west of England to fight
the decisive battle as soon as possible, before new local risings broke
out in support of Henry VI, once more a prisoner in the Tower of
London. Richard Beauchamp, constable of Gloucester Castle, gave
King Edward an opportunity to crush his opponents completely
when he refused to allow the fugitive Lancastrian army to enter
the city on Friday morning, 3 May. The news that the Lancastrians
had been utterly defeated at Tewkesbury on 4 May was sufficient
to prevent another Yorkshire rebellion against Edward IV,
although preparations by north-country malcontents were already
far advanced. A new insurrection in Kent, led by Thomas Nevill,
the Bastard of Fauconberg, which started on the morrow of Tewkesbury, was already too late to have any real prospect of success. The
dynastic struggle had at last been ended by the death at Tewkesbury
of Henry VI's heir, Edward, Prince of Wales, and the house of
Lancaster was politically extinct even before King Henry's murder
in the Tower on the night of 21 May.[128]

The majority of the English baronage remained aloof from the
dynastic struggle in 1471 and they regarded Edward V's fate with
similar indifference in 1483. Few peers were recipients of royal
grants made by Edward IV during his second reign,[129] and, unlike
the house of Lancaster, the Yorkist kings never succeeded in win-
ning deep-rooted or lasting loyalty from the English nobility. By
his arbitrary disregard of the rules of inheritance and traditional
property rights, Edward IV, once he was secure on the throne,
had injured some of the greatest families in the land. His annexa-
tion of the Mowbray dukedom of Norfolk, for the benefit of his

younger son, Richard (1473–83), duke of York, was carried out by legal means, in that it was ratified by an Act of Parliament passed early in 1483. But for this legislation, Lords Howard and Berkeley would have been co-heirs to the Mowbray estates after the death of the child heiress, the Lady Anne, in November 1481; they had to wait until the usurpation of Richard III before they could establish their rightful claims. In 1479 William Herbert (d. 1490), earl of Pembroke, had been obliged to surrender that earldom and almost all the Welsh lordships granted to his father in the 1460s. He was meagrely compensated with the title of earl of Huntingdon and thirteen manors in the west of England. The Welsh marcher lordships taken from the Herbert earl were given to the king's elder son, Edward, Prince of Wales. Already the earl of Pembroke had been deprived of the lordship of Gower and Kilvey, which his father had acquired in 1468 from the last duke of Norfolk, and this lordship was henceforth regarded as part of the Mowbray estates now vested in the king's second son, Richard, first as husband and subsequently as widower of the Mowbray heiress.

Other members of the nobility had their own grievances. Henry Stafford (1455–83), second duke of Buckingham, saw himself as the lawful claimant to the Lancaster moiety of the earldoms of Essex, Hereford and Northampton after the death of Henry VI in 1471. These three earldoms, the former de Bohun heritage, had been partitioned in 1421 between Henry V and his cousin, Anne (d. 1438), countess of Stafford. In order to retain Buckingham's loyalty in 1483, Richard III was even prepared to concede that demand. Lastly, the succession to the duchy of Exeter estates had been settled by Act of Parliament early in 1483 for the enrichment of Queen Elizabeth Wydevill's sons by her first marriage, Thomas (d. 1501), marquis of Dorset and Lord Richard Grey. In 1461 a large part of the lands forfeited by Henry Holland (d. 1475), duke of Exeter, had been granted to his wife, Anne, who was Edward IV's eldest sister. The duchess of Exeter obtained the dissolution of her marriage in 1472 and afterwards married Sir Thomas St Leger; their only child, Anne, who was contracted in marriage to the marquis of Dorset's heir, Thomas Grey, was made heiress to the Holland manors and lordships, which the duchess had held until her death in 1476 and which remained in St Leger's possession. The Act of Parliament passed in January 1483 to legalise these arrangements also ensured that the queen's second son, Lord Richard Grey, was to be provided for with a share of the duchess's estates worth 500 marks a year. But for Henry, duke of Exeter's forfeiture, his heir would have been his thrice-married sister, Anne (d. 1486), countess of Douglas, whose son by her second marriage, Ralph, Lord Nevill, succeeded in 1484 to the earldom of Westmorland. In view of the way in which the surviving descendants of the Holland dukes of Exeter had been legally disinherited for the advancement of the queen's family, it is not surprising that Ralph, Lord Nevill was regarded by Richard, duke of Gloucester, as one of his most trustworthy adherents. By 1483 there were too many English magnates who had a vested interest in the downfall of the children of Edward IV and Elizabeth Wydevill. By the assistance of such allies as Buckingham and Howard, Richard, duke of Gloucester, was able to seize power and take the crown from his nephew within three months of Edward IV's death.[130]

The death of Edward IV on 9 April 1483 resulted in a struggle for power which soon exposed the failure of Yorkist rule. His heir was a boy of twelve. Feuds among the Yorkist nobles made it impossible to organise a regency for the young Edward V. These rivalries were not a legacy of the Wars of the Roses; they were a consequence of Edward IV's irresponsible marriage with Elizabeth Wydevill and the aggrandisement of her family. For Richard, duke of Gloucester, the minority of his nephew was a situation full of danger. No doubt Gloucester genuinely feared that unless he seized control of the government he would before long be destroyed by the Wydevills and their kinsmen, the Greys. He received offers of support from two important magnates: William, Lord Hastings was the chief figure among the new Yorkist peerage created by the late king, and Henry Stafford, duke of Buckingham, was by far the greatest of the lords whose titles were older than 1461.[131]

After Edward V had been intercepted at Stony Stratford on 30 April while on his way from Ludlow to London, Duke Richard had no difficulty in asserting his claim to the office of lord protector, but his seizure of power was a revolution which solved no problems. The prospect before him was that of a few years of limited authority as lord protector. If the precedent of 1422 were followed, Gloucester would be merely a chairman of a council of regency, not a regent invested with the full exercise of royal power. When the young king came of age, Gloucester would be exposed to the revenge of the queen mother's family, who were not likely to forgive their exclusion from influence at court. In the second week of June Lord Hastings (formerly Gloucester's ally) may have joined forces with Queen Elizabeth's supporters in a conspiracy to overthrow the lord protector.[132] It was now clear that there was no security for Gloucester unless he became king. Moreover, he was dependent on men such as Buckingham and Lord Howard, who expected the rewards which only a king could give. The deposition of Edward V followed inevitably on 25 June. Fear for the future may have been just as important as ambition in bringing about the usurpation of Richard III.

In 1422 the aspirations of Humphrey, duke of Gloucester, to be regent had been defeated by the opposition of a united baronage.[133] By contrast, in 1483 the higher nobility was too weak and divided to prevent Richard, duke of Gloucester, from assuming the crown. If we exclude the near relatives of the queen mother (her eldest brother, Anthony, Lord Rivers, her eldest son, Thomas Grey, marquis of Dorset, and her youngest son, the child Richard, duke of York), the higher nobility consisted of only three dukes and six earls of full age when Edward IV died. Apart from Gloucester and his chief ally, Buckingham, the only English duke was Gloucester's brother-in-law, John de la Pole (1422–91), second duke of Suffolk, a man of whom little is known in his later years. In the politics of Richard III's reign the de la Pole family was represented by Suffolk's heir, John (c. 1462–87), earl of Lincoln, who emerged as one of the most trusted of King Richard's supporters.[134] After the death of Richard III's only legitimate son in April 1484 there was the prospect that the earl of Lincoln might eventually succeed to the throne. Three of the five other English earls were elderly men, and perhaps because of age or personal disinclination they had ceased to be active politicians; Arundel was sixty-five, Kent sixty-six, and Westmorland seventy-five. Far more important was Henry Percy (d. 1489), fourth earl of Northumberland, who had been Gloucester's retainer since 1474; Richard III's enthronement left him in an unchallenged position as the greatest magnate north of the Trent.[135] Lastly, there was the impoverished William Herbert, earl of Huntingdon, who had lost most of the Welsh lordships inherited from his father. He had little influence outside south Wales; although his first wife had been a Wydevill, he agreed early in 1484 to marry Richard III's bastard daughter, Katherine Plantagenet, a marriage which augmented his income by 1,000 marks a year.[136] In his account of the English revolution of 1483 Dominic Mancini stated that the lords were intimidated into submission to Gloucester's wishes.[137] If the membership of the higher nobility is considered, it is not difficult to understand why they acquiesced in the usurpation of Richard III.

Almost the whole of the English peerage was present at Richard III's coronation on 6 July 1483. Far more significant was the absence of most of the barons from the battlefield at Bosworth, where the king was attended by only ten lords, headed by John, duke of Norfolk, his heir, Thomas Howard, earl of Surrey, and William, earl of Nottingham.[138] Less than a quarter of the English peerage was sufficiently committed to fight for King Richard, and it is remarkable how little positive support he could inspire or compel after ruling England for more than two years. Norfolk and Nottingham (formerly Lords Howard and Berkeley) had gained much from Richard's usurpation; their rewards included their new titles, the Mowbray estates (which they had partitioned) and other royal grants. Francis, Lord Lovell was the king's personal friend, but the other active Yorkists among the peers were lesser barons, William Devereux, Lord Ferrers of Chartley, and Lords Dacre of Gilsland, Greystoke, Scrope of Bolton, and Zouche. Henry Percy, fourth earl of Northumberland, came to Bosworth, but only to watch the battle; his troops did not take part. Richard III was overthrown so easily because he had failed to enlist the co-operation of the English baronage. He had spared no effort to gain his subjects' loyalty and his grants were made at little cost to himself, because the fiasco of Buckingham's rebellion in October 1483 gave him a great fund of forfeited estates to dispose of. His largesse rivalled the prodigality of Henry IV. The majority of the lords benefited materially from his rule, in the form of grants of land, offices or annuities, but it was only a few families, especially the Howards, the Percies and the Stanleys, who did conspicuously well. Below the rank of baron, the best rewarded of Richard III's henchmen was Sir Richard Ratcliffe, who was given lands worth 1,000 marks a year. Far too much of what King Richard had to give was bestowed to enrich a small clique of trusted followers.[139] Like the inexperienced Edward IV during his first reign, Richard III had not discovered how to employ effectively the vast amount of patronage at the Crown's disposal. The house of York ruled England for less than twenty-five years because it remained throughout far too dependent on the loyalty of a few great magnate families.

The first Tudor king was too prudent to repeat that mistake. Sir William Stanley, whose intervention at Bosworth may have been decisive, was not rewarded with a peerage; he was executed for treason in 1495.[140] The English higher nobility numbered twenty families in 1485, but only half these titles survived when Henry VIII was crowned.[141] There was no rebellion after 1497 and few peers engaged in conspiracy against Henry VII, perhaps because the chances of success were so remote. No previous English king had ever realised so fully that money was power, but financial considerations did not always determine his policies. By 1509 all the royal revenues from the lordship of Denbigh were being consumed by life annuities which the king had granted early in his reign to eighteen persons, few of whom were Welshmen.[142] While seeking to repress unlawful retaining by any of his subjects, Henry VII aimed to make his dynasty more secure by retaining for life members of leading families among the English gentry in the Marches. Prince Arthur's own retainers in Herefordshire and Shropshire remained in the pay of the Council in the Marches after the prince's death in 1502. Unlike the hapless Edward V, Henry VII's heir was well befriended.[143] Far more important than the giving of such annuities was the distribution of the numerous lucrative local offices in the king's gift in the principality of Wales and the earldom of March. Most of these Welsh offices were obsolete long before the Act of Union of 1536, but, with their handsome fees, they served a useful purpose in English politics.[144] The survival of the new dynasty was no accident. The enormous concentration of landed property in Henry VII's hands included the duchies of Lancaster and York and all the possessions which had formerly belonged to Warwick the Kingmaker. Because the English Crown was now so rich, the early Tudor sovereigns had at their disposal a far greater fund of political patronage than any of their late medieval predecessors. They used it wisely. Although the royal finances were put on a firm basis, neither Henry VII nor Henry VIII was sparing in rewards to trusted supporters.[145] After a generation of Tudor rule, bastard feudalism was controlled and regulated by the Crown as a support to the royal power.[146] The Tudor dynasty ruled in six-sixteenth-century England because Henry VII had proved able to learn invaluable lessons from the fate of the houses of Lancaster and York.

Appendix
English peerages created by Edward IV (1461–83).

For information concerning these English peers, see *C.P.*, *passim*. Thomas (1450–1524), son and heir of William (d. 1487), earl of Arundel, was styled Lord Maltravers in 1465 (J. E. Powell and K.,Wallis, *op. cit.*, 516), although he was not summoned to Parliament until 1478. William Herbert (1455–90), who was made Lord Dunster in 1466 (see p. 87) was never summoned to Parliament by that title; he was still a minor in 1469 when he succeeded to the earldom of Pembroke. John (d. 1485), Lord Howard (later (1483–85) duke of Norfolk), is included in this list of peers created by Edward IV because he was already styled Lord Howard before 4 March 1470 (C. L. Scofield, *op. cit.*, 1,509), although he was not summoned to Parliament as a peer until the readeption Parliament of Henry VI, which met in November 1470. For the two holders of the Dacre barony after 1473 (Richard Fiennes (1425–83), Lord Dacre 'of the south' and Humphrey Dacre (1420–85), Lord Dacre 'of the north'), see J. E. Powell and K. Wallis, *op. cit.*, 520–1. The Gascon, Galiard Dureford, Lord Duras, is omitted from this list, although he was one of the lords who took an oath on 3 July 1471 to accept Edward IV's son, Edward, Prince of Wales, as heir to the throne (*ibid.*, 520), because he was never summoned to Parliament. For Irish peerages created by Edward IV, see *C.P.R.*, *1461–67*, 178, 185, and *C.P.R.*, *1476–85*, 120.

Duke	Clarence (1461)	George Plantagenet (1449–78)
	Gloucester (1461)	Richard Plantagenet (1452–85)
	Bedford (1470)	George Nevill (*c.* 1460–83; depr. 1478)
	York (1474)	Richard Plantagenet (1473–83)
	Norfolk (1478)	Richard Plantagenet (1473–83)
Marquis	Montagu (1470)	John Nevill (*c.* 1431–71)
	Dorset (1475)	Thomas Grey (*c.* 1455–1501)
Earl	Essex (1461)	Henry Bourchier (*c.* 1406–83)
	Kent (1461)	William Nevill (*c.* 1410–63)
	Northumberland (1464)	John Nevill (*c.* 1431–71) (surr. 25 March 1470)
	Kent (1465)	Edmund Grey (1416–90)
	Rivers (1466)	Richard Wydevill (*c.* 1405–69)
	Lincoln (1467)	John de la Pole (*c.* 1462–87)
	Pembroke (1468)	William Herbert (*c.* 1423–69)
	Devon (1469)	Humphrey Stafford (1439–69)
	Wiltshire (1470)	John Stafford (*c.* 1440–73)
	Northumberland (1470)	Henry Percy (*c.* 1449–89)

	Huntingdon (1471)	Thomas Grey (c. 1455–1501)
	Winchester (1472)	Lewis of Bruges (c. 1427–92)
	Salisbury (1478)	Edward Plantagenet (1476–84)
	Huntingdon (1479)	William Herbert (1455–90), formerly (1469–79) earl of Pembroke
Viscount	Berkeley (1481)	William Berkeley (1426–92)
	Lovel (1483)	Francis Lovel (1456–87)
Baron	Ferrers of Chartley (1461)	Walter Devereux (c. 1432–85)
	Hastings (1461)	William Hastings (1431–83)
	Herbert (1461)	William Herbert (c. 1423–69)
	Lumley (1461)	Thomas Lumley (1408–85)
	Ogle (1461)	Robert Ogle (1406–69)
	Stafford (1461)	Humphrey Stafford (1439–69)
	Wenlock (1461)	John Wenlock (c. 1400–71)
	Maltravers (1465)	Thomas Arundel (1450–1524)
	Dunster (1466)	William Herbert (1455–90)
	Dinham (1467)	John Dinham (c. 1433–1501)
	Mountjoy (1467)	Walter Blount (c. 1420–74)
	Morley (1469)	William Lovel (c. 1436–76)
	Howard (1470)	John Howard (1420–85)
	Dacre of Gilsland (1473)	Humphrey Dacre (c. 1420–85)
	Lisle (1475)	Edward Grey (c. 1435–92)
	Welles (1483)	Richard Hastings (1435–1503)

Notes

1 For example, *The Life of Edward II*, ed. N. Denholm-Young (1957), 1, 4, 5, 8, 99; *Bartholomei de Cotton Historia Anglicana*, ed. H. R. Luard (Rolls Series, 1859), 232. I am much indebted to Professor A. R. Myers, Dr A. L. Brown, Dr G. L. Harriss, Dr C. D. Ross and Mr W. R. B. Robinson for their helpful comments and criticisms of this paper.

2. J. E. A. Jolliffe, *The Constitutional History of Medieval England* (1937), 346–9; J. Enoch Powell and K. Wallis, *The House of Lords in the Middle Ages* (1968).

3 According to Mathew Paris, Henry III could recall the names of 250 English baronies (*Chronica Majora*, ed. H. R. Luard (Rolls Series, 1872–83), v, 617). Because of partition among co-heiresses, there were more barons than there were baronies in thirteenth-century England; the holder of a portion of a barony was still regarded as a baron. Powell and Wallis, *op. cit.*, 225; I. J. Sanders, *English Baronies: a Study of their Origin and Descent, 1086–1327* (1960).

4 *R. P.* iv, 135; Jolliffe, *op. cit.*, 435.

5 P.R.O., c. 66/512, m. 22; *C.P.R.*, 1461–67, 425–6.

6 *Annales rerum Anglicarum* (subsequently cited as 'William Worcester'), printed in *Letters and Papers illustrative of the Wars of the English in France,*

ed. J. Stevenson (Rolls Series, 1864), ii, part ii, 785–6. K. B. McFarlane, 'William
Worcester: a preliminary survey', *Studies presented to Sir Hilary Jenkinson*,
ed. J. Conway Davies (1957), 196–221, has shown that William Worcester was
not the author of these annals. For Archbishop Nevill's enthronement banquet,
see C. L. Scofield, *The Life and Reign of Edward IV*, i, (1923), 399–400, and
J. Leland, *Collectanea*, ed. T. Hearne, vi (1715), 1–14.

7 'William Worcester', 786; in his will, made on 16 July 1469, William
Herbert, earl of Pembroke, refers to 'my son Dunster' (Sir Thomas Herbert
(d. 1682) of Tintern, Co. Mon., *Herbertorum Prosapia* (Cardiff Free Library,
ms 5.7, f. 57).

8 *The Paston Letters*, ed. J. Gairdner, iii (1904), 204.

9 For information concerning these marriages, and all peerage families
mentioned in this chapter, see *G.E.C.*, *passim*.

10 A. S. Harvey, *The De La Pole Family of Kingston-upon-Hull* (East Yorkshire Historical Society, 1957); *C.P.R., 1388–92* 383, 513.

11 The daughters of a wealthy baron could each expect marriage portions of
at least a thousand marks, but far greater sums were paid in dowries by members
of the higher nobility; in 1434 Richard (d. 1460), earl of Salisbury, gave his
daughter, Cecily Nevill, 4,700 marks on her marriage with the earl of Warwick's
heir, Henry Beauchamp (W. Dugdale, *The Baronage of England*, i (1675–76),
239, 248). It is a measure of the relative poverty of Richard (d. 1469), Lord
Rivers, that his daughter, Elizabeth Wydevill, had only 200 marks as her portion
when she married Sir John Grey (d. 1461), heir of Edward, Lord Ferrers of Groby
(D. MacGibbon, *Elizabeth Woodville, 1437–1492* (1938), 29–30). One of the largest
sums known to have been paid by a nobleman in late-medieval England to buy a
husband for his daughter was the dowry of 4,500 marks which Richard, duke of
York, contracted on 10 August 1445 to give his eldest daughter, Anne,
on her marriage with the duke of Exeter's heir, Henry Holland (d. 1475); see
P.R.O., d.l.41/2/8. After the death of Humphrey, duke of Gloucester, in 1447,
John Holland (d. 1447), duke of Exeter, was Henry VI's nearest kinsman in
England. The prospects that Henry Holland (1430–75), third duke of Exeter,
might ultimately succeed to the Crown may have influenced the size of this
marriage portion.

12 John Montague (c. 1350–1400) earl of Salisbury, married, before 4 May
1383, Maud Francis (d. 1424), daughter of Adam Francis, mayor of London from
1352 to 1354. Her first husband, John Aubrey (d. 1380–81), had been a London
merchant; her second husband, Sir Alan Buxhall (d. 1381), was a knight of the
Garter. John Montague's marriage with Maud Francis may have taken place
before he became heir to the earldom of Salisbury (through the death of his
uncle, William (d. 1397), earl of Salisbury's only son, on 6 August 1382), but
he was at that time heir to the barony of Monthemer. See S. L. Thrupp, *The
Merchant Class of Medieval London, 1300–1500* (1948), 266–7, and A. R.
Wagner, *English Genealogy* (1960), 138.

13 *C.P.R., 1461–67*, 298. Anne (d. 1480), dowager duchess of Buckingham,
and Archbishop Bourchier, as executors of the late duke, sold to the king on
28 February 1464 the marriage of the Stafford heir, the young Duke Henry
(1455–83), in return for a grant of the custody of his estates to the dowager
duchess, without payment of the farm which she had previously been render-

ing. Katherine Wydevill (c. 1457–97) appears to have been the youngest daughter of Richard (d. 1469), Earl Rivers; see *Cal.I.P.M.*, *Henry VII*, I, No. 681. G. Smith, *The Coronation of Elizabeth Woodville* (1935), 16, 21, shows that Buckingham's marriage had already taken place before the queen's coronation on 26 May 1465.

14 'William Worcester', 785; the author of the *Annales* believed that Henry, duke of Buckingham, married Katherine Wydevill early in 1466.

15 The Yorkshire estates of the Nevills, held *in tail male*, were granted to Richard, duke of Gloucester, after the death of Richard Nevill, earl of Warwick (*C.P.R., 1467–77*, 260, 266).

16 That is, the male heirs of Thomas (d. 1487), earl of Arundel, Henry Bourchier (d. 1483), earl of Essex and Edmund Grey (d. 1490) earl of Kent; John Tiptoft (d. 1470), earl of Worcester's heir, Edward (d. 1485), was born c. 1468. John de Vere (1443–1513), earl of Oxford, had apparently married Margaret Nevill, sister of Richard (d. 1471), earl of Warwick, before he succeeded in 1462 to the earldom of Oxford.

17 *Waurin*, v, 458–9, appears to be the sole authority for the alleged attempt by Richard, earl of Warwick, in 1466 to arrange marriages for his two daughters with the king's younger brothers (C. W. Oman, *Warwick the Kingmaker* (1891), 168–9; P. M. Kendall, *Warwick the Kingmaker* (1957), 191–2, 346). For Warwick's failure in 1467 to obtain a papal dispensation for a marriage between George, duke of Clarence, and Isabel Nevill, see 'William Worcester', 788.

18 J. R. Lander, 'Marriage and politics in the fifteenth century: the Nevills and the Wydevilles', *B.I.H.R.*, xxvi (1963), 119–52 (especially 147); K. B. McFarlane, 'The Wars of the Roses' (the Raleigh Lecture on History), *Proc. Brit. Acad.*, L (1965), 97–8; *The Glamorgan County History*, III (1971), 198–9.

19 J. H. Ramsay, *Lancaster and York*, II (1892), 337–9; Scofield, *op. cit.*, I, 491–5.

20 For the peers summoned to the Parliament of 1453, see J. C. Wedgwood, *History of Parliament; Register of the Ministers and of the Members of both Houses, 1439–1509* (1938), and *The Fane Fragment of the 1461 Lord's Journal*, ed. W. H. Dunham (1935), 88–91. John de la Pole (1442–91), duke of Suffolk, was a minor in 1453; Humphrey (d. 1460), duke of Buckingham's heir was styled earl of Stafford, but he was never summoned to Parliament and died c. 1458; Henry Beaufort (c. 1436–64), duke of Somerset, styled earl of Dorset in the lifetime of his father, Edmund (d. 1455), duke of Somerset, was still a minor when he succeeded to the dukedom in 1455. John (d. 1461), duke of Norfolk's heir, John (1444–76), had been created earl of Surrey in 1451, but he also was a minor.

21 McFarlane, 'The Wars of the Roses', 115–17. In reckoning the English higher nobility as composed of sixteen families in 1455, the Nevills have been counted as two families: the main line of the Nevills was represented by Ralph (d. 1484), second earl of Westmorland, and the younger branch of the Nevills by Richard (d. 1460), earl of Salisbury, and his heir, Richard (d. 1471), earl of Warwick.

22 William Worcester, *Itineraries*, ed. J. H. Harvey (1968), 345.

23 *The Fane Fragment*, 93–4; John Mowbray (1415–61), duke of Norfolk,

was the only duke summoned to the Parliament of 1461; he died on 6 November, two days after its opening (*ibid.*, 91).

24 After the death in 1315 of Guy, earl of Warwick, there were only seven English earls of full age (Arundel, Hereford, Lancaster, Oxford, Pembroke, Richmond and Warenne). Thomas (d. 1322), earl of Lancaster, held five earldoms; he had inherited the earldoms of Lancaster, Derby and Leicester and he acquired the earldoms of Lincoln and Salisbury by his marriage with Alice de Lacy.

25 *C.P.R.*, *1461–67*, 332, 340–1.

26 See appendix.

27 K. B. McFarlane, 'Had Edward I a "policy" towards the earls?' *History*, L (1965), 145–59 (especially 146–8).

28 *The Handbook of British Chronology*, ed. F. M. Powicke and E. B. Fryde (second edition, 1961).

29 *Ibid.*

30 *C.P.R.*, *1461–67*, 327; A. J. Kirby (Mrs Pratt), 'George Plantagenet, duke of Clarence (1449–1478)', B.A. dissertation, University of Southampton (1967), 106–24.

31 *C.P.R.*, *1461–67*, 225; these estates, mostly in the west of England, were granted on 1 August 1462 to William Nevill (d. 1463), earl of Kent, and his heirs male, but Nevill had no legitimate son, and his wife, the mad heiress Joan Fauconberg (*c.* 1405–?1491) was too old to have more children. Nevill died on 9 January 1463, and part of his lands was granted on 25 January to George, duke of Clarence (*C.P.R.*, *1461–67*, 227).

32 *C.P.R.*, *1461–67*, *passim*.

33 R. I. Jack, 'A quincentenary: the battle of Northampton, July 10th, 1460', *Northamptonshire Past and Present*, III (1960), 21–5.

34 Scofield, *op. cit.*, I, 398; *C.P.R.*, *1467–77*, 19; *C.C.R.*, *1435–41*, 91, 141–2.

35 R.P., V, 250–3; Owain Tudor (as 'Owen FitzMeredith') had obtained letters of denisation on 12 May 1432, after the birth of his sons, Edmund and Jasper (*ibid.*, IV, 415; *C.P.R.*, *1429–36*, 212), but these benefits did not extend to his heirs.

36 *The Glamorgan County History*, III, 261, 624, n. 261, 689.

37 B. M. Cotton Vesp. F. XIII, 1, f. 99r; H. T. Evans, *Wales and the Wars of the Roses* (1915), 97–8, 101, 107, 109; E. F. Jacob, *The Fifteenth Century, 1399–1485* (1961), 511, 516. On 5 February 1460 Herbert was granted possession of the Welsh offices previously given him by Richard, duke of York, and Richard, earl of Warwick, but this grant does not prove that he had now aligned himself with the Lancastrians (*C.P.R.*, *1452–61*, 549).

38 'William Worcester', 777; William Worcester, *Itineraries*, 203; Evans, *op. cit.*, 126, 139.

39 Evans, *op. cit.*, 134–82; D. H. Thomas, 'The Herberts of Raglan as supporters of the House of York in the second half of the fifteenth century', unpublished M.A. thesis, University of Wales, Cardiff (1968).

40 N.L.W., Badminton MSS, Nos. 1501, 1502, and 1503, accounts of William, Lord Herbert's receiver-general, 1465–68.

41 For their dispute over the custody of the lordship of Newport during the

minority of Henry, duke of Buckingham, see *The Glamorgan County History*, III, 198.

42 Sir Thomas Herbert (d. 1682) of Tintern, Co. Mon., *Prosapia Herbertorum* (Cardiff Free Library MS 5.7) ff. 52–4, 57; *C.P.R., 1461–67, 533.* According to Scofield, *op. cit.*, I, 397, n. 3, the marriage of William Herbert, Lord Dunster, with Mary Wydevill took place at Windsor Castle in January 1467.

43 Scofield, *op. cit.*, I, 497–504.

44 For Warwick's propaganda against his enemies in 1469, see Warkworth's *Chronicle*, ed. J. O. Halliwell (Camden Society, 1839), 46–51.

45 See appendix.

46 Powell and Wallis, *op. cit.*, 436. Philip Despenser, who was summoned in 1388 for the first time, was a great-grandson of Hugh (d. 1326), earl of Winchester; he is regarded as representing a new family, because his father and grandfather, who had previously held his estates, had not been summoned to Parliament.

47 Sir Thomas West (d. 1405), who was summoned to Parliament from 19 June 1402 to 25 August 1404, apparently acted as deputy for his brother-in-law, Thomas (d. 1427), Lord de la Warr. He was a priest and in 1402 obtained royal licence to absent himself for three years from Parliaments and Great Councils (*ibid.*, 436; *G.E.C.*, II, 150–1; *ibid.*, XII, part ii, 520).

48 Wedgwood, *History of Parliament: Register, passim.*

49 *E.H.R.*, XLIX (1934), 614–18.

50 Francis Cornewall, last baron of Burford, Co. Salop, died in 1727: Lord Liverpool and Compton Reade, *The House of Cornewall* (1908), 243–4. The male line of the barons of Hilton, who were barons of the county palatine of Durham, survived until 1746; William (d. 1435), baron of Hilton, was summoned to Parliament in 1399 (G. Lapsley, *The County Palatine of Durham* (1900), 64–66; *G.E.C.*, VII, 19–35).

51 Powell and Wallis, *op. cit., passim.*

52 Robert Erdeswyke of Stafford, 'gentilman', so described himself *c.* 1414, and he is the first Englishman known to have adopted that usage; a statute of 1413 had laid down that in certain kinds of legal action 'the estate, degree or mystery' of the defendant must be stated, as well as his place of abode (Sir George Sitwell, Bt., 'The English gentleman', *The Ancestor*, I (1902), 58–103, especially at 73–6).

53 K. B. McFarlane, 'The English nobility in the later Middle Ages', *XIIe Congrès international des sciences historiques* (1965), *Rapports*, I, 'Grands thèmes', 337–45.

54 *Ibid.*, 341.

55 Thrupp, *op. cit.*, 269–78.

56 E. W. Ives, 'Promotion in the legal profession of Yorkist and early Tudor England', *Law Quarterly Review*, 75 (1959), 348–63.

57 H. L. Gray, 'Incomes from land in England in 1436', *E.H.R.*, XLIX (1934), 607–39; J. R. Lander, *Conflict and Stability in Fifteenth-century England* (1969), 173; K. Fowler, *The Age of Plantagenet and Valois* (1967), 38.

58 A. R. Wagner, *Heralds and Heraldry in the Middle Ages* (1956), 79–80.

59 *E.H.R.*, XLIX (1934), 633.

60 G. N. Clark, *The Wealth of England from 1496 to 1760* (1946), 13;
L. Stone, 'Social mobility in England, 1500–1700', *Past and Present*, 33 (1966),
24.

61 *E.H.R.*, XLIX (1934), 623.

62 T. B. Pugh and C. D. Ross, 'The English baronage and the income tax
of 1436', *B.I.H.R.*, XXVI (1953), 1–28.

63 For the taxable incomes of these fourteen peers (Humphrey, duke of
Gloucester, the earls of Huntingdon and Suffolk, and Lords Beaumont, de la
Warr, Ferrers of Chartley, Grey of Codnor, Harington, Scales, Scope of
Masham, Talbot, Tiptoft, Welles and Willoughby), see *E.H.R.*, XLIX (1934),
614–18. For the life annuities granted by these peers before 1436, and the
names of their annuitants, see *P.R.O.*, E.163/7/31, which consists of two files
of documents; included with them is a separate (and damaged) sheet of paper,
which records that Lord Tiptoft had granted life annuities worth £50 a year,
but the names of his annuitants have not been preserved in these files. The
taxable income of John Beaufort (1404–44), earl (and later duke) of Somerset
(£1,000), and the one life annuity which he had granted (£20), have not been
included in these calculations. As Somerset had been a prisoner in France since
his capture in 1421 (when he was still a minor), he had not had much opportunity to retain or grant fees. For annuities payable by the Crown *c.* 1433, see
P.R.O., E.101/514/6; the total sum of annuities charged on the Exchequer
(£7,823) included payments due to Queen Katherine (£2,125), Queen Joan
(500 marks), the king's cousin, the duke of Bavaria (1,000 marks) and other
members of the royal family. Annuities charged on the fee farms of the
counties totalled £2,978; some of these were grants during royal pleasure,
which would not have been taxable in 1436. J. L. Kirby, in *B.I.H.R.*, XXIV
(1951), 146, states that annuities charged on the Exchequer between 1422 and
1434 averaged more than £8,000 a year; in practice these payments cost the
Crown sums varying from £5,500 to £13,500 per annum.

64 Sir William Oldhall's tax return in 1436 (P.R.O., E. 163/7/31, part 2,
document 2) does not mention the annuity of £80 which Lord Willoughby
had granted him, in return for a loan, in 1431 (*The Paston Letters*, II, 33).
Oldhall was paying an annuity of £10 a year to his father's widow, Alice,
and another annuity of £5 a year to Robert Norwich. For Oldhall's career,
see the articles by C. E. Johnston, *E.H.R.*, XXV (1910), 715–22, and J. S. Roskell,
Nottingham Medieval Studies, V (1961), 87–112.

65 P.R.O., E.163/7/31, part 1, document 42, states that Sir John Popham's
taxable income in 1436 was £122, including £80 a year from his two annuities,
but according to P.R.O., E.179/240/269, m. 14(*d*), his lands in the counties of
Southampton, Oxford, Leicester and Huntingdon were valued at £40 a year
and his annuities totalled £82. For his career, see J. S. Roskell, 'Sir John
Popham, knight banneret, of Charford: Speaker-elect in the Parliament of
1449–50', *Hampshire Field Club Proceedings*, XXI (1958), 38–52.

66 P.R.O., E.163/7/31, part 1, document 42.

67 *Ibid.*, document 44. For his career, see J. S. Roskell, *The Commons in the
Parliament of 1422* (1954), 149–50.

68 P.R.O., E.163/7/31, part 1, document 44. By a scribal error, William
Pope's total taxable income was reckoned to be only £4, which may explain

why his name is not to be found in the tax returns for Middlesex printed in
E.H.R., XLIX (1934), 638.

69 *Ibid.,* 611 n. 1, 631–9.

70 P.R.O., E.163/7/31.

71 P.R.O., E.163/7/31, part 1, document 5.

72 *E.H.R.,* XLIX (1934), 636.

73 P.R.O., E.163/7/31, part 2, document 26.

74 *E.H.R.,* XLIX (1934), 619, 621.

75 *Ibid.,* 621; K. B. McFarlane, 'Parliament and "bastard feudalism"',
T.R.H.S., fourth series, XXVI (1944), 53–73, especially at 66–7; for a biography
of Sir Humphrey Stafford (d. 1442) of Hooke, Co. Dorset, see Roskell, *The
Commons in the Parliament of 1422,* 216–18.

76 *E.H.R.,* XLIX (1934), 616, 621.

77 *B.I.H.R.,* XXVI (1953), 23, 27; P.R.O., E.179/240/269, m. 9(d).

78 *T.R.H.S.,* XXVI (1944), 66; *Ec.H.R.,* second series, XVII (1965), 504.

79 P.R.O., E.163/7/31; the list of Lord de la Warr's annuitants is part 1,
document 28; for the returns made by John, Lord Scrope, of Masham and by
the earl and countess of Huntingdon, see part 2, documents 18 and 24.

80 *E.H.R.,* XLIX (1934), 610.

81 P.R.O., E.163/7/31, part 2, document 21.

82 Besides her own inheritance as heir to her father, Thomas Chaucer
(d. 1434), esquire, of Ewelme, Co. Oxon., the countess of Suffolk had the
dower interests acquired by her two previous marriages; her second husband
had been Thomas Montague (d. 1428), earl of Salisbury.

83 P.R.O., E.163/7/31, part 1, document 7; Elizabeth Mowbray, widow of
Michael de la Pole (d. 1415), earl of Suffolk, was a daughter of Thomas (d. 1399),
duke of Norfolk.

84. P.R.O., E.163/7/31, part 1, document 9. This annuity of £100, which
had been granted to John, Lord Talbot, in 1424, by Edmund (d. 1425) earl of
March (P.R.O., c.139, file 19, m. 36; I am indebted to Dr G. A. Holmes
for this information) was subsequently doubled by Richard (d. 1460), duke of
York (P.R.O., s.c.11/818, mm. 5, 7, 10, 12). Richard Legett, who was described as Lord Talbot's attorney-general in 1436, was appointed to be his
receiver-general in 1422; for his employment in Lord Talbot's service, see
A. J. Pollard, 'The family of Talbot, Lords Talbot and earls of Shrewsbury
in the fifteenth century', unpublished Ph.D. thesis, University of Bristol
(1968), 293.

85 P.R.O., E.163/7/31, part 2, document 22.

86 *The Household of Edward IV: the Black Book and Ordinance of 1478,*
ed. A. R. Myers (1958), 98. The fees and wages paid by Humphrey, duke of
Buckingham, are enrolled on the dorse of valors of his lands for 1441–42 and
1447–48 (Lord Stafford's MSS, deposited in Staffordshire County Record Office,
and Longleat MS 6411).

87 John Gage, 'Extracts from the household books of Edward, duke of
Buckingham (in 1507–08)'. *Archaeologia,* XXV (1834), 311–41; *infra,* 105–6.

88 J. M. W. Bean, *The Estates of the Percy Family, 1416–1537* (1958),
82–3, 93–4.

89 R. L. Storey, *The End of the House of Lancaster* (1966), 109.

90 *B.I.H.R.*, xxvi (1953), 12, 15.

91 P.R.O., e.163/7/31, part 1, document 14; *C.P.R., 1429–36*, 286, 515.

92 R. I. Jack, 'The Lords Gray of Ruthin, 1325–1490', unpublished Ph.D. thesis, University of London (1961), 156–7; H. L. Gray, in *E.H.R.*, xlix (1934), 616, 619, confused Sir John Grey (d. 1439) of Ruthin with the Lincolnshire knight Sir John Gray, whose estates were taxed as worth £87 a year in 1436 (P.R.O., e.179/240/269, m. 9(d); Roskell, *The Commons in the Parliament of 1422*, 81).

93 *E.H.R.*, xlix (1934), 635; Roskell, *The Commons in the Parliament of 1422*, 213–14.

94 *B.I.H.R.*, xxvi (1953), 27; P.R.O., e.163/7/31, part 1, document 29(d).

95 *E.H.R.*, xlix (1934), 638; Thomas Haseley, esquire, whose income in Co. Middlesex and other counties was rated at £100 a year in 1436, may have been the man of that name who had a life annuity of 40s from Humphrey, duke of Gloucester.

96 Roskell, *The Commons in the Parliament of 1422*, 215–16; in 1436 Sir John Skelton's income from his lands in Co. Cumberland and annuities in the counties of Dorset and Somerset was declared to be £118 6s 8d a year (*P.R.O.*, e.179/90/26).

97 See note 68 above.

98 *C.P.R., 1429–36*, 181; A Gooder, *The Parliamentary Representation of the County of York, 1258–1832*, 1, (Yorkshire Archaeological Society Record Series, vol. 91, 1935) 172–4; Ivo de Etton was the second son, and heir male, of his father, John de Etton (d. 1433).

99 Robert Sandford, esquire, was one of Humphrey, duke of Gloucester's feoffees in 1439 (*C.P.R., 1429–36*, 388; *ibid., 1436–41*, 319, 386, 576); his income in 1436 (including his annuity from Duke Humphrey) was taxed at £24 a year (P.R.O., e.163/7/31, part 1, document 41). For George Lampet of Thorndon, Co. Suffolk, see P.R.O. e.179/240/269, m. 11; Nicholas Wolfe is mentioned in 1438 as a feoffee of lands in Yorkshire (*C.C.R., 1435–41*, 175).

100 Roskell, *The Commons in the Parliament of 1422*, 71–2.

101 K. H. Vickers, *Humphrey, Duke of Gloucester* (1907), 303–5; *English Chronicle (1377–1461)*, ed. J. S. Davies (Camden Society, 1856).

102 John Mowbray (d. 1461), duke of Norfolk, would probably have rivalled the greatest English magnates in the extent of his possessions if the greater part of the Mowbray estates had not been held by his mother, the dowager duchess Katherine Nevill (d. 1483), who outlived all her Mowbray descendants. *C.C.R., 1429–35*, 204–5, 208–14; Dugdale, *Baronage*, 1, 130–1; she died shortly before 28 December 1483 (B.M., Harleian mss 433, f. 137b).

103 Longleat ms 6411; National Library of Wales, Peniarth ms 280 (*The Redd Booke of Caures Castell*) contains many extracts from a register of deeds of Duke Humphrey, as well as transcripts of some documents, including indentures of retainer.

104 N.L.W., Peniarth ms 280, ff. 6–7. Sir Edward Grey (d. 1457), who had meanwhile become Lord Ferrers of Groby, does not appear in the list of the duke of Buckingham's retainers in 1448 (Longleat ms 6411), but he had been in receipt of his fee of £40 a year in 1442 (Lord Stafford's ms, valor of Humphrey, duke of Buckingham's lands in 1441–2, Staffordshire County Record Office).

105 Wedgwood, *History of Parliament: Biographies*. The names and fees of Humphrey (d. 1460), duke of Buckingham's retainers are enrolled on the dorse of the valors of the duke's lands.

106 John Bourchier, esquire, was still receiving his annual fee of 40 marks from the duke of Buckingham as late as 1457. His elder brother, Henry, Lord Bourchier (d. 1483), later earl of Essex, was the duke of York's brother-in-law and had become a member of his council by 1450 (K. B. McFarlane, 'The Wars of the Roses', 104 n. 2).

107 *The Paston Letters*, II, 297.

108 T. B. Pugh, *The Marcher Lordships of South Wales, 1415–1536: Select Documents* (1963), 177–9; *C.P.R., 1446–52*, 323, 377.

109 Miss S. E. Hernon, 'The great household of the first duke of Buckingham, 1454–55', unpublished M. A. dissertation, University of Southampton (1970) estimates that the duke's household at Writtle, Co. Essex, cost over £2,000 in 1454–55. The total of the duke's household expenditure in that year cannot be calculated because the accounts of his receiver-general and the receiver of the lordship of Holderness, Co. Yorks., have not survived. The declarations of account of six of the duke's local receivers for 1454–55 show that they met part of the cost of the duke's household and that of his heir, Humphrey (d. *c.* 1458), earl of Stafford (Lord Stafford's MSS, Staffordshire County Record Office).

110 Humphrey, duke of Buckingham's daughter, Joan, married on 6 August 1452 William, Lord Bardolf, son and heir of John (d. 1460), Lord Beaumont. Her dowry was 2,300 marks and £443 was still unpaid in 1459. (N.L.W., MS 14803E, *The Stafford Great Chartulary*, f. 395(*d*)). Buckingham's widow, as executor of the late duke, was left with the task of paying his debts (P.R.O., s.c.6.1117/11, account of the receiver-general of Anne, duchess of Buckingham, 1463–64). These liabilities included the dowry of another of the duke's daughters, Katherine, who married John Talbot (1448–73), earl of Shrewsbury (see accounts of John Harcourt, esquire, receiver of Stafford, 1468–70: Lord Stafford's MSS, Staffordshire County Record Office).

111 *D.N.B.*, s.v.; C. A. J. Armstrong, 'Politics and the battle of St Albans, 1455', *B.I.H.R.*, XXXIII (1960), 1–72; *The Paston Letters*, III, 127.

112 *C.P.R., 1452–61*, 535, 548, 552, 571; the manor of Collyweston, Co. Northants., which Richard Nevill, earl of Warwick, had acquired from Ralph (d. 1456), Lord Cromwell's executors, was granted to his aunt, Anne, duchess of Buckingham. According to William Worcester, 7,000 marks had been spent on the building of Sir William Oldhall's manor house at Hunsdon, Co. Herts. (*Itineraries*, ed. J. H. Harvey (1969), 51).

113 *English Chronicle*, 96–7; W. Stubbs, *Constitutional History of England* fifth edition, 1903), III, 233.

114 K. B. McFarlane, 'Bastard feudalism', *B.I.H.R.*, XX (1947), 161–80, especially 164–6; Mr McFarlane estimated that about two-thirds of the indentures of retainer which had been published for the period 1327–1485 (fewer than 200 documents in all) are contracts made by John of Gaunt.

115 G. A. Holmes, *The Estates of the Higher Nobility in Fourteenth Century England* (1957), 5; R. Somerville, *History of the Duchy of Lancaster, 1265–1603* (1953), 90–3, 130. During Henry IV's reign the duchy of Lancaster lands were worth about £15,000 a year; this total includes the king's share of the

de Bohun heritage belonging to his first wife, Mary (d. 1394): see R. R. Davies, 'Baronial accounts, incomes and arrears in the later Middle Ages', *Ec.H.R.,* second series, xxi (1968), 229. A pension of 10,000 marks a year was paid to John of Gaunt after 1387 by the king of Castile; see P. E. Russell, *The English Intervention in Spain and Portugal in the Time of Edward III and Richard II* (1955), 506; and, for other sources of income in the duke's later years, see Somerville, *op. cit.,* 91 n. 1.

116 K. B. McFarlane, *E.H.R.,* lxx (1955), 110–11; *John of Gaunt's Register, 1379–1383,* ed. E. C. Lodge and R. Somerville (Camden Society, third series, lvi, 1937), especially xli, 6–13. Somerville, *op. cit.,* 131.

117 S. Armitage Smith, *John of Gaunt* (1904); Russell, *op. cit.*; Somerville, *op. cit.,* 62–4; A. B. Steel, *Richard II* (1941), 85.

118 Somerville, *op. cit.,* 162, 166, 187–8; P.R.O., DL.29/732/12028. In 1421 annuities payable at the Exchequer and those charged on the customs duties amounted to more than £12,000 a year (*P.O.P.C.,* ii, 314).

119 J. L. Kirby, *Henry IV* (1970), 128. *P.O.P.C.,* i, 154.

120 *E.H.R.,* lxx (1955), 108.

121 P.R.O., s.c.11/818.

122 Wedgwood, *History of Parliament: Biographies,* and note 64 above; Roskell, *The Commons in the Parliament of 1422,* 159–60. F. M. Wright, 'The House of York, 1415–50', unpublished Ph.D. thesis, Johns Hopkins University, Baltimore, Md. (1959), discusses the composition of Richard, duke of York's retinue (and confuses Reynold Grey, esquire, who deserted York at the rout of Ludford in October 1459, with Reginald (d. 1493), Lord Grey of Wilton). J. T. Rosenthal, 'The estates and finances of Richard, duke of York (1411–60)', *Studies in Medieval and Renaissance History* (1965), includes lists of Duke Richard's officials and annuitants. Among the Yorkists attainted in 1459 was John (d. 1464), Lord Clinton, the poorest of the English barons whose incomes were assessed for taxation in 1436; his taxable income was £60 (*R.P.,* v, 34–50; *E.H.R.,* xlix (1934), 618).

123 *C.P.R., 1452–61,* 548.

124 *The Historie of the Arrivall of King Edward IV,* ed. J. Bruce (Camden Society, 1838), henceforth cited as *The Arrivall*), 1–7; Somerville, *op. cit.,* 256 n. 2, confuses Nicholas Leventhorpe with Nicholas Sharpe, a former receiver-general of the duchy of Lancaster: see P.R.O. D.L.37/47/A2. *The Arrivall,* 6–7, attributes Edward's unpopularity in Yorkshire to memories of the slaughter of Yorkshiremen who had fought for Henry VI at Towton in 1461. Local hostility towards Warwick's brother, the Marquis Montague (who had held the earl-dom of Northumberland from 1464 until 1470) may have helped Edward IV in his progress through Yorkshire in March 1471, but *The Arrivall* concedes that a new rising, in order to restore Henry VI to the throne again, was imminent early in May (*ibid.,* 6, 31–32).

125 *C.Ch.R., 1341–1417,* 63; *C.P.R., 1350–54,* 258.

126 *The Arrivall,* 7–9; Wedgwood, *History of Parliament: Biographies.* Despite its Yorkist bias, *The Arrivall* (which was written in 1471 as the official history of Edward IV's restoration) seems more reliable than Warkworth's *Chronicle*; the author of Warkworth's *Chronicle* was strongly Lancastrian in his sympathies and his version of these events in 1471 dates from 1478 or later.

127 *The Arrivall*, 11; Warkworth's *Chronicle*, 15, states that George, duke of Clarence's force was 7,000 strong and made up half the army of 14,000 which Edward IV is said to have commanded in the battle of Barnet on 14 April 1471.

128 *The Arrivall*; Warkworth's *Chronicle*, 17–20. On 14 February 1471 Jasper Tudor, earl of Pembroke, had been appointed constable of Gloucester Castle for life (*C.P.R., 1467–77*, 236), replacing Richard Beauchamp, but this grant had not taken effect. If Warwick's government had been fully in control of the kingdom during the readeption of Henry VI, Gloucester would have been safely in the hands of Jasper Tudor in May 1471 and Queen Margaret and her son, Edward, Prince of Wales, might have been able to make good their escape across the Severn. Richard Beauchamp (d. 1503), succeeded in 1475 to the barony held by his father, John (1415–75), Lord Beauchamp of Powicke; as a reward for his services, he was granted for life the office of constable of Gloucester Castle, with an annuity of 40 marks (*C.P.R., 1467–77*, 315).

129 *C.P.R., 1471–85, passim*; William (d. 1487), earl of Arundel, was granted, for life, the office of constable of Dover Castle and warden of the Cinque ports on 1 March 1472, with £300 a year as his fee, and Lord Audley was granted a life annuity of £100 in 1474 (*C.P.R., 1467–77*, 310, 440).

130 *R.P.*, vi, 205–7, 215–18; *The Glamorgan County History*, iii, 261. Richard III's grant of the Lancaster moiety of the de Bohun estates to Henry (d. 1483), duke of Buckingham, is printed in Dugdale, Baronage, i, 168–9; for Richard, duke of Gloucester's letter of 11 June, 1483 to Ralph, Lord Nevill, see *The Paston Letters*, vi, 71–2.

131 'Historiae Croylandensis Continuatio', printed in *Rerum Anglicarum Scriptorum Veterum*, ed. W. Fulman, i (1684), 565–6; *The Usurpation of Richard III*, ed. C. A. J. Armstrong (1969) (henceforth cited as *Mancini*), 68–75, 115.

132 *Polydore Vergil's English History*, ed. Sir H. Ellis (Camden Society, 1844), 175–6, represents Lord Hastings as joining in a conspiracy at the beginning of May, immediately after Richard, duke of Gloucester, had taken charge of Edward V.

133 Roskell, *The Commons in the Parliament of 1422*, 98–100, 103–7.

134 It is improbable that John de la Pole (d. 1487), earl of Lincoln, was named as heir to the throne in 1484 (see *D.N.B.*), but he presided over the Council of the North during the latter part of Richard III's reign.

135 Bean, *op. cit.*, 133; *H.M.C.* sixth report, part i, 223; W. H. Dunham, 'Lord Hastings' indentured retainers, 1461–1483', *Trans. Connecticut Academy of Arts and Sciences*, 39 (1955), 1–175, at 140; W. Denton, *England in the Fifteenth Century* (1888).

136 The marriage contract, dated 28 February 1484, between William Herbert (d. 1490), earl of Huntingdon, and Dame Katherine Plantagenet is printed in C. A. Halstead, *Richard III*, ii (1884), 569–70.

137 *Mancini*, 96–7.

138 S. Bentley, *Excerpta Historica* (1833), 379–84; the list of peers said to have been present at Bosworth in B.M., Harleian MS 542, f. 34, is unreliable; W. Hutton, *The Battle of Bosworth Field*, ed. J. G. Nichols (1813), 209; Lander, *op. cit.*, 99 n. 1.

139 B.M., Harleian mss 433; Ramsay, *op. cit.*, ii, 534.

140 *D.N.B. S.V.*

141 In 1485 there were three dukes (Bedford, Buckingham and Suffolk), one marquis (Dorset) and sixteen earls (Arundel, Derby, Devon, Essex, Huntingdon, Kent, Lincoln, Oxford, Northumberland, Nottingham, Rivers, Shrewsbury, Surrey, Warwick, Wiltshire, and Westmorland). Jasper (d. 1495), duke of Bedford, and William (d. 1492), Marquis Berkeley (formerly earl of Nottingham), died childless and the earldoms of Huntingdon, Rivers and Wiltshire lapsed through the failure of heirs. John de la Pole, earl of Lincoln, was killed in the battle of Stoke on 16 June 1487 (and subsequently attainted in the Parliament of 1487). His brother, Edmund de la Pole (d. 1513), duke of Suffolk, surrendered his title of duke in 1493 and was henceforth earl of Suffolk until his attainder in 1504. Edward Plantagenet, earl of Warwick, was executed on 28 November 1499. After the death of Thomas (d. 1501), marquis of Dorset, his heir, Thomas Grey (1477–1530) was summoned to Parliament only by his lesser title of Lord Ferrers of Groby and he was not recognised as marquis of Dorset until 1511. Although Edward Courtenay, earl of Devon, survived Henry VII by a few weeks, dying on 28 May 1509, his heir, William Courtenay, had been attainted in 1504, and the earldom of Devon was not revived until 1511. When Henry VIII was crowned on 24 June 1509 the higher nobility consisted of one duke (Buckingham) and nine earls (Arundel, Derby, Essex, Kent, Oxford, Northumberland, Shrewsbury, Surrey (attainted on 10 December 1485 but restored in 1489) and Westmorland).

142 P.R.O., s.c.6. Henry VIII/4990, account of the receiver of the lordship of Denbigh, 1509–10; these annuities, which cost £115 a year, could not be paid in 1510 because the revenues of the lordship were insufficient.

143 B.M., Cotton Vitellius, C.I. f. 6; eight knights and ten esquires, whose annual fees cost £101 13s 4d, had been retained in Prince Arthur's service.

144 In 1518–19 the revenues of the earldom of March were worth £1,341, but fees and annuities amounted to £847 (B.M., Royal B. xxxviii); similar charges on the lands of the principality in north Wales and the earldom of Chester totalled £1,031, c. 1520 (P.R.O., e.101/519/24).

145 J. S. Brewer, *The Reign of Henry VIII*, i (1884), 69–71. For the Welsh offices held by Charles Somerset (d. 1526), earl of Worcester, and Henry Somerset (d. 1549), earl of Worcester, see W. R. B. Robinson, 'Early Tudor policy towards Wales', *Bull. Board of Celtic Studies*, xx (1964), 421–38; *ibid.*, xxi (1964), 43–74.

146 Dunham, *op. cit.*, 90–109. For a letter from Henry VII in 1505 to Henry Farington, steward of Penwortham and other lordships, Co. Lancs., forbidding the retaining of any of the tenants by anyone except the king himself, see *H.M.C.*, sixth report, 444; a similar letter was sent by Henry VIII in 1539 (*ibid.*).

R. L. Storey

Reader in History
University of Nottingham

6 The north of England

There is little need today to have to argue that the history of the
north of England is a worthy subject for our attention. For the last
six years the University of Leeds has amply demonstrated the
historical identity of the region, and put us all in its debt, by the
publication of its journal *Northern History*. One might say, of
course, that this journal only carries to a further level of communi-
cation the work of northerners in making their history known. I
need only refer to the fact that the oldest series of English local record
publications is that of the Surtees Society, founded in 1834 to
publish 'the unedited Manuscripts illustrative of the intellectual,
the moral, the religious and the social condition of . . . a region
which constituted the Ancient Kingdom of Northumberland'.[1] I
must confess, however, that, although a Northumbrian myself, I
would maintain that what makes the history of the region so important is not so much what is peculiar about it in isolation, what
makes the region different from the rest of England, but rather
the influence it exercised in the affairs of the kingdom as a whole.
For the historian of the fifteenth century this again is hardly a
point of view requiring much demonstration. The Lancastrian
dynasty was both established and destroyed by private armies drawn
largely from this area, and both Yorkist kings and Henry VII were
much concerned about its capacity to generate militant disorder.
  Of course, it was the character of the region which made it so
dangerous to the Crown. The influence of the north was disproportionate to its wealth and population. The six northern counties
occupy a quarter of the total area of England, but their adult population was only 15 per cent of the total recorded in the poll tax of
1377. The particulars for Yorkshire distinguish it from the five
other counties. Its size is not quite equal to the total area of the

others, but it accounted for two-thirds of the northern population. In other words, one tenth of the English population in 1377 were Yorkshiremen. Population density in Yorkshire was more like that in the Midland belt than it was in Lancashire and the other four, where obviously the distribution was thinner.[2] All the same, one can say that Yorkshire was part of the northern military complex. There was a line of castles running westward from the northern edge of the vale of Pickering into Wensleydale. Henderskelfe, Sheriff Hutton, Helmsley, Crayke, Middleham and Bolton were all built or extended in the later Middle Ages and show that their magnate owners were not inclined to follow their more southerly contemporaries in daring to sacrifice strength to comfort. Indeed, only twenty miles south of this line of fortresses the Percies built a far less defensible great hall at Spofforth. Two royal castles were at the ends of this line, namely Scarborough and Richmond. Architectural evidence thus indicates that this was the southern limit of a militarised zone prepared for defence in depth against Scottish invasion. In fact, Scottish incursions in the fifteenth century penetrated only Northumberland and Cumberland. When there was a threat of invasion, however, the men of Yorkshire—and of Nottingham and Derby—as well as their more northerly neighbours would be mustered by commissions of array, and so might the clergy of the province of York. Archbishop Bowet's appearance at the head of his martial priests is said to have scattered the Scots besieging Berwick in 1417.[3]

There were also important personal links between Yorkshire and the border country. For most of the century the two wardens of the Marches were the heads of the families of Neville and Percy. The biggest bloc of Neville territory was to the north and east of York city, and another was in Wensleydale. The Percies had large groups of manors around Beverley, in lower Wharfedale and the vale of York. Both families had lands in Cumberland, the Percies were well established in Northumberland also, and the Nevilles were the largest secular tenants in County Durham. Apart from the lords themselves, their followers from Yorkshire were employed in the Scottish Marches. One finds in the pardon rolls men whose aliases indicate that they were as well known in Cumberland as in Yorkshire, such as the John Story who was known as of both Cockermouth and Hunmanby. When there were no more Nevilles in Yorkshire their castle of Sheriff Hutton was the principal residence of their successors in the Marches, Richard of Gloucester and Thomas Howard, earl of Surrey. The Lords Clifford and Greystoke likewise preferred to have their main seats in Yorkshire rather than in Westmorland and Cumberland respectively.[4]

It would be no exaggeration to claim that the Anglo-Scottish frontier was the major factor in determining the political and social character of the north. This was not just because the feuding and raiding over the frontier were constant hazards to life and property in the most northern shires. It was also because the Crown preferred to entrust responsibility for guarding the border to those whom Parliament in 1388 described as 'les seignurs marchers del north'.[5] This use of the term 'marcher lords' in the northern context is interesting, but of course the only genuine marches in late medieval England were those bordering Scotland. Since the king gave considerable authority to these northern lords, he put them in command of military resources which they could use for their own ends; and these resources were the manpower of a population which had long experience of warfare and, because of its kind of existence, was not inclined to accept the overriding claims of the king to its loyalty. This was given to the lords who led them in war against the Scots and encouraged private forays into Scotland. As Dr Tuck has shown, border lords favoured such activities and were not sympathetic to royal efforts to improve relations with Scotland.[6] Moreover, such lords were more potent as protectors against private enemies in England. The king's justice was remote and ineffectual in the three most northern counties; there society had been conditioned by a century of border skirmishing to behave in a like manner at home. More than once in the few judicial records from this area the operations of Englishmen against their neighbours are likened to those of the Scots, or to the 'manner of war against the Scots'.[7] A gang of Westmorland men hunting a private enemy in Kendal in 1388 was said to have behaved 'modo guerre et modo Scottorum'. The reaction of the townsfolk is worth noting. Such was the commotion that the people of Kendal fled over the river into the woods and hills.[8] The town is fifty miles from the border but they obviously knew the drill for a Scottish raid. On the other hand, if I may digress, many individual Scots appear to have been accepted as settlers in the border counties. Bishop Langley's register records a few Scots being ordained in Durham and the less canonical international relations of a local knight with a Scottish mistress.[9] In 1449 the king permitted Bishop Neville to allow Scots

resident in the bishopric to remain, despite the war.[10] These resident
Scots were neither subject to the law nor protected by it. A Scot was
convicted of homicide at Newcastle, but the jury said that although
the crime occurred in England the victim also was a Scot. The
justices were unable to proceed further. They were again at a loss in
the case of a Scot said to have stolen a thousand sheep and whose
occupation was described as 'thefe'. In 1390 Alice Emson, of Holme
Coultram, was convicted for lighting a 'beken' to warn Scots in
Galloway that an expedition had sailed to raid them. She said that
she had been born in Galloway; she had lived in England for forty
years, married an Englishman and had children, but she had never
sworn allegiance to the king of England nor to his warden of the
March. The justices therefore dismissed her *sine die*.[11] English thieves
co-operated with Scots in robbery and in abducting fellow countrymen
to Scotland and holding them to ransom.[12]

For the society of the English border counties, the local lord commanded more respect than the distant king. The Tudor observation
that the people of the north knew no king but a Neville, a Percy or
a Dacre, echoes John Harding, who a century earlier had written
of the Percies that 'they have the hertes of the people by north and
ever had'.[13] It was a formidable consideration for the king that the
Percies, in particular, had command of such hardened followers, and
it may well be that the political belligerence of these northern lords
was encouraged by the quality and devotion of their followers.
Mr McFarlane warned us against under-estimating the influence
retainers might have upon their lords.[14] We need not presume that
their influence was necessarily conducive to the well-being of the
kingdom. In a society so disorderly, so physically remote from the
king and the central courts at Westminster, bastard feudalism
provided the squirearchy with its only hope of some kind of security.
It did not give immunity from violence, because both Neville and
Percy tried to recruit retainers in the same districts; the feuds of
the gentry continued and their scale increased with the support given
to rivals by other members of their respective lords' retinues, so that
it could be said of Cumberland in 1453 'that toon half of the shire
was divided from tother'.[15] At this date bastard feudalism was
probably more rampant in the north than at any time, as it was in
England generally. Bastard feudalism may have provided a limited
degree of social stability, in that 'good lords' did attempt to keep
the peace among their own followers,[16] but as the lords themselves

competed for regional dominance the scale of disorder was tending to increase until its eruption into the Wars of the Roses. Since the incompetent Henry VI had come of age in 1436,[17] his government had been corrupt, ineffective and powerless, unable to restrain over-mighty subjects and, if anything, more prone to exacerbate them by that flagrant partisanship in their quarrels which was largely responsible for polarising the 'ins' and 'outs' under the banners of Lancaster and York.[18] Serious disturbances in Yorkshire, Derby-shire, East Anglia and Devon, to name only the most notorious examples, reveal that Cumberland was not unique in demonstrating that bastard feudalism was inherently incompatible with the rule of law.

Despite the risks, the Crown had no real choice but to entrust the defence of the border to the marcher lords. It could not afford to maintain a military establishment under its own direct control. The likelihood of a large-scale invasion rarely arose, and when it did it tended to waste itself on sieges of Berwick, Norham, Rox-burgh and Carlisle. What was needed were means to repel sizeable raids mounted by Scottish border lords, such as Chevy Chase, and to police the frontier to prevent forays by Scots—and also by English-men into Scotland, lest these might compromise the precarious state of truce. For these more limited purposes it would be sufficient to array local levies, and consequently the Crown had to engage lords who had personal authority over these occasional forces. Moreover, the lords themselves were not willing to have their tenants at the disposal of any commander but themselves, nor that these tenants should be subject to the jurisdiction of warden courts held by others. Henry V and Edward IV both reversed Percy attainders and restored earls of Northumberland so that they could become wardens of the Marches at times when it was particularly necessary for these kings that the wardens should be lords 'who had the hearts of the people by north'. Henry VII likewise released the fourth earl from the Tower and restored him to his wardenship and life tenure of the shrievalty of Northumberland. The king's choice was very limited. There were no other magnates in the border counties but Percies and Nevilles. The other north-country peers—Cliffords, Dacres, FitzHughs, Scropes and the like—were in an inferior class, with revenues approximately a third of those of the comital houses, and they tended to attach themselves to one or other of these more powerful figures.[19]

The only safeguard which the Crown regularly took was to divide the border command between Percy and Neville. This policy was followed from the time of Richard II, when the office of warden achieved the form it kept for the following century. John of Gaunt, as the king's lieutenant in the Marches, tried to ease the earl of Northumberland from his border command and advance his own retainer, John Neville of Raby. Simultaneously, the office of warden came to be granted for a term of years to a single warden who contracted for an annual payment to engage as many troops as he deemed necessary; this meant, in fact, that he raised his own army at the king's expense. This system of indentured wardens lasted from 1388 to 1489. In this period there were Percy wardens of the East March for a total of eighty-one years, and the Nevilles held the West March for a total of fifty-nine years. We might note also that it was in Richard's reign that both families achieved their comital rank. The first Percy earl of Northumberland was created in 1377 and he established his family as the biggest tenant-in-chief in the West March with his marriage in 1381 to the heiress to the honour of Cockermouth and lordship of Egremont. Ralph Neville became earl of Westmorland in 1397, possibly on the recommendation of his new father-in-law, John of Gaunt. Neville also secured a foothold in the West March with a grant of Crown lands. Although this was a modest lordship compared with Cockermouth, it provided the site where Richard Neville built Penrith Castle in the 1420s.[20] If one may be allowed to dramatise, one could say that Richard II had set the scene for the north-country politics of the fifteenth century; he had formed the cast which was both to destroy and avenge him.

Enough has been written about the relations of the Percies and Nevilles with the kings of the fifteenth century to make their outline familiar. I propose to look at only one incident in this connection which has already been examined by Professor Bean in his article 'Henry IV and the Percies'. Dr Bean considered the various reasons usually produced for explaining why the earl of Northumberland and Hotspur rebelled, but in the end he could not accept them as sufficiently compelling motives. Dr Bean based his conclusion on the opinions of contemporary chroniclers and decided that 'the Percies' rebellion of 1403 is best explained as a further effort at kingmaking'.[21] I agree with this verdict, but I believe that there are two other factors which require attention; these support Dr Bean's conclusion but they also exemplify the general subject of baronial

politics in the fifteenth century. Dr Bean confined himself to the
relations of Northumberland and Hotspur with Henry IV. The
relations of both king and Percies with the Nevilles are also relevant.
One might make a general proposition at this point: that it is a
mistake to discuss royal relations with the baronage as if the king
on the one side and the lords on the other were single units. One
must consider the links and rifts among the lords themselves, as
these helped to determine their attitudes to the king. It is for this
reason that I cannot accept Mr McFarlane's suggestion that the
Wars of the Roses were due to the lords deciding to rescue the
country 'from the consequences of Henry VI's inanity'.[22] If the
lords had been united, there would hardly have been a civil war.

In 1403, as at other times, north-country politics can be seen as
a king–Percy–Neville triangle. The Percies had been given a mono-
poly of border offices as the price for their support of Henry in 1399.
It appears, however, that Henry soon resumed his father's pro-
gramme of advancing Neville as a watchdog on Percy. He retained
the earl of Westmorland as well as the two Percies to guard the
Marches against a threat of invasion in 1399, and he also gave him
the wardship of the Dacre estates in Northumberland's West March.
In 1402 Westmorland became keeper of Roxburgh Castle, although
in 1399 Hotspur had been appointed to keep the castle for ten
years.[23]

This advance of Neville's responsibilities on the border must be
linked with developments in central government. A third Percy
was involved in the rebellion of 1403. This was Thomas, earl of
Worcester, Northumberland's brother. According to Walsingham,
Hotspur was favourably impressed by the terms offered by the
king's envoys before the battle of Shrewsbury. He then sent Worcester to Henry, but the earl was apparently set in hostility to the
king and came back to the rebel camp with a jaundiced report, and
Worcester was thus responsible for the failure of these negotiations.[24] Worcester did not have the same northern interests as his
brother and nephew.[25] His career had been as a soldier in France,
as a member of Richard II's court, and most recently as the foremost
noble in Henry IV's immediate entourage; the report of a French
embassy which came to England in October 1400 suggests that
Worcester was then acting as president of the Council in England
while the king was in Wales.[26] For a year from 1401 Worcester was
steward of Henry's Household. Then he was diverted to duties in

Wales. His departure from court must be associated with other
changes among the leading personnel of the government. From late
in 1401 Henry was beginning to replace the former servants of
Richard's whom he had retained by men whose background was
solidly Lancastrian. First, Thomas Langley was appointed keeper
of the privy seal. A few months later William Heron replaced
Worcester as steward, and Henry Bowet became treasurer of
England. Henry completed this infusion of Lancastrian blood with
the appointment of Henry Beaufort as chancellor in February 1403.
A week later Worcester lost his Welsh command to the Prince of
Wales.[27]

Worcester's hostility to Henry five months later was more likely
to have been the consequence of his own loss of influence than the
grievances, real or imaginary, of his brother and nephew. In my
view, Worcester's dismissal from Henry's court was a major reason
for the revolt of the Percies. It was a serious blow to the family in
more than one respect. With Worcester established in the Council,
Northumberland and Hotspur could feel assured that their interests
had full consideration. Their suits for royal favour, for grants of
office to themselves and their clients, for windfalls like marriages
and wardships, had reasonable prospects of success. Dr Harriss has
shown how vital influence in the Council was to secure good assign-
ments on the dwindling royal revenue, and Dr Bean makes it clear
that the Percies were perhaps the most favoured of Henry's
creditors.[28] The consequences of the latest government changes in
terms of regional politics were no less serious for the Percies. The
new chancellor was Westmorland's brother-in-law, and for the
next forty years Bishop Beaufort's Neville nephews greatly profited
from his access to the royal bounty.[29] Westmorland's appointment
as keeper of Roxburgh was made six weeks after the last date
Worcester is known to have been steward. Within ten days of
Beaufort's becoming chancellor, a petition from Westmorland
resulted in the appointment of a tribunal to determine his dispute
with the Percies over the partition of Scottish ransoms ensuing from
the battle of Humbledon, instead of the matter being left in the
hands of the two Percies and Westmorland themselves.[30] We can
well believe that the Percies had cause to suspect the more obviously
Lancastrian regime of 1403; they may have expected a further attri-
tion of their dominance in the north to Neville's advantage. Thomas
Percy's place in Henry's Council had been the family's guarantee

of regional supremacy. He illustrates for us the link between local politics and central government. The pursuit of regional conse- quence which engaged fifteenth-century magnates required influence in the king's Council. Access to royal favour was the best means to gain control of local office and to prove that a magnate's 'good lordship' was worth having. This, of course, was the central issue in the Wars of the Roses. Like the Nevilles fifty-eight years later, the Percies in 1403 responded to their loss of influence in the king's Council by putting forward a Mortimer candidate to the throne. One reason why the Nevilles succeeded where the Percies failed is that by 1461 the Nevilles had behind them the fruits of half a century's exploitation of royal benevolence. Attainder had briefly deprived them of land and office, but it had not destroyed the long record of 'good lordship' which was the basis of their strength in manpower.[31]

The Lancastrian policy of guarding the north by setting Neville against Percy thus ended in disaster to the Crown because the ambitions and rivalry of these families led them into rebellion. This experience gave warning to the last medieval kings. The warden- ship of the Marches in the form it had developed under Richard II gave its holder more power than a wary king could tolerate. Richard III began to remove the teeth from the wardenship. He was holding the West March at his accession but he did not appoint a new warden; instead he appointed a minor local peer, Lord Dacre, as lieutenant, with a modest salary.[32] Henry VII did the same for the East March when the fourth Percy earl of Northumberland fell to mob violence in 1489. This murder was an unexpected stroke of fortune for Henry, as the earl's heir was a boy of twelve and the king was now free to reorganise the defence of the border without having to consult Percy or Neville interests. The Prince of Wales was given nominal command, but the responsibility was carried by a lieutenant anxious to redeem his Howard family estates from attainder. Another measure for the security of the north was initiated by Richard III. His council in Yorkshire was the model for the Tudor council of the north. The judicial powers of these councils not only made legal redress more readily available to northern society, but by the same token promised to reduce its dependence on baronial protection. The most obvious remedy for northern belligerence was peace with Scotland, and the treaty made by Henry VII in 1502 brought hope of its establishment.[33]

Two of the northern shires were regalian franchises, excluded from the national pattern of judicial and administrative dependence on Westminster. We might consider, however, that a fifteenth-century king could feel assured of the political loyalty of Lancashire and Durham. He personally held the palatine county of Lancaster, while Crown control of episcopal appointments enabled him to nominate the ruler of the bishopric of Durham. The two palatinates might therefore have upheld royal authority in the north. In fact such support was not always forthcoming. By mid-century personal ties of loyalty to the house of Lancaster were no stronger in the duchy than were those of Crown tenants elsewhere in England. Certainly in Derbyshire duchy tenants became retainers of the dukes of York and Buckingham; a Blount died fighting for Henry IV at Shrewsbury, but his grandson followed York.[34] Important Lancashire families such as the Stanleys and Harringtons were also attached to York.[35] The king was a stranger to Lancashire; his authority was exercised by his officers and the most influential of them were the effective rulers of Lancashire society. From 1456 to 1459 the chief steward in the north parts of the duchy was Richard Neville, earl of Salisbury.[36] Of course there were duchy tenants who defended Henry VI, but the point is that the landed society of Lancashire was as much divided in political allegiance as that of any other county. The same may be said about the bishopric of Durham. Four of its tenants-in-chief are known to have died on the day of Towton,[37] probably in the company of John Neville of Raby, who was killed fighting for Lancaster. In contrast, two more of the bishop's tenants, Robert Ogle and Thomas Lumley, were called to the peerage by Edward IV. Ogle had already shown his hand at the first battle of St Albans, when he 'took 600 men of the marchis and tok the market place'.[38] At that time the bishop of Durham was Robert Neville, Salisbury's brother, but Ogle's political connections were clearly not altered when Robert Neville was succeeded by Laurence Booth in 1457.

Booth's pontificate has special interest because it reveals the impotence of the bishop's franchise to preserve its immunity from external and internal pressures. When Queen Margaret secured Booth's provision to Durham she presumably expected to attach the bishopric to the royalist cause. In Robert Neville's pontificate the chief offices and revenues of the bishopric had been put at his family's disposal.[39] Booth certainly stopped this. The pensions

Neville had granted to Salisbury and other brothers and nephews whom he had retained for life died with him. William Neville, Lord Fauconberg, was replaced as chief steward by Thomas Neville of Brancepeth, a member of the senior branch of the Neville family; the Nevilles of Raby had little love for their cousins of Sheriff Hutton. Both, however, had no choice but to retain Geoffrey Middleton as sheriff of Durham, for Bishop Robert had granted him the office for life. Neville had also given Henry Preston a life grant of the office of constable of Durham Castle; Preston had been his temporal chancellor as well, and Booth retained him as such.[40]

It had been fortunate for Margaret that Robert Neville died before the outbreak of civil war in 1459. In the time of the Great Schism, popes had readily assisted successive ruling factions by translating suspect bishops; John Fordham from Durham to Ely, for example. This device was not practised during the Wars of the Roses, possibly because popes were less prepared to co-operate. Edward IV had to come to terms with the fact that the county palatine of Durham was ruled by a Lancastrian partisan. Booth had been keeper of the privy seal until the battle of Northampton. His relations with Edward, however, show that the liberties of the bishopric were no obstacle to royal authority. Exactly one week after the battle of Towton the palatine chancery appointed a commission of oyer and terminer to investigate all insurrections, rebellions, felonies, trespasses and every other kind of misdemeanour.[41] Unlike similar commissions in the kingdom, its terms of reference did not include treason. Was this perhaps because it was technically not possible to make such a charge in the bishop's liberty except for treason against himself? A commission of oyer and terminer was an exceptional occurrence in Durham and this one had presumably been ordered by Edward to trace his enemies in the county. He was in Durham city for a fortnight from 22 April 1461 and had work put in hand to strengthen the castle.[42] In June the men of the bishopric were arrayed to defend the kingdom and liberty from enemies, meaning the Scots and the remnant of Margaret's forces; and soon afterwards Booth was rewarded by Edward for repulsing a Lancastrian raid into Durham. It would appear that Booth had rapidly accommodated himself with the new regime. He had been dismissed from the commission of the peace in Yorkshire after the battle of Northampton but Edward restored him on 28 May 1461. The king

obviously made an effort to attach Booth and made him his con-
fessor, and in February 1462 he gave Booth life tenure of a manor
and, jointly with William Neville, life tenure of Northumberland's
former castle of Wressle. In this month Booth was appointed a
commissioner to treat with the lord of the Isles to instigate treason
against Margaret's host, the king of Scots.[43]

The correspondence of the contemporary priors of Durham suggests that Booth was a polished courtier who could hide hostility
under a fair mask. He could dine with the prior and give him
'right pleasant language' in the course of a serious dispute which
he would not mention at table.[44] Booth certainly did not inspire the
same confidence in his cathedral city as he had apparently done
with Edward. His relations with the chapter were strained from the
start, when the prior wrote apologising for the monks' conduct at
Booth's election.[45] Their distrust of the bishop persisted, because
whenever the convent required an influential champion it did not
turn to him but to George Neville, bishop of Exeter, 'in whom', as
Prior Bell once wrote, 'after Almighty God is our most trust'.[46]
The convent's choice of George Neville as its particular 'good lord'
is not surprising. His father, the earl of Salisbury, had been their
patron and lay brother for many years, since he was 'a young
husband and nought all redy purveyed' for and required a loan
of the prior's chariot.[47] The convent had appointed members of
Salisbury's needy brood to its temporal offices. Possibly this long
association inclined the convent to Yorkist sympathies. In November 1460 the prior wrote to Sir Thomas Harrington, 'thankyng God
that ye are past the trouble that ye were in'—a discreet reference
to a reversed attainder.[48] The priors' *registrum parvum* gives fascinating evidence that a great house was as conscious as a John Paston
of how the laws and prophets hung in the fifteenth century. Like
gentry retainers also, the convent transferred its allegiance to the
magnate who took the position of a fallen 'good lord'. After Barnet,
the prior of Durham turned to Richard of Gloucester; in 1475 he
wrote thanking Gloucester for his 'good lordship' and to ask him
'to desire the archbishop of York to be good and gracious lord and
tender father' to the prior and convent.[49] The archbishop was none
other than George Neville, but his 'good lordship' was then not
worth regular cultivation.

George Neville was thus interested in Durham affairs. In 1461,
as the prior wrote to him, Booth became 'heavy lord and doeth

strangely' to Master John Lound, who had been Robert Neville's
temporal chancellor. George called Lound to attend him, much to
Lound's comfort.[50] As George was Edward's chancellor, the king
may have been advised not to place too much reliance on Booth's
appearance of loyalty. In October 1462 Margaret, with French
help, captured Alnwick Castle. Edward came to Durham and on
7 December ordered the seizure of the bishop's temporalities.[51] His
commission gives no reason for the seizure. Its first clause suggests
that Edward's first interest was financial, as do the names of the
three keepers, who were the treasurer and controller of the household
and Thomas Colt. They were required to receive all the bishop's
revenues and account for them at the Exchequer.[52] In 1464 a valor
of the bishopric assessed its net annual profit at £2,788.[53] Edward
may simply have needed the money for his own expenses, but
equally he may have feared that Booth might give Margaret financial aid. Suspicion of Booth was the more likely reason for this
sequestration, for he was banished to his fellow's rooms in Pembroke
College, Cambridge.[54] The commissioners were further empowered
to appoint officers and justices. In fact, as Edward was detained in
Durham for several weeks with an attack of measles, he himself
appointed a sheriff of Durham, John Lound as chancellor, John
Neville, Lord Montagu, as steward, and a commision of the peace.[55]
Durham remained in the king's hands for more than two years,
until a month before the battle of Hexham and the final reduction
of the Northumbrian castles. On 15 April 1464, Booth was
permitted to live where he pleased in England and two days later
the temporalities were restored to him.[56] Thereafter, he appears to
have been faithful to Edward, even in 1470,[57] while the king's
nominees were left in possession of their Durham offices.

Booth's local difficulties continued. He celebrated his return to
Durham with a visitation of the convent, an event which alarmed
the monks,[58] and he claimed feudal prerogatives over the prior's
lands. This led the prior to appeal once more to George Neville.
Eventually, in 1467, the matter was taken up by the king's Council
and the king sent Booth a privy seal ordering him not to molest
the convent while the Council was considering the evidence.[59] The
prior's plea to the chancellor had thus led to a precedent for conciliar
intervention in the bishopric.[60] This was as serious a demonstration
of the bishop's inability to preserve his franchise as the seizure of
the temporalities by a direct exercise of royal authority. In 1433 a

substantial body of the bishop's subjects had attempted to destroy his regalian rights by arranging for a royal commission of enquiry to condemn them as usurped from the Crown. Bishop Langley had thwarted this constitutional rebellion by appealing to Parliament, but it was by submitting to the judgement of Parliament that he had the liberties of the bishopric reaffirmed. The fact remained that at least an influential proportion of the subjects of the bishopric wished to see an end of their ruler's palatine authority. Several of the richer Durham tenants had lands in other counties and sometimes served in their local administrations, and even as their shire knights.[61] Obviously they would not have considered the bishopric as an enclosed community. The Wars of the Roses also revealed that the political connections of the tenants of palatinates transcended county boundaries; whatever royal faction held the Crown, local men were always available for office. English society had outgrown the palatinates before Henry VIII's statute reduced their liberties.

Notes

1 A. H. Thompson, *The Surtees Society, 1834–1934* (Surtees Society cl, 1939), 2.

2 *An Historical Geography of England before* A.D. *1800*, ed. H. C. Darby (1963), 231–3.

3 *Rotuli Scotiae*, ed. D. MacPherson *et al.* (1814–19), ii, 294; *C.P.R. 1416–22*, 201; R. L. Storey, *Thomas Langley and the Bishopric of Durham* (Church Historical Society, 1961), 146, 152, 208.

4 R. L. Storey, *The End of the House of Lancaster* (1966), 106–8, 126–8 (inc. maps 3, 4,) 148; R. R. Reid, *The King's Council in the North* (1921), 42, 67, 78.

5 *R.P.*, iii, 251.

6 J. A. Tuck, 'Richard II and the border magnates', *Northern History*, iii (1968), 48.

7 Storey, *End of the House of Lancaster*, 117–22; 'Disorders in Lancastrian Westmorland: some early Chancery proceedings', *Trans. Cumberland and Westmorland Antiquarian and Archaeological Society*, new series, liii (1953), 69–80.

8 P.R.O., King's Bench, Coram Rege rolls (k.b.27), No. 518, Rex 17.

9 *The Register of Thomas Langley, Bishop of Durham*, ed. R. L. Storey (Surtees Society 1956–70), iii, Nos. 763, 827, 889–90; vi, No. 1582.

10 W. Hutchinson, *The History and Antiquities of the County Palatine of Durham*, i (1785–94), 337 n.

11 P.R.O., Justices Itinerant, Gaol Delivery rolls (j.i.3), No. 176, m. 28.

12. Storey, *Thomas Langley*, 140–1.

13 J. Hardyng, *Chronicle*, ed. H. Ellis (1812), 378.

14 K. B. McFarlane, 'Parliament and "bastard feudalism" ', *T.R.H.S.* fourth series, xxvi (1944), 70–3.

15 *R.P.* vi, 63; Storey, *End of the House of Lancaster*, 122–6.

16 E.g. J. T. Rosenthal, 'Feuds and private peace-making: a fifteenth-century example', *Nottingham Medieval Studies,* xiv (1970), 84–90.

17 No surviving record formally marks this event, but privy seal material and other details cited in Storey, *End of the House of Lancaster*, 31, suggest that October 1436 was probably the date.

18 R. L. Storey, 'Lincolnshire and the Wars of the Roses', *Nottingham Medieval Studies,* xiv (1970), 67–8; *End of the House of Lancaster, passim.*

19 H. L. Gray, 'Incomes from land in England in 1436', *E.H.R.* xlix (1934), 615–18; Storey, *End of the House of Lancaster*, 132.

20 *Ibid.*, especially 105–32; R. L. Storey, 'The wardens of the Marches of England towards Scotland, 1377–1489', *E.H.R.*, lxxii (1957), 593–615; *C.P.*, ix, 708–18 (Northumberland); xii, part ii, 544–7 (Westmorland).

21 J. M. W. Bean, 'Henry IV and the Percies', *History,* xliv (1959), 212–27.

22 K. B. McFarlane, 'The Wars of the Roses', *Proc. Brit. Acad.*, l (1965), 97.

23 Storey, 'Wardens', 903. Dr Bean does refer to the transfer of Roxburgh (p. 224).

24 *Thomae Walsingham Historia Anglicana,* ed. H. T. Riley (Rolls Series, 1863–64), ii, 257–8.

25 Dr F. W. Brooks pointed out, however, that Worcester built Wressle Castle, in the East Riding.

26 *Œuvres de Froissart,* ed. Kervyn de Lettenhove (1867–77), xvi, 366–72. For fuller details of Worcester's career, see Dr A. L. Brown's contribution to this volume.

27 *Handbook of British Chronology,* ed. F. M. Powicke and E. B. Fryde (1961), 75, 85, 92, 102. Worcester was retained as the prince's governor, but there is no evidence that he accompanied him to Wales (C. L. Kingsford, *Henry V* (1923), 35.)

28 G. L. Harriss, 'Preference at the medieval Exchequer', *B.I.H.R.*, xxx (1957), 17–40; Bean, *op. cit.*, 222–4.

29 Richard Neville, earl of Salisbury, the eldest son of Westmorland and Joan Beaufort, was the most favoured of their large family (see Storey, *End of the House of Lancaster*, 109–15). His brother Robert became bishop of Salisbury at the age of twenty-two, thanks to Cardinal Beaufort's influence (*Cal. Papal Letters,* vii, 32, 494, 571); and see note 39 below.

30 *C.P.R., 1401–05,* 213, 233; R. L. Storey, 'English officers of state, 1399–1485', *B.I.H.R.*, xxxi (1958), 85, 87.

31 Storey, *End of the House of Lancaster*, 190–5, which also points to the reversals of allegiances by the Nevilles and Percies in 1469–70.

32 Storey, 'Wardens', 608.

33 Reid, *Council in the North,* 41–91.

34 Storey, *End of the House of Lancaster*, 150–8.

35 *C.P.*, iv, 205–6 (Stanley, *sub* Derby); vi, 319–20 (Harrington), and *cf.* Storey, *End of the House of Lancaster*, 166, 186 n. See also J. S. Roskell, *The knights of the shire for the county palatine of Lancaster, 1377–1460* (Chetham Society, new series, xcvi, 1937), 193–201.

36 R. Somerville, *History of the Duchy of Lancaster*, I (1953), 420.

37 P.R.O., Palatinate of Durham, Chancery records, Cursitor's records (Durham 3), volumes of inquisitions *post mortem*, No. 4, ff. 7-8.

38 *C.P.*, VIII, 271-3 (Lumley); x, 29-31 (Ogle; especially 30 n. (*d*)).

39 Storey, *End of the House of Lancaster*, 115. The royal signet letter ordering the monks of Durham to elect Neville in 1437 commended him, *inter alia,* but firstly, for 'his birth and kynsmen there which been of right grete and notable estat' (Dean and Chapter of Durham, Locellus 25, No. 96; see also Storey, *Thomas Langley*, 144).

40 Dean and Chapter of Durham, Receiver-General's records, Nos. 189812, 189814; Hutchinson, *Durham*, I, 340-1 n., 360 n.; P.R.O., Durham, Chancery Rolls (Durham 3), No. 48, m. 2, 3.

41 *Ibid.*, m. 8.

42 Durham, Rec.-Gen. 189816.

43 P.R.O., Durham 3/48, m. 8; *C.P.R., 1452-61*, 682-4; *ibid., 1461-67*, 12, 73, 113, 115, 576; C. L. Scofield, *The Life and Reign of Edward the Fourth,* I (1923), 174, 186.

44 Dean and Chapter of Durham, Registrum parvum III, f. 131.

45 *Ibid.*, f. 92v; printed in *Historiae Dunelmensis Scriptores Tres*, ed. J. Raine (Surtees Society, IX, 1838), appendix, cccxliv.

46 Reg. parv. III, f. 134.

47 *Wills and Inventories*, ed. J. Raine, I (Surtees Society, II, 1835), 69; *Liber Vitae Ecclesiae Dunelmensis*, I (Surtees Society, cxxxvi, facsimile, 1923), f. 73v.

48 Reg. parv. III, ff. 86, 91, 95v; *R.P.* v, 348-9.

49 Reg. parv, III, f. 161v; *Script. Tres*, appendix, ccclvi.

50 Reg. parv. III, f. 105v; for Lound, see A. B. Emden, *A Biographical Register of the University of Oxford to A.D. 1500* (1957-59), II, 1164-65.

51 Scofield, *op. cit.*, I, 261-4.

52 P.R.O., Durham 3/48, m. 11; printed in Hutchinson, *Durham*, I, 347-8n.

53 Dean and Chapter of Durham, Rec.-Gen. 189817.

54 A. B. Emden, *A Biographical Register of the University of Cambridge to 1500* (1963), 78-9.

55 P.R.O., Durham 3/48, m. 11, 12.

56 *Ibid.*, m. 15; *C.P.R., 1461-67*, 374-5; Hutchinson, *Durham*, I, 348 n.

57 Booth was dismissed from the commission of the peace for the North Riding, the only commission he held, in November 1470. He and William Gray of Ely were the only bishops so treated in the readeption of Henry VI (*C.P.R., 1467-77*, 609, 622, 637). Booth became Edward's chancellor in 1473 and was promoted to the archbishopric of York in 1476.

58 Dean and Chapter of Durham, Cartulary III, ff. 300, 311.

59 Reg. parv. III, ff. 128, 131, 133-4.

60 For intrusion by the Council of the North, see G. T. Lapsley, *The County Palatine of Durham* (1924), 260-3.

61 Storey, *Thomas Langley*, 116-34.

R. A. Griffiths

Senior Lecturer in History
University College, Swansea
in the University of Wales

7   Wales and the Marches

In the mid-1430s that early essay on 'strategic studies' *The Libelle
of Englyshe Polycye* summed up what many Englishmen felt about
Wales:

> Beware of Walys, Criste Ihesu mutt us kepe,
> That it make not oure childes childe to wepe,
> Ne us also, if so it go his waye
> By unwarenesse; sethen that many a day
> Men have be ferde of here rebellione
> By grete tokenes and ostentacione.[1]

The great majority of contemporary Englishmen regarded Wales
with fear and suspicion. Most English historians have been content
to disregard her. Stubbs did not even deign to mention Wales in the
third volume of his monumental *History*, while for Professor Du
Boulay relations between Englishmen and Welshmen in the later
Middle Ages rarely rose above a crude and mutual contempt. Few
Welshmen nowadays would wish to echo G. M. Trevelyan's flattering
list of priorities: 'The Wars of the Roses [he declared] were to a
large extent a quarrel between Welsh Marcher Lords, who were also
great English nobles, closely related to the English throne.'[2] Nevertheless, if Yorkshire and the north were to demand recognition of
their uniqueness in this period, then Wales (to put it ungrammati-
cally) was even more unique. It certainly demanded special treatment
from the English State. Looked at more broadly, Wales displays
many of the pressures to which English kings responded in formu-
lating their policy, and also some of the assumptions underlying their
attitude to regional problems.

The term 'Wales and the Marches' in the fifteenth century had an
air of vagueness about it even thicker than that surrounding until

recently the term 'Wales and Monmouthshire' in the twentieth century. The 'Principality of Wales and the Marches' would have been more precise and certainly more comprehensible to modern readers of, for example, the Parliament rolls. To the west of the English shires lay two distinct forms of government still full of meaning in the fifteenth century: the shires of the principality of Wales and Flint, and the Welsh Marches or marcher lordships.[3] Contemporaries appreciated the difference, and it received careful acknowledgement from the Crown. The principality shires, organised in two groups centred on Carmarthen and Caernarvon, with Flint attached by history and convenience to Chester, were vested in the king and his heirs as kings of England. They were governed directly by the king or prince through his appointees, headèd both in the south and north by a justiciar and chamberlain, but they stood quite separate geographically and constitutionally from the shires of England.[4] The marcher lordships, on the other hand, were quite different in their origin and development. Ultimately held of the Crown, into whose hands on occasion they fell by escheat, forfeiture or wardship, they were franchises of the most independent kind. Every function of government in each lordship was the sole responsibility of its marcher lord: his courts had power of life and death over his tenants, he could impose his own taxes, royal officials from neighbouring English or Welsh shires had no authority there, and even bishops with letters of excommunication in their pocket sought the support of the lord's secular arm (and not the king's).[5] This was the public framework within which Welshmen lived and English marcher lords and kings ruled in later medieval Wales.

The maintenance of public order in the shires and lordships of Wales depended on the vigour of the Crown and marcher lords and on the responsibility of the local population. Furthermore, Edward I had specifically declared it to be the Crown's sovereign responsibility to guarantee justice to every subject. The effort to achieve order and justice against almost insurmountable odds by these means was the continuing theme of fifteenth-century Wales. I have therefore adopted it as the theme of this paper.

The Crown's response to the rebellion of Owain Glyndŵr, which broke out in 1400, reveals how carefully those features of Welsh government already mentioned were respected, and yet also how Wales's relationship to the English State could be modified in the interests of order. In Parliament on 15 October 1399 Henry IV invested his eldest son and heir with the estate, honour and dignity of Prince of Wales. The king put a circlet on his head, a gold ring on his finger, a rod of gold in his hand; he kissed him on the cheek, handed him his charter and young Henry became thus Prince of Wales. The income of the principality and the reality of government were transferred some weeks later, on 8 November.[6] Such was the uncertainty of 1399, and such perhaps the exclusively seignorial experience of the new king, that Henry IV was not prepared to delegate complete control over the principality (nor indeed over Chester) to his son. Rather was a community of government forged between king and prince which did not give to Prince Henry the freedom enjoyed by the Black Prince. On 20 October 1399 the king had appointed Hotspur justiciar of north Wales and Chester for life, and ten days later William Beauchamp, lord of Abergavenny, became justiciar of south Wales also for life. Six months later, on 24 April 1400, it was again Henry IV who nominated Hotspur to be constable of Chester, Flint, Conway and Caernarvon castles and sheriff of Flint, again during his lifetime.[7]

The Glyndŵr rebellion may have fortified the king's inclination to supervise his son's principality; indeed, it was vital that he should do so if a unified command were to be created and financed to crush the rebels. It was in this spirit that Henry IV's government often paid for the safe keeping of the principality's castles early in the revolt, and despatched ordinances before April 1401 to Hotspur as justiciar of north Wales and Chester.[8] At first this exercise in joint government gave rise to friction. There is no more telling instance of this than the Conway incident of 1401, when the agreement concluded by Prince Henry and Hotspur with the Welsh captors of Conway Castle was angrily repudiated by the king. Henry IV reminded his son that it had been *his* officers who had lost the fortress and *his* financial responsibility to regain it—although the royal treasury would inevitably have to foot part of the bill.[9] Only gradually did the prince shoulder responsibility for more than the routine business of governing his shires; but from 1405 onwards his father rarely assigned money for operations in the principality and hardly ever made internal appointments there.[10]

To gear the marcher lordships for the suppression of rebellion was a more difficult task. It was too dangerous to override marcher privileges after the manner of Edward I and Hugh Despenser;

in any case, it was not in the nature of a man who until recently
had himself been a great magnate and powerful marcher lord.[11]
Even under the strain of rebellion, Henry time and again confined
himself to urging the marcher lords to visit their lordships and
garrison their castles.[12] Too often their assistance fell short of expec-
tation, as the petitions presented in Parliament made clear, and,
no doubt urged on by the Commons in the Parliaments of 1401
and 1402, the king resorted to more radical measures from November
1401. Henry then appointed lieutenants for north and south Wales,
both distinguished magnates, to co-ordinate civil and military rule
temporarily in the principality and in the Marches. Thomas Percy,
earl of Worcester, was the first, appointed for south Wales in
November 1401 after the king had returned from a chastening
expedition to Wales. Percy's nephew, Hotspur, joined him on
31 March 1402 as lieutenant of north Wales. They did not supersede
shire and seignorial custom, but they could organise the military
campaign and punish or pardon the rebels.[13]

    This royal intervention was justified by rebellion and treasonable
war against the king. Only he could pardon high treason and,
according to the statute of 1352, receive the forfeitures of the convicted, whether they were tenants of the king himself or of any other
lord. Henry IV continually exercised this prerogative as sovereign
in the principality and in the Marches, either directly or through
the lieutenants of north and south Wales.[14] When Prince Henry
became royal lieutenant in January 1406 there existed throughout
Wales a measure of unity similar to that achieved by the later
prince's Council in the Marches, though in the lordships at least
it scarcely extended beyond the temporary needs of a military campaign. His commission was renewed on several occasions and he
was still the king's lieutenant in September 1411.[15]

    Two pressure groups existed which urged more radical measures
to crush Glyndŵr and contain future Welsh uprisings: they were
the border English shires and the Commons in Parliament. The
border communities were convinced that they were witnessing an
upheaval as serious as the Edwardian conquest, to which episode
they resorted in the search for precedent in dealing with the troublesome Welsh.[16] The number of petitions presented in Parliament
on their behalf betray an extreme apprehension of their Welsh neighbours, even xenophobia; this is likely to have given to the border
representatives coherence and persistence as a lobby in a Parliament

exasperated with marcher particularism during a war which the Commons partly had to finance.[17] Costs sharpened their minds and their tongues. The parliamentary experience of men such as Sir Ralph Stafford (M.P. for Worcestershire in 1383, 1384 and 1401), Sir Thomas Fitz Nicol (M.P. for Gloucestershire in six Parliaments before he sat in 1401 and 1402), and Roger Thornes and Thomas Pryde (who between them represented Shrewsbury on six occasions before they did so together in 1401 and 1402) must have been invaluable in discussing the border's problems.[18] Henry IV, however, resisted most of such demands in 1401 and 1402 as went beyond precautions for the present and the enforcement of established and reasonable custom: he parried the more extreme or far-reaching of them with 'the king wishes to preserve his right' or 'let this petition be committed to the Council'. Thus, if he was prepared in 1401 to agree by statute that no Welshman should purchase land in England or in the Welsh plantation towns (presumably of Edwardian foundation), in 1402 he declined to interfere with local privileges by prohibiting all Welshmen from trading elsewhere in Wales than in the market towns. Moreover, when he agreed to a petition that no Welshman be an officer in Wales or a councillor of an English lord there, he inserted an important, open-ended reservation that excluded bishops and all loyal lieges from the measure.[19]

If the Crown was not prepared to impose major modifications on the political structure of Wales in an emergency like this, it certainly did not do so after Glyndŵr had withdrawn into obscurity. Henry V was as careful of marcher susceptibilities as his father, but his experience of Welshmen, his statesmanship and, soon after, his need for a tranquil Wales which would pay subsidies and array its men for the French war, dictated a policy combining conciliation and firmness.[20] Whole communities of Welshmen purchased collective pardons during the next four years, albeit with hefty fines: 1,600 marks was imposed on those of Caernarvonshire, Merioneth and Anglesey in November 1413.[21] A certain degree of economic recovery and social stability was induced by royal ordinance when the earls of March and Arundel, the lords of Powys and the chamberlain of south Wales were ordered to return to the principality shires in north Wales tenants who had fled from Anglesey, Caernarvonshire and Merioneth; the king in 1413 even assigned £200 to be spent on cows and sheep for the re-stocking of the Caernarvonshire and Merioneth countryside.[22] Furthermore, corruption and oppression by the king's own servants in the principality were swiftly investigated, and in July 1413 the earl of Arundel headed a commission in north Wales to enquire into treasons and riots committed by royal officials; it was as a result of this investigation that Thomas Barneby, chamberlain of north Wales, was removed from office in the following March.[23] Even the Welsh law of inheritance was guaranteed in the royal territories, while in north Wales debts to the Crown incurred before 5 November 1411 were cancelled and everyone restored to the lands they had held before the revolt broke out.[24]

But Henry V could also be firm. He guarded against further insurrection, especially in north Wales, where the poor and inaccessible county of Merioneth was seen as the key to future peace in the region.[25] He also enlisted the aid of the great lords to ensure order in the Marches, and lordships in his own hand were circumspectly disposed of, frequently to members of his own family.[26] It was a notable achievement: no large-scale rising occurred even when the fugitive Sir John Oldcastle proposed a Celtic alliance in 1417, and many Welshmen fought for their king in France.[27] War taxes were paid even in north and west Wales, whilst in the duchy of Lancaster lordships the degree of recovery was such that local officials were eventually able to realise 98·8 per cent of the potential revenue for the years 1411–17.[28] The king's policy in Wales had been eminently successful, and the brevity of his reign scarcely allowed time for its more oppressive features to ripen into protest.[29]

After the rebellion neither the Crown nor the marcher lords were capable of displaying the vigour they had shown during it; and as time passed the local population exercised less and less responsibility. The Welsh squirearchy, brothers-in-arms of the gentry and knights of England, were the leaders of local society, the moulders of opinion, patrons of the Welsh Church and Welsh culture, and, in a society bereft of a substantial mercantile community, also the main repository of landed wealth. Above all, they provided political leadership as public servants of the Crown and the marcher lords.[30] They were a gregarious and enterprising body of men, whose unusually durable ties of kinship enabled them to play a crucial part in fifteenth-century politics. They had held the key both to the temporary success of Glyndŵr and, after they had deserted him, to the ultimate failure of his enterprise.[31] For all the repressive instincts of Henry IV's early Parliaments, the Crown needed these squires to administer its estates, collect its revenue and preserve the peace. As Welshmen, they were excluded from the most prestigious positions in the principality; thus, between 1400 and 1461 no Welshman born of Welsh parents was appointed to the post of justiciar or chamberlain of south Wales. But men such as Gruffydd ap Nicholas in Carmarthenshire and William ap Gwilym ap Gruffydd in Caernarvonshire deputised so regularly for the English officials that this was a hollow restriction. The former was deputy justiciar of south Wales by August 1437 and again between 1447 and 1456 in the inevitable absence of magnate justiciars like Lord Audley, Humphrey of Gloucester and Sir John Beauchamp of Powick; Gruffydd extended his service by acting as deputy chamberlain for Sir Edward Stradling, Lord Sudeley and Lord Audley. At the other end of Wales, William ap Gwilym's achievement was only a whit less noteworthy, for he had become deputy chamberlain of North Wales by 1457.[32] Both men took the precaution of securing by letters of denizenship ultimate legal protection against the largely moribund legislation of Henry IV, for the abrupt end to the career of Sir John Scudamore, Glyndŵr's son-in-law, only a few years earlier had indicated that what lay dormant on the statute book could, if desired, be roused to endanger an official position.[33]

The Welsh squire may have been even more vital to the marcher lords than he was to the Crown. The vast complexes of estates in England, Wales and overseas of, for example, Duke Richard of York, Richard Neville, earl of Warwick, and Duke Humphrey of Buckingham were staffed from a much smaller pool of retainers, servants and councillors than that available to the king. The local man was consequently enlisted as steward and receiver, and not simply as an effective deputy paying lip-service to the harsh enactments of Henry IV's early Parliaments; like William ap Thomas and his son William Herbert in Usk, Glamorgan and Monmouth, he often enjoyed seignorial power by default of the lord himself.[34] Such a man was capable of providing peaceful and efficient government, but equally his selfishness and neglect could create resentment among his less powerful neighbours and promote anarchy in his locality.

The greatest opportunity for the Welsh and English squirearchy in Wales came during Henry VI's reign—even for erstwhile rebels. For several reasons, central control over Wales was weaker then than at any time since the Edwardian conquest. Already in the late fourteenth century, some marcher houses were losing their direct interest in Wales, and this continued to be so in the early fifteenth century. The Bohun inheritance was divided, and the Mortimers' attention was diverted elsewhere, especially to Ireland before the turn of the century.[35] The Despenser, Mortimer and Stafford families were blighted by minorities: for forty-one of the sixty-five years between 1349 and 1414 the head of the Despenser family was a minor; for thirty-four years in the period 1382–1432 most of the Mortimer properties were in youthful hands, and Humphrey, earl of Stafford and lord of Newport, was under age from 1403 to 1423.[36] Some inheritances, like the duchy of Lancaster lordships, the Mortimer estates, the county of Pembroke and the lordship of Glamorgan, were incorporated into such large landed complexes that their lord could devote only a fraction of his time to the Welsh properties and their officials. Aristocratic households could be remarkably sophisticated and organised, but an older organisation may have undertaken additional commitments less easily than a newer one, and, as the case of William, Lord Herbert shows, a frequently resident magnate probably supervised his estates more effectively than an habitual absentee.[37] Moreover, the Crown's territories in Wales after 1399 were so large and so widespread that to supervise effectively the duchy of Lancaster, the principality, and lordships in royal hands, each with its own customs and traditions, was a heavy burden for a monarchy increasingly racked by faction and ultimately overwhelmed by civil war. In 1461 the earldom of March was added.[38] Nor could the problem be eased by transferring at least the principality and Chester to a capable young prince: between 1413 and 1509 there was a prince for only thirty-seven years and at no time was he an adult.[39]

There was, then, a certain inevitability about Wales's detachment from its rulers in the fifteenth century. This was accentuated by the fear of Wales which many Englishmen felt after the revolt and which the *Libelle of Englyshe Polycye* expressed.[40] In addition, Wales's principal attraction for its lords—its revenue—had become much attenuated of late. Lords such as the king, the duke of Lancaster and the earl of March found it difficult to maintain their Welsh income in the late fourteenth century; after the rebellion their fortunes were in marked decline. In Glamorgan, for example, the lord's revenue never recovered from the experience of the revolt;

in Denbigh the yields of the late fourteenth century had been possible only with considerable strain and by judicial pressure which could not be sustained after Glyndŵr's rebellion; in the southern counties of the principality the extraordinary subsidies that Richard II had demanded in the 1380s and 1390s could not safely be emulated by Henry VI, whose income there declined sharply.[41] The same story can be told of the earl of Shrewsbury's border manor of Blackmere (Salop), where 'the whole history of the estate in the late Middle Ages is dominated by one event: the sacking of Whitchurch and the surrounding country by the Welsh rebels in 1404'.[42] Increasingly, lords resorted to financial expedients, exploiting their precious judicial privileges, but no longer could this be done without concessions to the Welsh population. This explains why most marcher lords followed the Crown's rapidly established practice in Carmarthenshire and Cardiganshire of frequently allowing the annual great sessions or sessions in eyre in each lordship to be prematurely suspended—even completely terminated—in return for a substantial grant from the community.[43] The principle of a subsidy from the great sessions of these two counties was firmly established during the reign of Henry IV, when a concession of such magnitude had to be offered to the local population if a substantial grant were to be extracted from them. It was not without the occasional precedent elsewhere before 1399, but now it became a habit difficult to break. During the period 1422–85 only twelve of the fifty-two Carmarthenshire sessions for which some sort of record survives ran their proper course and were not prematurely dissolved in return for a 'general fine'. During these decades 'dissolution of the sessions' spread like a contagion to almost every marcher lordship in south and central Wales, and to Denbigh at least in the north.[44] As a fund-raising device it was immediately profitable, but its impact on government in the widest sense was ultimately disastrous. Justice was too often subordinated to financial gain, and seignorial and royal authority to local squirearchical power. Its damaging effects could, perhaps, be obviated by a resident lord or a conscientious official, but both were rare phenomena. As it was, Richard of York rarely visited his Welsh estates other than at times of personal crisis; Richard Neville's and Duke Richard of Gloucester's interests were remote from Glamorgan, and at Pembroke Humphrey of Gloucester must have been little more than a tourist.[45] It is difficult to prove that the preoccupations of marcher lords were greater in the fifteenth century than in the fourteenth. But it is incontrovertible that the small number of aristocratic families which dominated Wales made it impossible for lords to give personal attention to their estates. Nor, one suspects, was this peculiar to Wales.

The result of royal and seignorial withdrawal, judicial paralysis and squirearchical power was to intensify the disorder for which Wales had long been a by-word. Lawlessness is impossible to quantify in an age which was not statistically minded, and it is therefore difficult to speak comparatively about it. However, its prevalence is indicated by the steps taken by the Crown to curb it in its own territories in Wales, by the appeals to the king's Council from both royal and seignorial lordships, and by the complaints of the border shires in Parliament. Underlying Welsh disorder in the fifteenth century was, first, the deep resentment of the conqueror which Glyndŵr had recently brought to the surface once more. The aftermath of revolt was keenly and bitterly felt by loyalists in the border English shires as well as in Wales itself.[46] In an age of absentee lordship, it was directed especially at the plantation towns and their privileged burgesses—still very largely of English extraction in the northern shires and maintaining their 'colonist' mentality to the end of the century: it was their protests in 1445 which temporarily brought to an end the granting of letters of denizenship.[47] The bitterness was directed also at the inhabitants of the neighbouring English shires, who were subjected to acts of revenge after the revolt—raiding, cattle rustling and holding to ransom.[48] Second, marcher privilege had always been a source of potential injustice and disorder. Distress taken indiscriminately by aggrieved tenants outside their lordship in retaliation for destructive acts within it, the opportunity for criminals to escape their just deserts by disclaimer into another lordship, and the localised hostilities which periodically engulfed any frontier community—these exasperations contributed to the mass violence of later medieval Wales.[49]

A diversity of laws need be no more conducive to disorder than a uniform, centralised system such as the common law of England provided. Moreover, in Wales means existed to control turbulence without involving the sovereignty of the Crown: 'love days', 'parliament days', 'days of redress', or 'days of the March' were proclaimed at traditional meeting places on the border between adjacent jurisdictions for the purpose of composing their differences, while virtual extradition treaties were periodically concluded by neighbouring marcher lords and their officers.[50] But too often they could be subverted by kinship loyalties, negligent officers and lack of forceful direction. The Severn Valley was especially turbulent, with the Welsh from nearby lordships descending on its river traffic, killing, destroying, and blackmailing traders who frequented the wealthy commercial centres as far south as Bristol.[51] Nor were the royal territories more orderly. Carmarthenshire and Cardiganshire were falling more and more out of the control of the central government between 1430 and 1455. In 1435 one complainant to the king's Council claimed that he dare not 'suy the Com[on]e lawe' out of fear of violence because Morgan ap Dafydd Fychan, recently a royal official in Carmarthenshire, 'drawyth un to hym utlaws and diverse mysrewlede men the whech obey not zour lawe ther nethyr zowyr officers'. Even a wayward deputy justiciar was singled out for dismissal in 1436. Moreover, Gruffydd ap Nicholas, for all his willingness to curb lawlessness in others, forged a career for himself in west Wales which cut through the restraints of royal authority as cleanly as a knife through butter.[52] In the north of Wales that termagant among Welsh shires, Merioneth, had become ungoverned and ungovernable by the 1450s: it was noted in July 1452 and August 1453 that the county had persistently failed to produce rents and hold audits and sessions since 1449, while for years its tenantry had been a plague on the neighbouring lordships of Powys and Mawddwy.[53] To judge by the exasperation expressed in Parliament and by the commissions issued by the government, the 1420s, '30s and '40s saw public order in Wales deteriorate alarmingly. Existing agencies for its preservation were now woefully inadequate: the links in what Professor Glanmor Williams has described as 'the chain of command' in government had become perilously weak. A petition presented to the Commons in Parliament in 1449 could maintain that even in the royal territories the population 'dayly habundeth and encreseth in misgovernaunce'.[54]

Various remedies were devised by the late Lancastrian, Yorkist and early Tudor governments to replace outmoded and unworkable procedures. In the first place, the Crown was the only superior authority which could re-establish order and stability in Wales. Its responsibility to do so had been clearly enunciated by Edward I, and where treasonable activity was involved it could even override the protection ordinarily afforded by seignorial custom. King Henry IV's intervention had been in such an emergency, prompted by what he regarded as Glyndŵr's treason. Thus most of the commissions of oyer and terminer which Henry V and Henry VI sent into the principality and Marches carried the same justification in law: the breathless catalogue of 'felonies, misprisions, oppressions, extortions, conspiracies, confederacies, maintenances, champerties, concealments, ambidexterities, falsities, contempts and deceptions, and other trespasses, offences and negligences' was prefaced by 'treasons, insurrection and rebellions'.[55] But such intervention was now less effective against an increasingly autonomous Welsh squirearchy. The colourful story of Gruffydd ap Nicholas's cavalier treatment of a royal commissioner, who was plied with drink, robbed of his commission, and despatched home in Gruffydd's livery, may be apochryphal in detail but it is redolent of the true state of mid-fifteenth-century Wales. It was a society coming adrift from its former loyalties.[56]

Second, Edward I had guaranteed to every subject the right of appeal to the king.[57] During Henry VI's reign the normal means of securing justice by common law or marcher custom were so paralysed that complaints were received by the Council and Parliament from humble subjects in the royal shires and occasionally the Marches. In reply to the harrowing petition presented in the 1439 Parliament on behalf of Margaret Malefant, who was kidnapped in the lordship of Gower and taken into Glamorgan, the king agreed that the kidnappers should be arraigned before King's Bench, provided the rights of the marcher lords were safeguarded.[58] But when the local agencies of law enforcement had to be relied upon, even the Council and Parliament fulminated in vain.[59]

Third, King Edward had outlined his responsibility to intervene in private warfare between Welsh lords or lordships by his treatment of the earls of Hereford and Gloucester.[60] It is true that the fifteenth century did not witness the worst excesses of violence between marcher lords of a century earlier, but there were many occasions when communities of a shire or lordship descended on a neighbouring lordship to wage localised war. The growing ineffectiveness of the customary march days and mutual agreements to curb these outrages was evident in the 1430s and '40s, when the Crown had to command their use by royal and seignorial officials. In October 1442 the marcher lords were firmly ordered by the king and his

Council to meet together and agree on a remedy for the disturbances that were prevalent in Wales; and in a particular case, in 1448, several marcher lords (or their officers) and the king's justiciar and chamberlain of north Wales were required by Henry VI to stop the wholesale theft that inflamed the borders of Merioneth, Caernarvon, Powys and Mawddwy.[61] On occasion, the traditional means of settling local disputes were even adopted in desperation on the initiative of the communities themselves to deal reciprocally with criminals and stolen property.[62]

These were the avenues open to a king who wished to deal with Wales as a whole. If they were paved with good intentions, they were also pitted with local custom and privilege. Only the most courageous of kings would launch a frontal attack on these. When the Commons petitioned that the border J.P.s be empowered to try Welshmen from adjacent lordships, Henry VI temporised, put his faith in marcher custom and issued cloudy statements. The most that could be achieved was that in 1442 the J.P.s were allowed to try Welsh raiders provided an appeal to the marcher lords had been made and failed—but these lords should receive any forfeitures that might result and the statute was to last for only six years.[63] Even in the king's own lands the government was reluctant to tamper with age-old custom. Instead, officers were ordered to their posts and lords to their lordships, futile steps in an age of persistently absentee officials and preoccupied lords. Small wonder that by September 1453 negligent officers and extortionate officials had become the subject of an enquiry in the three northern shires of the principality.[64] Under Henry VI the aim was to tighten up the existing machinery for law enforcement. Only reluctantly did the king and the marcher lords accept the need for a more radical solution imposed by the Crown's sovereign power.

Collective action by the king and marcher lords, with the advice of prominent local gentry ('six, five or four at least of the notablest of their lordships'), was proposed by the Crown in 1437–38 and 1442–43 to re-establish what it described as 'the good governance of Wales'.[65] The degree of co-operation achieved during the rebellion may have been in the proposers' mind, and the warnings of the *Libelle of Englyshe Polycye* may have influenced the government in this as in several other instances. Moreover, Henry VI's own initiative may perhaps be seen in the threat made in October 1442 that he himself would act in the Marches if the lords failed to do so: it has the ring of a personal ultimatum about it.[66] But so long as exhortation was supported by conservative methods and the local officialdom, there could be little improvement. There was none as aristocratic faction and civil war overwhelmed the provinces: York replaced Somerset, and Jasper Tudor replaced York in the principality shires; in 1453 Warwick fought Somerset in Glamorgan; Sir William Herbert and Sir Walter Devereux, tenants and probably councillors of York, captured Edmund, earl of Richmond, in west Wales in August 1456; and Jasper Tudor strove thereafter to rally much of Wales to the house of Lancaster.[67] Moreover, the bewildering changes of lordship in Wales, intensified by the political tergiversations of the 1450s, and the bloody battles in which Welshmen were involved sapped the strength of men's loyalty to their absent lords.[68] Such ties were fast becoming an irrelevance: the squirearchy's personal instinct for power transcended responsibility to a lord.

Duke Richard of York, during his two protectorates, may have wished to remedy the worst excesses of misgovernment in Wales and the chronic weakness of the Crown's authority there. Certainly his several manifestos evinced a concern for effective government and the reformation of justice. But these months were so full of personal problems and political difficulties for the duke that in Wales no headway was made in the principality—let alone in marcher lordships other than his own. One enthusiastic writer said of York during his first protectorate that 'for one whole year he governed the entire realm of England well and nobly, and miraculously pacified all rebels and malefactors . . .' In Parliament in July 1455, shortly after his victory at St Albans, a committee consisting of marcher lords (*Domini Marchearum*) and the Crown's legal advisers was set up to investigate means of establishing 'restful and sad rule in Wales'. Yet in his dealings with the lawless gentry of west Wales the duke showed how futile a distant government's efforts could be.[69]

This pattern of intermittent discussion about ensuring public order in Wales was overtaken by the civil war and its aftermath. Edward IV's most urgent need in 1461 was not for experiment which might antagonise his aristocratic allies but for a strong regime that would re-establish order and loyalty in a traditional setting. This was provided by William Herbert, the son of Sir William ap Thomas, 'the Blue Knight of Gwent', and Gwladys Ddu, daughter of the famous Welsh commander, Dafydd Gam, who was killed

in Henry V's service at Agincourt. With such an upbringing, it is
hardly surprising that Herbert came to inspire devotion from Welsh
propagandists, while around him were grouped both family and
friends who were enlisted in Edward IV's service as a core of loyal
officers.[70] In nine months between May 1461 and February 1462
Herbert gathered into his and his relatives' hands the southern
counties of the principality and practically all the southern marcher
lordships apart from Glamorgan, Abergavenny and the earldom
of March.[71] By 1468 there were few areas in Wales as a whole
(Glamorgan is again the principal exception) of which he was not
either lord, custodian or principal official. One Welsh poet fittingly
described him as 'King Edward's master-lock'.[72] It was far from
the king's mind to modify drastically marcher custom and privilege,
for he actually created two new independent lordships for Herbert
himself: Crickhowell and Tretower were detached from the earldom
of March in June 1463 and erected into a fully-fledged marcher lordship, and so was Raglan (formerly part of the lordship of Usk) in
March 1465.[73] Rather was Herbert's position akin to that of Henry
IV's lieutenants, although his personal control over all the lordships
which came into the king's hands was unique. But elsewhere in
the Marches and the border English shires he only headed commissions of traditional scope encompassing treason, rebellion or
counterfeit money, all of which violated the Crown's sovereignty.[74]

The death of Herbert in 1469 created a vacuum which not even
Duke Richard of Gloucester could fill, with the result that 'the outrageous demeanyng of Walsshmen' continued. Although Gloucester
became justiciar of north and south Wales, and chief steward,
approver and surveyor of the principality of Wales and earldom of
March in 1469–70, his authority was not revived after the readeption
of Henry VI.[75] During the 1470s, therefore, Edward IV was driven
to attempt a more constructive solution to the problem of order
which would bring the king's sovereignty more to the fore. But
it took time. Created Prince of Wales in June 1471, Edward of
Westminster did not secure full control over his inheritance until
November 1472, when the income of the principality and of Chester
was made over to him.[76] During the next four years a Council
managed his affairs for him very much as Councils had done for
princes in the past. In the meantime, conditions in Wales were made
perfectly plain to the king by Parliament in 1472 and 1473. Once
more the men from the border English shires were feeling the

brunt of the disorder—or so it was claimed on their behalf by the Commons.[77] Responding to their plight, Edward conferred with the marcher lords in 1473, and at Shrewsbury in June he concluded agreements with them.[78] These indentures codified current customary and statutory methods of preserving public order in the marcher lordships and border shires, and the king sealed them as earl of March and not as sovereign. The familiar expedients of a conscientious and resident officialdom, and a satisfactory relationship between neighbouring lordships, were the basis of these agreements.[79] As in the past, the king's Council was made available only as an appeal court or to settle disputes between marcher lords. In its details, this was a conservative code which rationalised and publicised existing procedures; even the placing of the chief officers of each lordship, both royal and seignorial, under a financial surety to observe its provisions was not a novelty.[80] But at last the king had advanced from mere exhortation to securing from the marcher lords a promise to fulfil ancient responsibilities. The absence of any method of correcting a lord who failed to do so was now that much more obvious. This is just what the prince's Council could provide.

According to Dominic Mancini, Prince Edward in Wales 'devoted himself to horses and dogs and other youthful exercises to invigorate his body'.[81] His affairs were managed by an impressive body of prominent advisers. Even before he undertook full responsibility for the government of his possessions, Queen Elizabeth and her brother, Lord Rivers,.the king's brothers, the dukes of Clarence and Gloucester, the archbishop of Canterbury and ten other persons had been nominated in July 1471 to administer the principality and his other properties for him until he reached the age of fourteen. On 20 February 1473 this group was increased in size from fifteen to twenty-five and specifically entrusted with full powers of government in Prince Edward's name; in the following winter it was strengthened by a small household of permanent and influential councillors appointed during pleasure.[82] About the same time they received authority to deal with disturbances in Herefordshire and Shropshire, and in February 1474 the prince and his Council were provided with assistance from the border population to arrest some felons who had fled into Wales; but these were commissions designed for a specific purpose.[83] It was not until the early months of 1476 that more thoroughgoing measures were being discussed which would give continuity to the Crown's supervisory power in

Wales, the marcher lordships and the border shires. The prince's Council would be its instrument in an act of governmental devolution which was by no means unique in Yorkist England.

On 2 January 1476 the prince was given a commission of oyer and terminer throughout Wales and the neighbouring English shires of Gloucester, Hereford, Worcester and Salop; in March he, or certain of his councillors, was instructed to enquire about franchises in the Marches and the border shires which were suitable for resumption by the Crown, and about criminals who escaped justice in the same area.[84] Moreover, the importance which the king attached to his son's Council is indicated by the conference he arranged at Ludlow in March 1476 between it and the marcher lords to discuss the punishment of crime in Wales and the Marches. One probable outcome was the commission issued on 29 December to the prince during pleasure to appoint judicial commissions in Wales, the marcher lordships and the four border shires, to array men if necessary to punish criminals, and to enquire into negligent officials. This was a notable accession of authority outside the principality and royal lordships, and evidently the basis on which the prince's Council in 1478 issued ordinances for future peace in Shrewsbury 'and for good Rule to be kepte [amongst] thofficers' there.[85] The Crown's responsibility as sovereign in Wales and the border country was being delegated semi-permanently to the prince's Council settled in the Marches at Ludlow. It was doubtless part of the design that the earldom of March was gradually transferred to the prince's hands, as also was the county of Pembroke in 1479 'for the reformation of the wele publique, restfull governaunce and mynystration of Justice in the said parties of South Wales'.[86] There now existed in Wales an authority which had complete powers of government in the principality, the earldom of March and other royal lordships, together with a supervisory jurisdiction in the English shires and private marcher lordships when justice should falter or officials were negligent. The prince's Council even entertained, probably *ad hoc* and for reasons of sheer convenience, a few complaints ordinarily heard by the king and his Council at Westminster. Twice in 1480–82 appeals were made to Prince Edward at Ludlow by men from Coventry, a city well outside the territorial scope of his earlier commission but one which had a long connection with the princes of Wales. On each occasion the prince acted in his father's name and with his authority, while in June 1481 Edward IV specifically asked his son to assume the task of raising men from Coventry for the projected Scottish campaign. The king was delegating his sovereignty to young Edward's councillors for specific purposes and for reasons of convenience in a city which had a special attachment to the king's heir. The commissions of 1476 in no way provided the authority under which the prince and his advisers intervened in Coventry.[87]

In May 1483, barely three weeks after Edward V left Ludlow as king, Protector Gloucester at one stroke tried to perpetuate at least the concept of delegated prerogative.[88] He assigned to his ally, Duke Henry of Buckingham, for life the government of all the royal lands in Wales: he became justiciar and chamberlain of north and south Wales, steward and receiver of Pembroke, and either custodian or principal officer of all the king's lordships throughout the length and breadth of Wales. To this was added

the oversight of oure [i.e. the king's] subgettes now being or herafter to be in Southwales, Northwales and in the merches of Wales and in the countees of Salop, Hereford, Somerset, Dorset, and Wiltshire, and also power and auctorite by his discrecion in oure name for oure defence and the defence of oure realme and for the defence and keping of oure peaxe of and in the said parties to assemble oure said subgettes defencibly arreied and them conveie or sende to suche place or places and fro tyme to tyme as shalbe thought to the same duc expedient and necessarie in thet behalve . . .[89]

This 'oversight' was equivalent in nature to that exercised by the prince's Council before 1483, but territorially it was much wider. That it reposed in the hands of one man was probably due to the delicate political position of the Protector. Buckingham combined the personal ascendancy of Herbert with the judicial and administrative authority of the late Council. But he enjoyed them for only five months, for on 15 October the duke was proclaimed a rebel and less than three weeks later he was executed.[90]

The problems which faced the first Tudor king in Wales were the same as those which had confronted the last of the Plantagenets. Neither the use of the so-called dragon banner of Cadwaladr nor the king's Welsh harp and part-Welsh ancestry could alleviate them.[91] Jasper Tudor doubtless inspired admiration for his tenacity over twenty-five years if for nothing else. Since 1461 he had first plotted and campaigned in the interest of Henry VI, and then advised and protected in exile his young nephew, Henry Tudor.[92] But in Wales conditions had not fundamentally changed: Brecon castle was attacked and ransacked by rebels in 1486, and twelve years later there was insurrection in Merioneth.[93] The new government's response followed essentially the lines laid down by Edward IV. In order to reactivate the Crown's authority in Wales, on 11 March 1486 Henry VII empowered his uncle Jasper, during pleasure and in terms identical with those of 1476, to oversee the workings of justice in Wales, the Marches and the three English shires of Hereford, Gloucester and Worcester, to array men to provide assistance if necessary, and to keep watch on the abuse of office.[94] The code of public behaviour of which Jasper was now the guardian was that contained in Edward IV's indentures. But Henry did not give his uncle the breadth of responsibility for the internal administration of Wales's shires and lordships which Buckingham had enjoyed. It is true that Jasper, now duke of Bedford, was the most powerful personage in the south of Wales: he had Caldicot, Pembroke, Cilgerran, Llanstephan and other lordships in the south-west returned to him, and he received the lordships of Glamorgan, Haverford and Abergavenny *in tail male* by grants issued in March 1486 and March 1488. Moreover, by virtue of his marriage to Katherine Woodville, the duke of Buckingham's wealthy widow, he controlled Newport, and by May 1491 seems to have been in possession of Builth as well.[95] Elsewhere in Wales, most notably in the earldom of March and the principality, authority was diffused.[96] Indeed, the co-ordination of royal administration was achieved gradually during the reign by the king himself, not by Duke Jasper or by Prince Arthur's Council.

By 1485 the majority of marcher lordships belonged to the king, and others came his way by death or forfeiture. The administrative separateness of the earldom of March was duly abolished as from 2 February 1489, so that thenceforward every kind of grant from the earldom's estates would pass under the great seal of England 'as it is used in all othir thinges concernyng the Crowne by the Cours of the comen Lawe'.[97] Stewards of Welsh lordships who had been appointed by Edward IV or Richard III were removed in Parliament in 1487, and in the later years of the reign charters of liberties to the northern lordships ensured uniformity of law, particularly of the common law relating to property, and guaranteed uniformity of privilege and opportunity throughout the royal territories by the annulment of Henry IV's penal legislation.[98] Yet, apart from Duke Jasper, no one was allowed to enjoy hereditary

possession of any of the lordships in the king's hands. Viscount
Welles, who was given the lordships of Usk and Caerleon for life
in August 1490, was Henry's own uncle, whereas Prince Arthur,
his son, held the lordships of the earldom of March from November
1493 during the king's pleasure.[99] Once his immense debt to Uncle
Jasper had been paid, Henry VII, probably for financial reasons, was
reluctant to delegate his powers of government completely and
permanently.

After the creation of Arthur as Prince of Wales in November
1489 his Council exercised this authority, although Jasper seems to
have hung on to his position as the prince's alternate.[100] The means
of ensuring peace and good government were still those of Edward
IV's indentures. These were now supplemented to emphasise the
crucial importance of the steward, and they were used more exten-
sively by Henry VII than hitherto. It is likely that by 1491 not only
had the marcher lords been made party to them, but so also had the
stewards of every royal lordship in Wales; and they were concluded
with Henry as king. As far as a written and sealed undertaking
with a financial penalty clause could do so, the Crown had established a machinery for order and justice in Wales. The prince's
Council, or Jasper Tudor in its absence, was specifically required to
superintend its working.[101] A wide-ranging commission on the
Yorkist model was issued to Arthur and Jasper on 20 March 1493
to superintend the execution of justice throughout Wales and the
shires of Salop, Worcester, Hereford and Gloucester; at the same
time Arthur received military powers to facilitate law enforcement
and he was authorised to replace unsatisfactory officials. This was
the authority under which the prince and his Council acted in 1494
to stop a dispute between the Worcestershire towns of Bewdley and
Kidderminster and to insist that differences between them in the
future should be referred to Arthur and his councillors; the commission also enabled the prince to urge Shrewsbury's bailiffs to
remedy a complaint received from the local Dominican priory.[102]
Again, as in 1476, Arthur was to enquire into further private
franchises in the Marches which deserved to be resumed by the
Crown and thereby be put under uniform administration.[103]

The cardinal weakness of Prince Edward's Council as a political
and judicial instrument had been its dependence on the existence of
a prince. This defect was finally removed in 1502, when Prince
Arthur's Council remained in being until the creation of his brother

as prince two years later restored its customary form. Arthur died on 2 April, but on 18 June the Council 'within the principality of Wales', under the presidency of Bishop William Smyth of Lincoln, was given the now familiar commissions of oyer and terminer and of array in north and south Wales, Chester, the Marches and the four border shires.[104] As at periods in the past when there was no Prince of Wales, from the beginning of 1503 most of the revenue of the principality was taken to the king at Westminster, but 'his commissioners in the parts of the March of Wales' stayed on at Ludlow or Bewdley to exercise other aspects of his sovereignty.[105] The machinery at their disposal was now a generation old. There was nothing novel in the recommendation of these commissioners that 'all lordes marcheres be bowndon by indentures to the kynge's grace for the good rule and ordre of the lordschippes, accordyng to the good and laudable usage and customes ther'; the result, in the case of Edward, duke of Buckingham, at least, was the renewal in 1504 of the 'olde indenture' with the king.[106] The royal prerogative was now permanently delegated to ensure law and order throughout Wales and the English border land, and to bind all lords and major officers formally to discharge their obligations. It was a job still only partly done by 1509.[107]

The fifteenth century in Wales had seen a struggle to preserve peace, stability and justice. They were imperilled by social and political changes. On the one hand, the feudal position and political power of the aristocracy were decaying to the point where they increased the disorder common to many a frontier or marchland. On the other hand, the rising Welsh squirearchy was eager to shoulder the responsibilities of government and political leadership. To enable these developments to take place peacefully, the Crown needed to realise its sovereignty in Wales more consistently than hitherto. It did so not by revolution but by hesitant and often painful steps in an effort to marry the traditional privileges of English and Welsh lords in Wales with effective royal supervision. It was truly a long struggle, and the imperfections in the achievement were to provide much of the justification for the momentous changes of the 1530s.

Notes

1 *The Libelle of Englyshe Polycye*, ed. Sir George Warner (1926), 40.

2 F. R. H. DuBoulay, *An Age of Ambition* (1970), 25–6; G. M. Trevelyan, *History of England* (third edition, 1945), 259.

3 W. Rees, *An Historical Atlas of Wales* (second edition, 1959), plate 53.

4 W. H. Waters, *The Edwardian Settlement of North Wales in its Administrative and Legal Aspects, 1284–1343* (1935); J. G. Edwards, 'The early counties of Carmarthen and Cardigan', *E.H.R.*, xxi (1916), 90–8; Ralph A. Griffiths, 'Royal government in the southern counties of the principality of Wales, 1422–85', unpublished Ph.D. thesis, University of Bristol (1962).

5 J. G. Edwards, 'The Normans and the Welsh March', *Proc. Brit. Acad.*, xlii (1956), 155–77; *The Marcher Lordships of South Wales, 1415–1536*, ed. T. B. Pugh (1963), 4; F. D. Logan, *Excommunication and the Secular Arm in Mediaeval England* (1968), 114–15; R. R. Davies, 'The law of the March', *Welsh History Review*, v, No. 1 (1970), 9–15.

6 *R.P.*, iii, 426; *C.P.R., 1399–1401*, 61. Cf. J. G. Edwards, *The Principality of Wales 1267–1967* (1969), especially 16–20.

7 *C.P.R., 1399–1401*, 37, 33, 28.

8 *P.O.P.C.*, ii, 264; i, 148–50 and *passim*; *Issues of the Exchequer, Henry III–Henry VI*, ed. F. Devon (Record Commission, 1837), 299; *Anglo–Norman Letters and Petitions*, ed. M. D. Legge (Anglo–Norman Texts, iii, 1941), 301–2.

9 *P.O.P.C.*, i, 145; *Royal and Historical Letters during the Reign of Henry IV*, ed. F. C. Hingeston (Rolls Series, 1860), i, 69–72.

10 E.g. *Issues of the Exchequer*, 314; *C.P.R., 1405–08*, 359; *Royal and Historical Letters*, ii, 15–17, 22–4.

11 Henry, as the husband of Mary Bohun and the heir to the duchy of Lancaster, was lord of the marcher lordships of Brecon, Kidwelly, Monmouth and the Three Castles in 1399: R. Somerville, *History of the Duchy of Lancaster, 1265–1603*, i (1953), 639–54; R. R. Davies, 'The Bohun and Lancaster lordships in Wales in the fourteenth and fifteenth centuries', unpublished D.Phil. thesis, University of Oxford (1965).

12 E.g., *R.P.*, iii, 476 (1401), 612 (1407), 624 (1409–10); *S.R.*, ii, 129 (1401).

13 *P.O.P.C.*, i, 173–76; *C.P.R., 1401–5*, 53; J. E. Lloyd, *Owen Glendower* (1931), 43–4

14 *S.R.*, i, 320; *C.P.R. 1399–1401*, 396, 451–2; *ibid.*, *1401–05*, 299.

15 *C.P.R., 1405–08*, 156, 169, 215, 445; *ibid.*, *1408–13*, 202, 306. The king's personal influence in the Marches was considerably enhanced by the unprecedented number of marcher lords who were under age after 1405 and thus came into Henry's custody.

16 *R.P.*, iii, 457, 476, 509.

17 *Ibid.*, iii, 439, 472–3, 474, 476, 615, 663–4; iv, 52. For the Commons' contribution to financing the war, see *ibid.*, iii, 547, 580, 609, 624, and T. Kido, 'English government finance, 1399–1413', unpublished Ph.D. thesis, University of London (1965), 177–86.

18 W. R. Williams, *The Parliamentary History of the County of Worcester* (1897), 21, 24; *id.*, *The Parliamentary History of the County of Gloucester*

(1898), 27, 31; E. Edwards, *Parliamentary Elections of the Borough of Shrewsbury* (1859), 7.

19 *R.P.*, III, 476, 508–9; *S.R.*, II, 129, 141. A comparison of the petitions relating to Wales presented in the Parliaments of 1401 and 1402 with the resultant statutes is instructive.

20 *R.P.*, IV, 10–11 (1413); *S.R.*, II, 171–2.

21 Ralph A. Griffiths, 'The Glyndŵr rebellion in north Wales through the eyes of an Englishman', *Bull. Board of Celtic Studies*, XXII (1966–68), 152; *C.P.R., 1413–16*, 137, 195; W. T. Waugh, *The Reign of Henry V*, I (1914), 108.

22 P.O.P.C., II, 231 (2 May 1417); Griffiths, 'The Glendŵr rebellion', 152. For Henry V's sensitivity to hardship in south Wales, see R. R. Davies, 'Baronial accounts, incomes, and arrears in the later Middle Ages', *Ec.H.R.*, second series, XXI (1968), 224.

23 Griffiths, 'The Glyndŵr rebellion', 151–2; *C.P.R.*, 1413–16, 114.

24 Griffiths, 'The Glyndŵr rebellion', 153, 166–7; *R.P.*, IV, 90–1; *C.P.R., 1413–16*, 380, 405.

25 In May 1417 Henry ordered sheriffs to be resident in Anglesey, Caernarvonshire and Merioneth, and that castle constables should be equally conscientious and of English birth. J. B. Smith, 'The last phase of the Glyndwr rebellion', *Bull. Board of Celtic Studies*, XXII (1966–68), 253–4; *P.O.P.C.*, II, 231–2.

26 *C.P.R., 1413–16*, 347; *ibid.*, 170, 192, 229, 306–7, 395; P.R.O., Ministers' Accounts, 1165/11 m. 1; 1165/12 m. 3*d*; 1166/1 m. 1; 1166/2 m. 1; 1222/10 m. 4.

27 Smith, 'The last phase of the Glyndŵr rebellion', 254–5; H. T. Evans, *Wales and the Wars of the Roses* (1915), 43–6, 63–4; Waugh, *Henry V*, I, 113–14; A. D. Carr, 'Welshmen and the Hundred Years' War', *Welsh History Review*, IV, No. 1 (1968), 35–41. For negotiations to reconcile Maredudd, son of Owain Glyndŵr, see Lloyd, *Owen Glendower*, 143–4, and Smith, 'The last phase of the Glyndŵr rebellion', 255–6.

28 P.R.O., Ministers' Accounts, 1216/3 m. 2; 1223/1 m. 1; Davies, 'Baronial accounts', 226–7; Pugh, *Marcher Lordships of South Wales*, 42, 148.

29 I am grateful to Mr T. B. Pugh for a timely reminder on this point.

30 For a study of this important class in one area, see Ralph A. Griffiths, 'Gentlemen and rebels in later mediaeval Cardiganshire', *Ceredigion, Journal of the Cardiganshire Antiquarian Society*, V (1965), 143–67.

31 R. R. Davies, 'Owain Glyn Dŵr and the Welsh squirearchy', *Transactions of the Honourable Society of Cymmrodorion* (1968), 150–69; Griffiths, 'Gentlemen and rebels', 153–8.

32 Ralph A. Griffiths, 'Gruffydd ap Nicholas and the rise of the House of Dinefwr', *National Library of Wales Journal*, XIII (1964), 256–68; *id.*, 'Gruffydd ap Nicholas and the fall of the House of Lancaster', *Welsh History Review*, II (1965), 213–31; J. R. Jones, 'The development of the Penrhyn estate up to 1431', unpublished M.A. thesis, University of Wales, Bangor (1955), ch. IV.

33 *R.P.*, IV, 440. Gruffydd ap Nicholas's letters of denizenship probably date from March 1437, whereas William ap Gwilym secured his in two stages: on 26 November 1439 and 24 January 1443. P.R.O., Ancient Petitions 130/6464–5; *R.P.*, V, 16, 45, 104; Griffiths, 'Gruffydd ap Nicholas and the rise of the House of Dinefwr', 258; *C.P.R., 1436–41*, 416; *ibid., 1441–46*, 164.

34 *Dictionary of Welsh Biography*, 101, 354; Evans, *Wales and the Wars of the Roses, passim*; D. H. Thomas, 'The Herberts of Raglan as supporters of the House of York in the second half of the fifteenth century', unpublished M.A. thesis, University of Wales, Cardiff (1967), chs. i–vi; Somerville, *op. cit.*, 650.

35 G. A. Holmes, *The Estates of the Higher Nobility in Fourteenth-century England* (1957), 18–19, 24–5; A. J. Otway-Ruthven, *A History of Mediaeval Ireland* (1968), 13–38, 362–3.

36 *The Glamorgan County History: Medieval Glamorgan* ed. T. B. Pugh (forthcoming), 182; *C.P.*, iv, 273–82; viii, 448–53; D. H. Owen, 'The lordship of Denbigh, 1282–1425', unpublished Ph.D. thesis, University of Wales, Aberystwyth (1967), 82ff; Pugh, *Marcher Lordships of South Wales* 151–2.

37 *Ibid.*, 180.

38 For the declining efficiency of government in the southern counties of the principality under Henry VI and in the duchy of Lancaster, see Griffiths, 'Royal government in the southern counties of the principality', ch. xi; Somerville, *op. cit.*, i, 190–8; Davies, 'Baronial accounts', 228. See also Pugh, *Marcher Lordships of South Wales*, 9–10, 21.

39 Edwards, *Principality of Wales*, 29.

40 As in the excerpt which opened this paper.

41 Pugh, *Medieval Glamorgan*, 185, 202; Holmes, *Estates of the Higher Nobility*, 97–101; Owens, 'The lordship of Denbigh', 202; Griffiths, 'Royal government in the southern counties of the principality', chs. viii, ix; P.R.O., Ministers' Accounts, 1306/4 m. 3; 1210/5 m. 1d; 1222/6 m. 6d.

42 A. J. Pollard, 'The family of Talbot, Lords Talbot and earls of Shrewsbury in the fifteenth century', unpublished Ph.D. thesis, University of Bristol (1968), 359 and table facing 388.

43 T. B. Pugh and W. R. B. Robinson, 'Sessions in eyre in a marcher lordship: a dispute between the earl of Worcester and his tenants of Gower and Kilvey in 1524', *South Wales and Monmouth Record Society*, iv (1957), 113; Pugh, *Marcher Lordships of South Wales*, 36–43; Griffiths, 'Royal government in the southern counties of the principality', 50–67.

44 Pugh, *Marcher Lordships of South Wales*, 17–20, 37–40; P.R.O., Ministers' Accounts, 1222/12 m. 2; 1222/14 m. 2; Griffiths, 'Royal government in the southern counties of the principality', 649–58. The phenomenon cannot be detected in the principality's sessions in north Wales.

45 J. T. Rosenthal, 'The estates and finances of Richard, duke of York (1415–60)', *Studies in Medieval and Renaissance History*, ii, ed. W. M. Bowsky (1965), 197–200; Pugh, *Medieval Glamorgan*, 201.

46 *R.P.*, iv, 10–11 (1413), 52 (1414), 329 (1427); v, 104 (1445); *S.R.*, ii, 171–2, 188–9.

47 *R.P.*, v, 104, 138–9; J. B. Smith, 'Crown and community in the principality of north Wales in the reign of Henry VII', *Welsh History Review*, iii, No. 2 (1966), 156, 170–1. There seem to have been no such grants during the remainder of Henry VI's reign.

48 *R.P.*, iv, 52 (1414); v, 53–4 (1442), 104 (1445), 151 (1449); *S.R.*, ii, 188–9, 317–18, 331, 351.

49 *R.P.*, III, 615 (1407), 663–4 (1411); v, 137 (1447), 154–5 (1449), 200 (1449–50); *S.R.*, II, 159–60, 356; Pugh, *Marcher Lordships of South Wales*, 13, 15 (1415).

50 Davies, 'The law of the March', 29–30; J. B. Smith, 'Cydfodau o'r bymthegfed ganrif', *Bull. Board of Celtic Studies,* XXI (1964–66), 309–24, whose conclusions are expressed in English in *id.*, 'The regulation of the frontier of Meirionnydd in the fifteenth century', *Journal of the Merioneth Historical and Record Society*, v (1965–68), 105–11.

51 *R.P.*, IV, 332–3 (1427), 351 (1429), 379 (1431); *S.R.*, II, 265–6.

52 P.R.O., Exchequer, T.R., Council and Privy Seal, 55/40; 56/29; Ministers' Accounts, 1166/11 m. 7*d*; 1166/12 m. 3*d*; 1167/3 m. 6*d*; 1167/2 m. 8; 1167/5 m. 1; Griffiths, 'Gruffydd ap Nicholas and the fall of the House of Lancaster'.

53 *C.P.R.*, *1446–52*, 581; *ibid, 1452–61*, 124; P.R.O., Exchequer, T.R., Council and Privy Seal, 52/55 (10 July 1430); 78/1–3, 94 (26 November 1448); Smith, 'The regulation of the frontier', 106–10.

54 *R.P.*, v, 154–5; *C.P.R. 1416–61, passim.*

55 *C.P.R., 1441–46*, 106. See also *ibid., 1413–16*, 114, 179; *ibid., 1416–22*, 76, 270; *ibid., 1422–29*, 218, 362; *ibid., 1429–36*, 130, 200; *ibid., 1436–41*, 452; *ibid.,1446–52*, 585; *ibid., 1452–61*, 120, 444, 564–5.

56 Griffiths, 'Gruffydd ap Nicholas and the rise of the House of Dinefwr', 261–2.

57 'And this is to be intended in all Places where the King's Writ lieth. And if that be done in the Marches of Wales, or in any other Place, where the King's Writs be not current, the King, which is Sovereign Lord overall, shall do Right there unto such as will complain.' *S.R.*, I, 31 (Statute of Westminster, 1275); T. F. T. Plucknett, *Legislation of Edward I* (1949), 30.

58 *R.P.*, v, 14–16. For petitions to the Council, see Griffiths, 'Gruffydd ap Nicholas and the rise of the House of Dinefwr', 260–1, and above, p. 155 (from the principality); P.R.O., Exchequer, T.R., Council and Privy Seal, 44/38 (Llanstephan, 1424); 59/20 (Traean, 1438); 72 (Denbigh, 1444).

59 Griffiths, 'Gruffydd ap Nicholas and the fall of the House of Lancaster', 220–4. Abuse of official position was a frequent source of complaint in the mid-fifteenth century. P.R.O., Exchequer, T.R., Council and Privy Seal, 59/20 (Traean, 1438); 59/71 (Cardiganshire, 1439); 63/66 (Kidwelly, 1440); *R.P.*, v, 366–67 (royal counties of Wales, Chester and Flint).

60 H. M. Cam, 'The decline and fall of English feudalism', in *Liberties and Communities in Medieval England* (1963), 207; J. E. Morris, *The Welsh Wars of Edward I* (1901), 220–38.

61 *P.O.P.C.*, v, 211; P.R.O., Exchequer, T.R., Council and Privy Seal, 78/1, 2, 3, 94; Smith, 'The regulation of the frontier', 109. See also *R.P.*, v, 137 (1447), 154–5 (1449), 200 (1449–50).

62 National Library of Wales, Kentchurch Court MS 1027 (29 November 1451, involving Hay, Clifford and Elfael.)

63 *R.P.*, IV, 329, 332–3 (1427), 351 (1429), 379 (1431); v, 53–4 (1442); *S.R.*, II, 265–6, 317–18.

64 *P.O.P.C.*, v, 3 (1436); VI, 60 (1447); P.R.O., Exchequer, T.R., Council and Privy Seal, 41/110 (1423); 78/237 (*c.* 1436–38); *C.P.R., 1452–61*, 173.

F C E—M

65 *P.O.P.C.*, v, 82, 95, 211, 213, 215; Evans, *Wales and the Wars of the Roses*, 36.

66 G. A. Holmes, 'The *Libel of English Policy*', *E.H.R.*, LXXVI (1961), 193–216; *P.O.P.C.*, v, 211 ('or elles ye Kyng lateth hem wite that he wol ordeine a remedy').

67 *C.P.R.*, *1452–61*, 245, 340; R. L. Storey, *The End of the House of Lancaster* (1966), 135, 239–40, 179–80; Griffiths, 'Gruffydd ap Nicholas and the fall of the House of Lancaster', 225–8; Evans, *Wales and the Wars of the Roses*, 75ff; R. S. Thomas, 'The political career, estates and "connection" of Jasper Tudor, earl of Pembroke and duke of Bedford (d. 1495)', unpublished Ph.D. thesis, University of Wales, Swansea (1971), ch. IV.

68 Glamorgan and Pembroke passed in turn to half a dozen different families between 1400 and 1485.

69 *The Paston Letters*, ed. J. Gairdner (1904), I, 97–8; II, 177–8; Trinity College, Dublin, MS E.5.10, *f*. 187 (translated); Griffiths, 'Gruffydd ap Nicholas and the fall of the House of Lancaster', 218–24; *R.P.*, v, 279–80.

70 *Dictionary of Welsh Biography*, 354; Thomas, 'The Herberts of Raglan', ch. VIII; Evans, *Wales and the Wars of the Roses, passim*; *Mynegai i Farddoniaeth y Llawysgrifau*, ed. E. J. L. Jones and H. Lewis (1928), 130, 143, 205, 208, 243.

71 *C.P.R.*, *1461–67*, 7, 13, 30, 34, 43, 114, 119; Somerville, *op. cit.*, 644–5, 648. Thomas Vaughan, Herbert's uterine brother, became receiver of Brecon, Hay and Huntington during a minority in August 1461: *ibid.*, 43; *Dictionary of Welsh Biography*, 996–7.

72 *Gwaith Lewis Glyn Cothi*, ed. J. Jones and W. Davies (1837), 64; *Gwaith Lewis Glyn Cothi*, ed. E. D. Jones (1953), 4; *C.P.R.*, *1461–67*, 271, 352, 526–7, 533; *ibid.*, *1467–77*, 22, 25, 62, 41, 154, 163.

73 *C.P.R.*, *1461–67*, 268, 425–6.

74 E.G., *ibid.*, *1461–67*, 38, 280; *1467–77*, 54, 57, 58, 102; *S.R.*, I, 320.

75 *R.P.*, VI, 8–9; *C.P.R.*, *1467–77*, 179–80, 185, 275.

76 *C.P.R.*,*1467–77*, 283, 361.

77 *R.P.*, VI, 8–9, 159–60.

78 While in the border country, he referred certain cases to King's Bench because local jurors were afraid to speak out. *R.P.*, VI, 159–60; C.L. Scofield, *The Life and Reign of Edward the Fourth*, II (1923), 60.

79 P.R.O., Exchequer, Augmentations, Miscellaneous Books, 40/75 (3 June 1473). The 'olde composicion betwene the lordshipps of Glamorgan, Neuporte and Brekenok' was still in force at the end of the century, although even in 1476 it was difficult to produce in the court of one lordship offenders who lived elsewhere. Pugh, *Marcher Lordships of South Wales*, 23–6, 32–3, 256, 272.

80 In a Welsh context the bond or recognisance had been employed after Glyndŵr's rebellion to ensure that officials discharged their responsibilities properly (Davies, 'The Bohun and Lancaster lordships', ch. V, quoting P.R.O., Duchy of Lancaster, 41/9/8 m. 5; 42/16, ff. 16v, 74v; 25/3489). For the similar use of sureties or pledges for the receiver of Brecon in 1451 and for even minor officials in the principality shires from 1454, see Pugh, *Marcher Lordships of South Wales*, 246 n. 2; N.L.W., Badminton manorial records, 1561; P.R.O., Ministers' accounts, 1168/8–9; 1169/1.

81 *The Usurpation of Richard III,* ed. C. A. Armstrong (second edition, 1969), 71.

82 *C.P.R., 1467–77,* 283, 366, 401, 414, 417.

83 *R.P.,* vi, 160–1; *C.P.R., 1467–77,* 429 (26 February 1474).

84 C. A. J. Skeel, *The Council in the Marches of Wales* (1904), 26–7; *C.P.R., 1467–77,* 574–605. Worcestershire was omitted from the latter commission.

85 *C.P.R., 1467–77,* 574; *1477–85,* 5; Skeel, *op. cit.,* 21–2, 27; Williams, *Council in the Marches,* 9.

86 The earldom was tranferred piecemeal between 1477 and 1483 (*C.P.R., 1477–85,* 59–60, 94, 339). Pembroke was exchanged with William Herbert, earl of Huntingdon, as from 25 March 1479 (*R.P.,* vi, 202–4).

87 *The Coventry Leet Book,* ed. M. D. Harris, ii (Early English text Society, 1908), 432–42, 474–7, 484–510; T. F. Tout, *Chapters in the Administrative History of Medieval England,* iv (1928), 319 n. 2. Professor A. R. Myers brought this matter to my attention. For a similar connection with Coventry of Prince Edward (*c.* 1479–80), Prince Arthur and Prince Henry (*post* 1504, not 1502), see M. D. Harris, 'Unpublished documents relating to town life in Coventry', *T.R.H.S.,* fourth series, iii (1920), 104–6; *H.M.C.,* fifteenth report, appendix, part x, 147.

88 The new king left Ludlow about 24 April 1483: E. F. Jacob, *The Fifteenth Century* (1961), 611.

89 *C.P.R., 1477–85,* 349, 356, 361; *Grants of Edward V,* ed. J. G. Nichols (Camden Society, 1854), 33. On that day, 16 May, Buckingham became steward and receiver of the Welsh lordships of the duchy of Lancaster, and constable of their castles: *ibid.,* 32; Somerville, *op. cit.,* 640–2, 648.

90 Jacob, *Fifteenth Century,* 625–6.

91 C. Morris, *The Tudors* (1955), 60–1. The symbolic propaganda which Henry VII directed at Welsh hearts, if not Welsh heads, has been coldly and sceptically analysed by S. Anglo, 'The *British History* in early Tudor propaganda', *Bulletin of the John Rylands Library,* xliv (1961–62), 17–48, and in *Spectacle, Pageantry and Early Tudor Policy* (1969), 16, 44–5.

92 These were often the qualities for which Jasper had been praised in verse before 1485.

93 Smith, 'Crown and community', 166–7; Pugh, *Marcher Lordships of South Wales,* 242 and n. 2; P.R.O., King's Bench, Ancient Indictments, 957/8; B.M., Egerton roll 2192 m. 2*d,* 5. (I am grateful to Dr R. S. Thomas for drawing my attention to these documents.)

94 *C.P.R., 1485–94,* 84. Already on 18 February Jasper had headed a commission of oyer and terminer in the Welsh lordships of the earldom of March, while as justiciar of south Wales he had been exercising the king's authority in Carmarthenshire and Cardiganshire since 13 December 1485: *ibid.,* 47, 85–6.

95 *R.P.,* vi, 278–9; *C.P.R., 1485–94,* 64, 220, 345; Pugh, *Marcher Lordships of South Wales,* 241.

96 E.g. *C.P.R., 1485–94,* 5, 10, 24, 55, 65, 88, 299, 316, 365.

97 *S.R.,* ii, 538–9 (1489); C. A. J. Skeel, 'Wales under Henry VII', in *Tudor Studies presented to A. F. Pollard,* ed. R. W. Seton-Watson (1924), 3.

98 *R.P.,* vi, 403; *C.P.R., 1494–1509,* 434, 464–5, 471, 523, 534–5, 586–7;

Smith, 'Crown and community', 145–71. Dr R. R. Davies pertinently quotes the Welsh poet Sion Tudur's comment that Henry VII was 'the one who set us free': 'The twilight of Welsh law, 1284–1536', *History* LI (1966), 153 and n. 60.

99 *C.P.R., 1485–94*, 316, 453.

100 For the appearance of the prince's Council as early as the end of 1489, and its activities in the principality shires of north Wales during 1489–91, see Smith, 'Crown and community', 160–1.

101 P.R.O., Exchequer, Augmentations, Miscellanea, 15/37 (with Jasper Tudor, 1 March 1490); Cardiff Free Library MS 5.7, ff. 78–9 (with the earl of Huntingdon (d. 1490)), 80 (the steward of Usk, June 1488); Pugh, *Marcher Lordships of South Wales*, 29–30, 257–8, 279–81 (the steward of Clifford, Winforton and Glasbury, March 1490). The existence of a book of recognisances at Newport, which recorded bonds between the duke of Buckingham and some of his prominent tenants, indicates that an indenture was concluded with the duke too. *Ibid.*, 244–6. For a glimpse of Prince Arthur's Council dealing in traditional fashion with disputes involving Buckingham's lordships, see *ibid.*, 257–8, 272, 274–5.

102 Williams, *Council in the Marches*, 10; Skeel, *op. cit.*, 29, 30; *C.P.R., 1485–94*, 438–9, 441.

103 *C.P.R., 1485–94*, 439. For the more general encroachment on franchises under Henry VII, see Cam, *Liberties and Communities*, 214–19, and I. D. Thornley, 'The destruction of sanctuary', in *Tudor Studies*, ed. Seton-Watson, 182–207.

104 *C.P.R. 1494–1509*, 295. Williams, *Council in the Marches*, 10, gives the composition of this Council.

105 Smith, 'Crown and community', 167–8.

106 Pugh, *Marcher Lordships of South Wales*, 29–30; T. B. Pugh, 'The "Indenture for the Marches" between Henry VII and Edward Stafford (1477–1521), Duke of Buckingham', *E.H.R.*, LXXI (1956), 436–41.

107 Williams, *Council in the Marches*, 10–11; Skeel, *op. cit.*, 31–7. For its continuation under Henry VIII, see P. R. Roberts, 'The "Acts of Union" and the Tudor settlement of Wales', unpublished Ph.D. thesis, University of Cambridge (1966); Pugh, *Medieval Glamorgan*, ch. XII, section 2.

Index